T3-AJK-984

READING
THE ENTRAILS
AN ALBERTA
ECOHISTORY

By
NORMAN C. CONRAD

BRESCIA UNIVERSITY
COLLEGE LIBRARY
7/8//

University of Calgary Press

© 1999 Norman C. Conrad. All rights reserved.

University of Calgary Press
2500 University Drive NW
Calgary, Alberta, Canada T2N 1N4

Canadian Cataloguing in Publication Data

Conrad, Norman C. (Norman Charles), 1947-
    Reading the entrails

    Includes bibliographical references and index.
    ISBN 1-55238-012-2

    1. Natural history—Alberta. 2. Nature—Effect of human beings on—
Alberta—History. 3. Human ecology—Alberta—History. 4. Alberta—
Environmental condition—History. I. Title.
QH106.2A4C66 1999   508.7123   C99-911174-4

 We acknowledge the financial support of the Government of Canada through the Book Publishing Industry Development Program (BPIDP) for our publishing activities.

 Publication and promotion of this book has been made possible by financial support from the Alberta Foundation for the Arts.

COMMITTED TO THE DEVELOPMENT OF CULTURE AND THE ARTS

All rights reserved. No part of this work covered by the copyrights hereon may
be reproduced or used in any form or by any means—graphic, electronic or
mechanical—without the prior permission of the publisher. Any request for
photocopying, recording, taping or reproducing in information storage and
retrieval systems of any part of this book shall be directed in writing to
CANCOPY, One Yonge Street, Suite 1900, Toronto, Ontario M5E 1E5.

Printed and bound in Canada by Veilleux Impression à Demande Inc.
∞ This book is printed on acid-free paper.

Cover design by Doyle Robert Buehler.
Typesetting and page design by Cliff Kadatz.

With hope, Verity and Felicity.
In memory, Mother and Father.

CONTENTS

Acknowledgements

y intent is to provoke thought, so this work suffers the usual problems of the brash and brazen—wanting in respects, indelicate in places and perhaps wrong in yet others. But the main themes seemed so important I felt they must be presented this way.

Over the years Ed Wolf provided ideas and attitude, some of which found its way into print. Discussions with Richard Thomas, Dave Mayhood, Mike Sawyer, Mike Judd, Tony Hall and Peter Fitzgerald-Moore helped in concept formation. Vanessa Porter, Elaine Conrad, Phil Elder and Brian Horejsi reviewed and constructively commented on a number of chapters. When I was lost in the desert with manuscript in hand, George Melnyk gave me directions and good advice. Ian Clarke provided critical comments that focused and improved the document in many ways. Walter Hildebrandt efficiently encouraged me along in the final stages.

Several people aided me just by being supportive neighbours, family and friends. Members of the Western Affairs Committee (WAC), particularly Bob Johnston, Jennifer Bobrovitz and Donn Lovett, gave me encouragement, as did my good friends Clint Cawsey, Rod and Catherine Keelty, Trevor and Sonya Ross, Arthur Caldicott, Bob Price, Larry and Eileen Peltier and my never-to-be forgotten neighbours on Barnes Road, Kay and Tony Wiersma, the Cunnins, the Zurrers, Charles Poole and the Reiners. They were supportive without really knowing what I was up to and without in any way endorsing the product. My brothers and sisters were the same, no doubt thinking, "There goes Norman, again." And my mother and late father have always been there for me, even as they pass from this life.

The project was demanding. Heavy burdens were borne by my children. It is dedicated to them, Verity and Felicity, with love in my heart and hope. That does not make it right but I tried my best doing what I thought best. The faults, errors, excesses and deficiencies are mine and mine alone.

Calgary, September 1999

PROLOGUE

NEIGHBOURS (1993)

I live in sight of the Calgary Tower. For a time it was the tallest freestanding manmade thing in the west. Later, with the vertically ambitious thrusting higher all around, it became just a tall pointy thing with a saucer in a neighbourhood of higher things. It is not strictly my neighbour. It is just in my sight. Happily so, because my neighbourhood is nicer. An ordinary inner city community in one way, it is a fascinating crossroads in other ways.

My lawn is a standard commercial mix of grasses brought in from Kentucky and California or wherever and "blended" for local conditions, hoping I guess that it looks like someplace else, maybe California or Kentucky. Out front is an old cottonwood, female, and so we tolerate her mid-June bursts of cottony seeds. She is the only remnant wild thing on this narrow lot. A couple of Manitoba maples are struggling to become the dominant near-exotic trees in the backyard. We live next to June.

The narrow lot is sliced and boxed from lands that underlay front lines in the battle of the ice giants 20,000 years ago. Cordilleran ice thrust out from the Rocky Mountains, grinding eastward down the Bow Valley toward my house. Looming in from the east was the massive colossus of the Laurentide Ice Sheet, a mile thick, horizon-wide and advancing southwest. Would either have toppled that Calgary Tower thing if it were then standing? That would be a popcorn, beer and lawnchair event!

Slipping down an ice-free corridor between these hulks, right over my lawn, might have come the first Americans. From Eurasia with a stopover in Beringia, they brought along state-of-the-art tools, spears, stone pounders and the like. And wow, what a biorama—mammoths, camels, wild asses and sabretooth tigers—right there, milling around in my backyard.

Sometimes, when tending my flowers in the backyard (exotics and not happy about their place), I turn to these earlier times. Other times I think about the future. Maybe someday, in 100 years or so, somebody will be standing out here watering petunias and wonder about me, the guy who let the feral maples go and left the cottonwood to stand and rot. What will become of that person? Anyway, if there is one real purpose in writing the following stuff, it is because of worries for neighbours.

Timescape/landscape neighbours include the Stoney, Cree, Blackfoot and those before them. What became of them? How is it that a pasty little white guy like myself holds title to bison lands, even if only 10 by 40 metres? Not long ago the bison and Native people had it all: land, lots of rich land; life, lots of wonderful life; and then, what is more, they got great gifts from their new European friends. With liberal immigration policies, Native people opened their world to new high technology, free trade and global competition. They got rich and then, just over a century ago, they lost it. Maybe they overshot and collapsed? Maybe they did not understand what they were doing? Maybe they listened to their hunters too much?

Their forefathers enjoyed a similar bonanza 11 millennia earlier. Back then the new species, man, assayed pristine America with its myriad animals. Neither nature nor nurture prepared Quaternary creatures for the gangs of rock-throwing, sharp-stick-poking, cunning, puny bipedal predators. Eden was easy pickings—except for a couple of nightmarish predators, giant short-faced bears and ghastly cats. With all kinds of unwitting and tasty animate resources to exploit, humans, the new king of beasts in the New World, became wonderfully well off. They got rich and plentiful; then it stopped. Maybe they overshot and collapsed. Maybe they did not understand what they were doing? Maybe they listened to their hunters too much?

Immigration, they say, brings new human resources, new tools, new ways, new ideas and new energy to build the land and to make it strong and just. Was that the effect of that first immigration or our last? During the most recent influx, the coming of Europeans, Native people shared their lands with their new neighbours and adopted many of their ways. Guns and horses slew bison like never before. Other techniques levered their power higher, enriching the instant while devouring their future. Did these new tools plunder first Americans?

How could charming trade consume these first people? Its magic was to turn things one had too much of into things one had too little of. Excess solved deficiency as bountiful bison were turned into scarce guns, flour and axe heads. Trade encouraged specialization, dependency and galloping consumption. The words of an anonymous Hudson's Bay Company memo from May 22, 1822 keep ringing in my ears:

> I have made it my study to examine the nature and character of Indians and however repugnant it may be to our feelings, I am convinced they must be ruled with a rod of iron to bring

and keep them in a proper state of subordination, and the most certain way to effect this is by letting them feel their dependence upon us . . . . In the woods and northern barren grounds this measure ought to be pursued rigidly next year if they do not improve, and no credit, not so much as a load of ammunition, given them until they exhibit an inclination to renew their habits of industry. In the plains however this system will not do, as they can live independent of us, and by withholding ammunition, tobacco and spirits, the Staple articles of Trade, for one year, they will recover the use of their Bows and spears, and lose sight of their smoking and drinking habits; it will therefore be necessary to bring those Tribes round by mild and cautious measure which may soon be effected.[1]

Alongside came European appetites, ambitions and diseases. While things seemed the same only better, everything changed. Soon the bison disappeared, Native people and their lands withered to near nothingness. I wonder about that time and the people, and if they understood what was happening.

And now today we have the same wonders coming our way: liberal immigration policy and a clamour for more; all kinds of new technology and the clamour for more; and wonderfully expanding markets and international trade and we clamour for more. We (or some, or more realistically a decreasing few) are getting very rich but those few say there is more wealth to come, more than enough for everyone. Things are different now because we are smart, just, democratic and besides, our hunters tell us there is lots left. More than enough for us and future generations.

Those things come to mind when I pull dandelions. I worry about my other neighbours, the nonhuman kind. As I watch a robin (one of the only native wildlife species now common in my yard) pull out another worm, I think "What a wonderful array there once was." That splendid pageant is over; halted by the trappers, bison hunters, wolfers, railroaders, farmers, oil men, foresters and the florescence of consumers. As we grind nature down, eliminating first the mega-faunas, then exploiting succeeding trophic levels in a mad dig to entropy, I wonder how smart we are and reflect on the words of a noted thinker, Michael Polayni, in *The Study of Man*[2]:

Animals have no speech, and all the towering superiority of man over the animals is due almost entirely to man's gift of speech. Babies and infants up to the age of 18 months or so are mentally not much superior to chimpanzees of the same age; only when they start learning to speak do they rapidly outdistance and leave far behind their simian contemporaries. Even adults show no distinctly greater intelligence than animals so long as their minds work unaided by language. In the absence of linguistic clues man sees things, hears things, feels things, moves about, explores his surroundings and gets to know his way about, very much as animals do . . . .

A great connoisseur of rat behaviour, E. C. Tolman, has written that a rat gets to know its way about a maze as if it had acquired a mental map of it. Observations on human subjects suggest that a man, however intelligent, is no better at maze-running than a rat, unless assisted by notes, whether these are remembered verbally or sketched out in a drawing.

It sets me to think. Do humans really think often, well, or deeply? Certainly we are an inventive lot, but for all that, the thinking we do usually feeds more base objectives (Maslow's hierarchy speaks to the issue). If the end is cheese, how superior is man to Tolman's rat?

Human knowledge and sentience is of what? Not of nature, at least not in essential ways. Mostly our grasp of nature is of the kind the butcher feels when contemplating beef—where to find it, grow it, kill it, cut it, sell it and, if truly prudent and sustainable, how to do it all over again. Religion and philosophy in the European envelope are positively stunted, profoundly insentient when it comes to nature and human relationship with nature. World views without the world—a vast problem to any intelligent life form? For example, in his modern liberal classic *A Theory of Justice*, John Rawls summarily deals nature away, perhaps for another day when it might better be made to fit with contemporary constructs:

No account is given of right conduct in regard to animals and the rest of nature . . . . They are outside the scope of a theory of justice, and it does not seem possible to extend the contract doctrine so as to include them in a natural way. A correct conception of our relations to animals and to nature would seem to depend upon a theory of the natural order and our place in it. One of the tasks of metaphysics is to work out a view of the world which is suited for this purpose; it should identify and systematize the truths decisive for these questions.[3]

Fortunately, since Rawls wrote this in 1971, others have turned their minds to the issue, so that religion and philosophy now have back eddies of thinkers who are grappling with them. If it takes several centuries for a philosophical idea to leap from thinker to mass mentality (it took the Pope 350 years to apologize to Galileo), we may look forward to some broader social enlightenment on these matters in the 23rd century.

Tired of pulling dandelions, I get a beer. So sentience and reason are, at best, doled out to humans in spare quantity and quality. Where does that leave human divinity? Well, just as God's divinity plunged a few centuries ago, human divinity dives lower in my mind. The closer I get to the bottom of my beer and the more science looks at it, man is another breathing, living-dying, peeing-pooping, reproducing beast. His brain only starts to look really clever when one amasses the products of billions of such minds, assembled over tens of thousands of years, with good thoughts captured by means of extrasomatic systems to record and propagate them to those coming after. Yes, throw in some mutant minds, geniuses and the fortunate products of many stupid mistakes. Add it all together, mix it up and attribute the product to each individual. Then each of us looks very smart. The fallacy of attribution turns idiots to savants.

This brings up the past—how do we treat our chronological neighbours? Good things from the past we accept as deserving inheritors of their benediction. Newton acknowledged his debt to the past with his "I stand on the shoulders of giants." But his taking from the past was extremely selective. Like us, when harvesting the past he took only the beneficial, avoiding its burdens. Whatever bad happened in the past we dismiss as "That was them, then." We detach from it as if it were leprosy. While sitting comfortably on aboriginal or bison lands, we recents say that the genocidal treatment of first Americans, the biocidal treatment of the bison or many other past wrongs are not our problems. Ethical burdens we shift to our forefathers, saying they were unsophisticated, ignorant or even evil, back then. In this high-grading, a form of time-externalization, the benefits remain untainted and current, while the guilt and burdens sediment out in the past. Take the gold, leave the slag.

What about time-neighbours to the future? Equipped with another beer, they get sort of fuzzy in my mind. I know the party line. They are not really there, but I wonder. With no future, what happens to now? Is the present not diminished without a future? And if the future for future people is terrible because of us now, ought there not to be a future reckoning, now? This intergenerational equity thing is all new and no one has it figured out yet. We live on Groucho Marx's insight—"Do something for posterity? What have they ever done for me?" Or we use Newtonian shoulders to help us shrug; tomorrow's people will have the shoulders of our giants to stand on. With this handy time warp, today's people glory in making a better world for next generations.

It seems grossly unfair. A bunch of people present now can exploit and pillage the only life-sustaining system, nature—the mother of mankind and every other kind—and leave another bunch of neighbours—future neighbours—without, just because of the iron shackles of unidirectional time. What a getaway, "You won't get me because I passed on. Ha ha!" Of course when I walk by the mirror I cringe; I am a product and practitioner of nearly everything I rail against. Past-exploiting, future-forgetting; it is pretty much all there.

On sunny Saturday afternoons I relax around the yard with a gin and tonic, and revel in nature. Kind of harmonizing. Big black squirrels (melanistic greys) hang out, looking cute, helping you feel a part of nature, waiting for a handout or testing you for what they can steal. Over 60 years ago these husky rodents captured the fancy of a traveller in eastern Canada who felt sure he could improve on Calgary's nature. Why not displace the more retiring red squirrels by bringing a volley of these fearless, prolific rodents to Calgary and release them at the Calgary Zoo? They now have the run of the city.

Kids like them until bitten. Adults go into some kind of trance when they are around, a time-place transport back to Eden's harmony. Feed a squirrel and achieve oneness with God and nature. Grey/black squirrels know a good thing when they find it, so they happily dispense indulgences to these desperate, not too clever beasts, urban humans. A neighbour, more forthright than most, calls them bushy-tailed rats. A congregation of them invaded her attic.

I lift world-weary eyes from a fresh gin and tonic to observe another neighbour's handiwork. Adroit with the saw and hammer and longing for the halcyon days of youth when he trudged the dusty streets of some prairie Mecca or from furrow to furrow on a rural monoculture, this neighbour has created a half-metre-high grain elevator birdhouse. He raised it high above the clothesline pole, positioning it so that no cats could prey on its precious feathered tenants. What a nexus, nostalgia for his past prairie youth coupled with a lost Eden, architecturally provided for in a miniature grain elevator. Of course, the inhabitants are not local yokels but those feisty continental sojourners, English sparrows. These tiny Churchills dominate this and nearly every other elevator in the land.

A few blocks away is one of those boutique stores that sells wild bird stuff; feeders, feed, decoys, wind chimes and other wholesome and backyardsy clutter. Birdseed sells by the wagonload, but do feeders do any good? One winter I bought a backyard bird feeding station. Its remnants still litter the area. I should clean up better. Think of it—shivering, starving cold little birdies, without anyone to care for them. They needed me. I took a stand for Mother Nature. I would right the imbalance, defend the wild kingdom. I put out a pile of seeds on this store-bought, guaranteed to bring the birds, sure to make me harmonize with nature, feeding station.

The squirrels got the good stuff first. English sparrows and starlings performed cleanup. There may have been leftovers for that connoisseur of songbird eggs, the blue jay, but for our other wild local friends, the ones in desperate trouble, nothing. And worse! For the few remaining local songbirds, the bird feeding station operates as a bird sink, a feline feeding station. Warblers make a colourful entree. Some think an exotic is as good as a wild native animal, and, in practical ways, domestic animals have greater rights than wild animals, so they like this affirmative action program for introduced English sparrows, starlings and neighbourhood cats, but I prefer the finches and true sparrows. As predators go, give me a good short-tailed weasel.

While there are more jays around my neighbourhood, there are wildly more of their cousins, the magpies. A population explosion is under way, directly related, I suspect, to ambient garbage, unprotected dog food dishes and fast-food outlets. Also, magpies relish a fresh roadkill. About this time of the year, early fall, there are lots of those. The annual population bomb of grey squirrels explodes on the city. Carrying capacity exceeded, parents drive their children off with no invitation to return. "Go out into the world, son, and make your fortune, but be wary, the journey is dangerous." Streets and automobiles get most of them. Tires squash squirrels and a horde of magpies squawk and flap to the feast. I sometimes think of lawyers when I see this snappy, flashy, black and white attired, loquacious, opportunistic, somewhat clever and always aggressive flock arrive at a fresh roadkill. I know it would offend some, but it does take me back to disrobing in the barrister lounge at the courthouse.

Two blocks north is a schoolyard. At summer's end, before the fall migration, the schoolyard is the ring-billed gull's meeting place. They stand out there feeding and squawking all day—at least until the football team comes along—likely discussing matters of importance, like the abundance of worms, the laziness of their younger generation or competition from starlings. Inside the school, educators instruct young humans that they must be more competitive; that the young in other lands learn to produce more, faster, and consume more, faster. If you want more, which you must, you must get rid of the stuff in your education that limits your ability to be good producers and consumers—distractions like art, poetry, literature, philosophy and such. Be an engineer, be in management, be any factor of production that you want but forget this being a being stuff.

Living close to the centre of the city makes for convenient exploration of its fauna and flora. Sometimes I bicycle or jog along the river. People connect to nature down by the water, feeding mallards, about the only waxing species of duck, and the wildly prolific Canada geese. The zoo is a few kilometres away along river paths. I have a membership so I get one kind of nature on the way there and another inside its gates. I go to the zoo mostly for the people. Young women with large families tend to go, perhaps some atavistic need to connect with non-human life. It must be disappointing for them because you do not really find much non-human life at the zoo. Young people on their first few dates go, I presume to show how sensitive and loving they are; a kind of foreplay. Christian families go on Sundays, undoubtedly expressing their love of God's creation with little or no remorse over their blessed killing of it. And then there are the macho guys with tattoos and tarts, going from cage to cage, fascinated in their boyish minds with what they would do to this beast or that one, if they only had their gun along.

Meanwhile, the zoo itself, forgetting the bloody past of zoos and uncritical of their present roles, preaches a limited conservation—one that largely ignores habitat and ecosystems, praises direct human intervention and sustains the idea that it is good enough if we maintain biodiversity, if only in zoos. They also provide a delightful and forgiving stage for industry to throw a few dollars at the zoo in a public gala, while trashing the world outside. Kind of like Jack the Ripper's $5 donation to a women's abuse shelter. The part I like best is the human's cage. Above the bars is the caption "World's most dangerous animal."

Closer to home now, two doors down and across the street is another schoolyard. It has an old school, built in 1920, and a yard that is bounded on the west by a bushy escarpment that separates my transitional neighbourhood from the rich and famous in Calgary's Mount Royal. One hundred years ago the hillside was full of splendid native vegetation. Now exotic grasses, shrubs and trees have taken over. Itinerant, urban poor sometimes dwell in the bushes. You can tell by the remains of their scavenged garbage bags, empties and used hypodermic needles. Contemporary hunter-gatherers. Teenage kids go into the bushes for their first sexual encounters; used prophylactics indicate that. But at a distance this hillside still looks nice.

Farther along the hill, one little patch of native shortgrass prairie remains. It is small, very small, perhaps only a few hundred metres square now. Every year runaway crabgrass and shrubs encroach, looming in from all sides. It still has a startling array of autonomous and fragile flowering herbs in the spring—crocus, shooting stars, yarrow, buttercups and one little pincushion cactus. I could not find the intensely brilliant pinkish, purple cactus blossom this year. I could not even find the cactus. Gone, I guess.

At its top, near the path, is a shrinking bed of the most exquisite, and by context, resilient, gentian. How they remain mystifies me. It fills me with hope that somehow beauty will survive. But every year, as this abused bed of bliss shrinks, so does my hope.

At noontime, children from the school play on the hill. These coddled little animals scour its magic side, a jungle, desert or mountain, to fight the Hun, pirates and cavalry. All dwell there in their mindscapes. But they are killing the last of the grass and the fragile gentian. Sometimes I think if justice was limited to here, now and humans, it is all right that these kids stomp these remnants because their forefathers stomped most other things. I want to tell these children to fight for their gentian and native shortgrass. I want them to know that the new ice age is looming over them and it is unlike the others; not a cycle in nature, but out of nature. It is a dangerous experiment that affects all life, including theirs. But I know that they would not understand and I do not want to end up like Holden Caufield. So what to do?

OF ICE AND MEN

Later, in my study, I open E.C. Pielou's *After the Ice Ages*[4], in which she tells of the ending of North America's last great glaciations and the return of life. Her story stops short at the most recent invasions—waves of Eurasian peoples flooding in—but as her prologue indicates, her concern does not:

> The development of human history has always been governed by the setting—the natural environment—in which it has taken place. In the past this setting changed so slowly that it could be regarded as static. Predictions about humanity's future did not need to take account of changing climate, spreading deserts, rising sea levels, disappearing forests and the like. Now, as we are all aware, changes of these kinds are likely to affect our future profoundly. We are now well into the population explosion that has threatened us at least since the time Thomas Robert Malthus (1766-1834) first published his dire warnings, and the exploding population is quickly degrading its own environment.

She ends her book on this troubling note:

> From the time the European invaders of North America established themselves ... the natural history of northern North America began to deviate from its "natural" course. The continent was no longer isolated. The foreign invaders multiplied rapidly, destroying native ecosystems at an ever-increasing rate. In time, the byproducts of technology began to poison earth, water and air and have now begun to influence the climate. The measured responses of biosphere to climate, and climate to astronomical controls have, for the foreseeable future, come to an end. And the story told in this book comes, at least temporarily, to a close.

The arguments presented in the following pages also begin with the end of the recent ice age, but have a different focus.

Early this century the Russian scientist Vladimir Vernadsky used the term "Biosphere" to indicate the realm of autonomous life (nature) and "Noosphere" to indicate the human managed realm, the anthropogenically altered world. This story spans three recent Alberta morphological influences—ice, life and human—the period from the end of the ice age to the most recent convulsion, the "development of Alberta." It observes the retreat of the Biosphere and the advance of the Noosphere, changes resulting from anthropogenic influences.

CHAPTER 1

ICY BEGINNINGS

L ong ago, far to the north and east of Alberta, high in the Keewatin, snow fell and did not melt. Accumulating year upon year, new buried old, concreting into strata, forming an ever-thickening overburden of enduring ice. Fanning deeper and wider by years, centuries, millennia, it came to be a continent itself, a continent of ice. Upward it reared and outward it overrode, burying the ancient Laurentia plate and displacing life. Ice starts this story, civilized men end it.

GLACIAL MECHANICS

Plate tectonic theorists tell us that long ago Earth's crustal movements, the so-called continental drift, slid North America's plate northwesterly overtop the Pacific plate. Millions of years of migration carried the American landmass into cooler climes at higher latitudes. Running under the same boreal winds, buoyed on the same magma seas, Eurasia sailed slowly northward, rafting with North America close in around the pole, circling and squeezing the Arctic Ocean. Greenland, islands and the Bering Sea shallows chinked in gaps. Wandering lands ran in under more stable weather, staunching warm oceanic flows to polar regions. Average temperatures settled lower, often below freezing. It has been that way for the Quaternary Period, the last two million years, and it will continue so for the next eight million.[1]

Beginning 1.75 million years ago, a series of immense glaciers grew out of high latitudes, draping down over America. Ponderous sky-high massifs of ice overthrust the mid-latitudes of the Northern Hemisphere for tens of thousands of years at a time. But glaciation was not continuous. Interglacial periods occur. We repose in one now. Earlier this century a Serbian mathematician, Milutin Milankovitch, observed that apparently regular progressions in orbital shape, axis tilt and axis rotations of Earth relative to the sun coincided with glacial periods. These Milankovitch cycles predicted glacial reoccurrences just in excess of every 100,000 years, involving glaciations of 60,000 to 90,000 years with corresponding interglacial periods of 40,000 to 10,000 years. The Wisconsinan Glaciation is most recent, beginning less than 100,000 before present (often referred to as "BP" in scientific convention).

Perhaps the Wisconsinan Glaciation started with winds blowing off temperate seas. Streaming northward, these warm, wet winds encountered land and lifted. Increasing altitude and latitude cooled and rarefied this flow, stripping it of moisture. If cold enough, precipitates turned to snow and gathered on the land. Mirror-like, snow reflected solar radiation into space, cooling and further speeding an icy accumulation.[2] Increasing elevations and decreasing temperatures forced yet more snow from the overpassing air, settling on an expanding core of ice. Around this swirled feeder forces of wind and water. As Laurentide conditions neared perfection, a colossal ice machine growled to life, ultimately amassing a dome five kilometres high over the Keewatin.

A crown so high required an empire wide. Gravity's effect on the agglomerating dome squeezed its central mass with immense pressure, causing it to squash outward, toward the margins. An ocean-sized gelatinous egg broke and spread onto a continental plate. At glacial pace this egg flattened, the white spreading out from the high yolk-dome in a slow breaking tsunami. This overriding, viscous continent's lead edge thinned to mere kilometer-high massifs of turgid white and blueness at its frontier. There, travelling plateaux and marching mountains of ice tumbled and broke over meltwater lakes.

SHEETS OF ICE

The Wisconsinan Glaciation's largest component was the Laurentide Ice Sheet, centred over Hudson Bay, a present-day modest liquid remnant. There cold and moisture enjoyed a frigid, yet fruitful conjugation; this offspring grew outward with hulking power. It spread through the Arctic, the Northwest Territories, Keewatin District and Labrador, draping down over the Canadian Shield to the plains and woodlands beyond. At its maximum, 18,000 years BP, the Wisconsinan Glaciation covered 15 million square kilometres of North America. Part of the Laurentide Ice Sheet, the Keewatin Sheet, overran western Canada.

Cordilleran ice sheets formed high in Canada's western mountains, nurtured by both altitude and latitude. Growth pushed and gravity pulled them from their mountain nurseries downslope to the oceans, to the plains, and southward. Together, the Laurentide and the Cordilleran ice sheets over-ran nearly all of Canada. Their walls, a thousand metres high and thousands of kilometres wide, were backed by millions of cubic kilometres of expansive ice. Towering ramparts of ice advanced, razing and levelling hills, scouring and scarifying the plains, ploughing and pulverizing mountains to mere boulders and rockflour. Lead edges of these enormities collided along Alberta's foothills. With cyclonic winds swirling round, rearing and roaring giants warred over barren rock. In this dreamscape spectacle, continents of ice battled for dominion over land.

Earth's surface sagged beneath this overhumping mass. Just beyond the ice, non-glaciated lands bobbed up to new heights as if in a waterbed. Oceans retreated, shrinking as ice's empire captured water from evaporating seas, placing it in terrestrial cold storage atop northern lands. And abiotic ice had ambition. It hungered to overrun more distant lands, to extend its dominion farther, into the mid-latitudes.

REFUGIA

After ice swarmed and swallowed the land, no longspur sang, no larkspur flowered: no brilliant bird, no blossoms seen. No fern, no fen, no bog. Even seasons froze. Ice rebuffed summer's blazing sun, reflecting it back into the void. Winter's sun scarcely lit the overarching sky—a shaded blue-white moonscape. But close by this frozen shroud, huddled in refuge, life waited.

Occasional mountain horns or high plateaux punctuated this ice sea. These rocky islands, nunataks, jutted above its viscous flood. Too high for ice to reach, too dry for ice to form, spring timidly returned there each year. A distant struggling sun warmed stony soils enough to germinate last season's seeds. Birth, growth, reproduction and death played in quick time, each sprout seeking to keep its species-hope alive. Flowers still bravely blossomed, perfuming cold-purged air. Above the grind, boom and roar of ambitious ice, adventurous birds trilled defiance and warmed their next generation's eggs.

Sometimes, unique local conditions—aridity, warmth or geographical circumstances—left enclaves unglaciated at lower elevations. Life hunkered down here "in refugia" awaiting the thaw. In the farthest northwest reaches of North America another refuge appeared. Perhaps anticipating Moses, amassing glaciation "made the sea dry land and the waters were divided."[3]

It happened like this. At maximum, Quaternary glaciations occupied nearly 30% of Earth's land surface. With oceans crystallizing as ice on land, water no longer ran back to sea; saltwater bodies shrank. Reallocation of the planet's water supply on this scale had global effects. Sea levels receded about 100 m, creating the relative illusion of lands rising from the sea (eustatic change). Lands underlying the ice sheet sank under its massive weight. Depressing Earth's surface in one location raises it elsewhere, usually nearby, in hydraulic response (isostatic change). Shoals arose from the sea, dividing the waters and making the sea dry land.

Together, rising seabeds and falling sea levels split the waters, levitating the Bering Sea shallows from out of the sea. Named Beringia, these lands bridged Asia to the Americas, providing a way for life to migrate intercontinentally, to leap the "seams of Pangaea."[4]   But the bridge was long and the leap slow. Like Utnapishtim's barque or Noah's ark, Beringia became a vessel carrying species through the tempest of the ice ages. For thousands of years generations of terrestrial life used Beringia as a bridge, an ark, a home.

The glaciation that lifted Beringia from the shoals also heaped up an impenetrable wall of ice, closing this bridge's eastern exit, the gateway to the Americas. Biotic ambitions lured some life forms east from Asia to this wall. But when ice retreated the oceans rose, resubmerging the land and flushing life from the bridge. Fortuitously for Beringian life, glacial retreat also melted open a gateway to the east. Like the pulse of a pump, Beringia sucked Asiatic life in from the west and, at the pace of glacial melt, expelled it to the east, into the Americas.

Sun on Ice

But what of the thaw? Could the transition from a continent of ice to an ocean of meltwater be other than cataclysmic? Along ice's southern frontier heat/cold, water/ice and life/death battled. War zones shifted with the weather: sometimes the sun won, laying bare denuded lands; other times King Winter advanced, submerging the stony earth with his icy battalions. Along this front lay meltwater mush, mess, monstrous proglacial lakes and other detritus of siege and assault. South of the battle zones lay windswept, rocky, barren and cold deserts, casualty to earlier glaciations and the devastating effects of continental climates colliding with a near eternity of ice.

While ice still reigned, 18,000 years ago, the most fantastic life forms waited in America's mid-latitudes. Glaciation drove tundra, taiga, northern mixed forest and prairie zones south into strange biomic clumps and mixed blobs of life, clustered together in unique ecosystemic combinations maintained, strangely, with some stability. The peculiarity is that during glaciation's toughest times species diversity survived; but with later climatic amelioration, diversity diminished. This host of species served out their expulsion from the north, awaiting a day they might reclaim their realm, their ancient habitats and relict ranges.

Meanwhile, Earth orbited, tilted and wobbled round the sun, progressing through this 100,000-year Milankovitch cycle, warming the north. Finally, immensely and messily, cold gave way to heat. Ablation is part of any ice sheet's daily struggle. Its presence is felt strongest at its edges so glacial margins are mucky affairs. But when rates of ablation vastly exceed accumulation, when glaciation is in wild retreat, the edges become maelstroms of awesome aquatic forces. The Great Flood!

Meltwater torrents engulfed lowlands, building temporary lakes larger than seas. Then, overfilling banks, they probed out a low or breach point, violently carving out an escape channel. Out cascaded pent-up walls of wild water, flooding everything below. Today's coulees and their trickling little seasonal streams hold little hint of the wild and raging rio grandes brimming their channels during the great meltdown. Then, they were surging, fluid furies.

Alberta's southern highlands, from the Milk River Ridge to the Cypress Hills, halted the Laurentide Ice Sheet's earlier advance and blocked the flood's escape to the south later, when the meltdown came. Mountains stopped meltwater's escape to the west. Glaciation's ice massifs, now receding northeast and liberating oceans of meltwater, formed another horizon-bracketing dam to these swelling seas. Surrounded, impounded and nurtured this way, temporary proglacial lakes of enormous size surged higher and higher. A few low points along the highlands, one the Milk River Canyon, uncorked, bursting forth seas, flooding south into the Missouri/Mississippi basins.

Glacial withdrawal to the northeast opened lower elevation drainages farther east. All along the sheet's receding walls proglacial lakes formed. When the containments farther northwest overswelled, water erupted outward in nearly spasmodic deluges downward, usually to the southeast, along the retiring face of the Laurentide Ice Sheet. Like opened liftlocks, out flooded monstrous outpourings, forming new ephemeral lakes—gigantic proglacial lakes such as Lake McConnell and Lake Agassiz. Today's Great Bear Lake, Great Slave Lake, Lake Athabasca, Lake Winnipeg and the Great Lakes are leftover puddles from these freshwater giants.

The Laurentide Ice Sheet's final stand was back at the dome. When that collapsed, divided in two, the Hudson Bay Lowlands flooded, becoming a gargantuan meltwater sea called the Tyrrell Sea, many times larger than its modern relic, Hudson Bay. This opened drainage to the Atlantic. Lands farther northwest could now empty up the Mackenzie River into the Arctic Ocean. Writhing, frigid fever gone, the Ice King quieted, then died. The retreat lasted about 10 millennia, from 18,000 years BP to 8,000 years BP. Alberta was virtually ice free by the beginning of the Holocene. Except at highest altitudes in the coldest Cordilleran regions, glaciation surrendered up Alberta to the sun and life.

LIFE'S RETURN

Each drainage shift in this dynamic watery world provided new freshwater highways for aquatic life. Waterways along the length of the Laurentide's retreating face connected the living southeast (south of the present-day Great Lakes) to the barren northwest. Each drainage change—first south into the Missouri and Mississippian systems, then east through what are now the Great Lakes, then later through Hudson Bay and north to the Arctic—opened ways for aquatic life to venture into new waters. Fishes and their fellows fought against the flood, driving upstream to occupy the northwest. In this diaspora, tribes of aquatic life pioneered and settled Alberta.

Sixty millennia of glacial activity ravaged the underlying land. The hammer and chisel of ice sculpted new visages. Glaciers gouged and meltwater rivers incised precipitous valleys throughout the Cordilleran plateaux, pointing the peaks and sharpening the horns of the Rockies. Floodwater drainages cut deeply and widely into the plains, today's river valleys and coulees. Everywhere lay glacial litter—eskers, erratics, gravels, tills, sands, loess and flour—a mineral junkyard.

With hurricane force, postglacial windstorms howled through the dissipated land, turning day to night, blasting earth's unprotected surface with loess and sand. When they came, rains were torrential and the runoff, having little to hold it, knifed through unconsolidated litter, carrying ice's grindings away. Downstream, as waters slowed, minerals settled out, forming alluvial fans and plains. Wind and water now scrubbed and scoured Earth's face. It was a harsh, barren, lonely land.

After the flood, the sodden land consolidated and dried, readying itself. Some glacial deposits and recently drained lake beds, protosoils, provided a medium for terrestrial life. Plants pioneered, led first by those reliant on the wind to cast their seed. Southwesterlies carried their germ to the northeast, setting them back to Earth for Alberta's greening. Sometimes tundra dwellers—moss campion, blueberries, crowberries and the willow—leapt to the advance. Other times plants typical of a boreal forest, spruce and poplar, ventured forth first.

Those having valuable nitrogen-fixing characteristics—avens, dryads and alder—enriched the soil for more particular homesteaders yet to come. Juniper, buffaloberry and wolfwillow hungrily followed in repossessing the land. This melange differed from that broad north-south ecosystemic spectrum we now see—tundra, then boreal forest, parkland and grasslands. Thousands of years would be required to establish those biomes, a rainbow of relative stability and dynamic harmony that characterized Alberta until last century.

Plant life, the bottom rung of the food chain, formed the first terrestrial successions. Then animate life filed from Noah's ark—grazers, browsers and their predators. Snakes slithered and frogs hopped back from nunataks, refugia and the south. Birds flapped and fluttered in. On wing with them came insects in their many kinds. A wild biological medley retook the land.

Separated by glaciation, populations of some species evolved unique characteristics. It seems in the west flickers became red-shafted; their eastern counterpart, yellow-shafted. Ice may have divided the myrtle from the Audubon subspecies of yellow rumped warblers and the slate-coloured from the Oregon subspecies of dark-eyed juncos. Northern shrikes and bohemian waxwings, having survived glaciation in Beringia or Siberian refugia, rejoined their southeastern cousins, the loggerhead shrike and cedar waxwings, over former ranges. Other geographically distinctive species or subspecies now resided side by side, sometimes hybridizing.[5]

Even while ice reigned, new species from the Old World found their way down Alberta's ice-free corridor, an icy-walled valley that lured life from cold to warmth, from subsistence to plenty.[6] Some Eurasian and Beringian emigres—the modern moose, elk (wapiti), wolf and grizzly bear—arrived near glaciation's end. Others crossed during Beringia's earlier levitations. These joined in with native North American species and South American life (which ventured north after the Americas' terrestrial union several million years earlier) to form a profound diversity. Among these were the most spectacular and unusual large animals, creatures from the imagination of Dr. Seuss. But the return was not merely of species. It was a restoration of this most miraculous empire, life. Life changed the land and land changed life so that neither was the same and both were better. This epochal springtime was celebrated by a stupendous efflorescence.

TRIUMPHANT LIFE

Woolly mammoths survived the icy seige in Beringia and along glaciation's southern margins. Adapted to cold climates, they lived in proximity to the ice sheets on tundra-like lands. Well-furred with long outer hair and cosy compact fine inner wool, protectively insulated with fat and having smaller extremities than most elephantines, inhospitable extremes were quite to their liking. About 2.7 m high at the shoulder, they were the largest tundra mammals. They fed on the sparse herbs and shrubs characteristic of dry, cold ecosystems, using their trunk and tusks to scrape for low browse. With glaciation's retreat, a vast area of habitat opened to these large herbivores—tundra and boreal forest enough for droves of these reddish-brown animals.

South of the ice cap another mammoth persevered. This was the larger imperial mammoth, some 3.5 m high at the shoulder. Unlike its tundra-loving cousin, it grazed the steppes and browsed the forest. Like its woolly cousin, the imperial mammoth followed its favoured biomes north as they advanced into the Laurentide vacuum. Its size and demeanour suggest the African elephant of today, emperor of the plains and newly forested lands.

Though more common in eastern North America, the American mastodon also inhabited postglacial Alberta. Similar in size and appearance to the woolly mammoth, mastodons represent the earlier evolved elephantine family *Mammut*. Different in habits from mammoths, they occupied distinctive niches, browsing forests, primarily spruce but nearly any conifer would do; again a herbivore niche scarcely occupied today.

Life was large and luxuriant. Some creatures appeared nearly familiar, others exotic and bizarre. Family packs of peccaries, each animal the size of a modern Eurasian wild boar, foraged, grubbed and snorted through nearly all of early Alberta. Bear-sized giant beaver padded the early woods and paddled their waterways. With gigantic gnawing incisors but lacking the flattened tail, this mega-beaver pursued a more terrestrial lifestyle than our modest, modern beaver and in those ways was more like our muskrat.

Three species of ground sloth lumbered about Alberta after the flood. The Shasta ground sloth, a large creature weighing up to 180 kg, furrowed for roots and browsed shrubs, eating berries and seeds on plains and open forests. It was stunted compared with the giant ground sloth. Nearly Volkswagen-sized, this mammal foraged the woods, not arboreally as modern sloths do, but with powerful hind legs firmly planted on the ground and grasping foreclaws shaking and ripping boughs from trees. A large kind of llama might have come to Alberta. Wide-ranging migratory herds of dromedary-like camels traversed the new land. The western camel and another giant camel did as well. And bighorn sheep were bigger.

Rolling herds of giant bison animated the landscape. Bodies were larger and horns longer than today's magnificent and intimidating animals. Oversized stag-moose and other equally large cervids dwelt in woods and muskeg. These monster deer competed with our more moderate modern mule deer.

Deeper yet in the forest, also browsing, hid the furtive shrub ox and the snorting, stomping and stinking wood muskox.

Alongside this parade of giants trailed humbler life forms. One among several species in the unique American line of antelopes, the four-horned antelope dashed about the grasslands. That shrunken family is now represented by only one species, the pronghorn. Five species of horses trotted the plains. The Mexican wild ass was common.

Splendid carnivores pursued this menagerie of herbivores. The dire wolf, a ferocious animal with a larger body and far more powerful jaws than today's grey wolf, was the paramount canid. Recently arrived from Asia via Beringia, the grey wolf might have competed directly with the dire wolf, perhaps ultimately winning. Smaller canids included American jackals.

The cat family, felids, was wildly more diverse. Cheetahs, in America? Yes! Some cat species were nearly mythical in features and scale. The scimitar cat, just smaller than a modern lion, attacked with its long canines. This specialized killer preyed on the very young and old of large animals. Larger again, with even longer canines, was the fabled sabretooth tiger—*Smilodon*. It too hunted the largest herbivores. Sword-like teeth pierced vulnerable organs, killing its prey by stabbing. Largest of all cats was the American lion. It weighed nearly twice as much as modern lions.

The most fearsome of all, the apex predator, was the giant short-faced bear. Moose-high on all fours, its long powerful legs were made to run, and run fast. A compact face, therefore its name, permitted broad powerful jaws to grasp, hold and crush nearly any prey. This cursorial hunter was a complete carnivore. Loping through open forests and plains, it tested herds of nearly any species for individuals with weakness, disease or inattention. Failure to pass its test resulted in rapid pursuit, capture and kill. Even in this land of giants, with its size, power and speed, most gave it way.

Life charmed this land 12,000 years ago. In the forests, meadows and tundra flowed a vibrant vital tide. Streams of antelope avoided rivers of gigantic, fearsome-looking bison. Beyond these eddied groupings of diminutive horses, tall camels and moose-size deer; mastodons stripped trees, their trunks grasping high, with young mimicking to the side. Browsing beyond might be several towering imperial mammoths and a giant sloth. Not far away, in faithful attendance, lay their predators.

From concealment, a sabretooth tiger schemed its attack on a mammoth calf frolicking in a nearby coppice of poplar. Resting dire wolves eyed herds of grazers looking for their next opportunity. Farther away, testing nearly every living thing, terrorizing all, coursed a giant short-faced bear. Giant hyenas awaited the bones. On columnar updraughts thousands of metres above the land—as high as the ice sheets once were—floated lazy condors and giant teratorns on five-metre wings, hungrily anticipating the scraps of this richness. There was a time, not long ago, when the land had everything it has today and far more; when wonderful life seized and populated it with a tropical intensity and fervour. With the tyrant king in defeat for the interglacial period (the next 10,000 to 30,000 years), it was a rich and exciting new age for Alberta.

CHAPTER 2

FIRST
PEOPLES

ADRIFT

A bout 200 million years ago, the supercontinent Pangaea broke up. Its pieces, the continents—Antarctica, Africa, the Americas, Australia and Eurasia—separated, drifting apart, sailing their own courses out into the single global ocean. With continental drift came biological drift. Plants and animals floated off atop their respective plates, disconnecting their common root, each tacking on toward its particular evolutionary destination. Stretches of water isolated the continents, insulating each one's terrestrial life forms from the others. As a result, each continent evolved its unique convention of complex, dynamic, interdependent life. Isolated in Africa and Eurasia were the lines that would evolve to *Homo sapiens sapiens*. But that would not last.

Early humans migrated out of Africa over the land bridge to the Middle East, until, as in Africa, they reached limits and had to innovate or emigrate. When emigrating, their technology, cultures, ambitions and dispositions moved with them. More potent replaced the more benign in a rough "red in tooth and claw" technological and cultural evolution. Itinerant biological baggage—dependent, domesticated or habituated species of disease, parasites, plants and animals—came along in what would become a rule of human migration; the export of exotics and the displacement and destruction of the indigenous.

Like the gigantic dome of ice centred over Hudson Bay during the Wisconsinan, the Middle East became humanity's great dome on Earth, a hub of trade and traffic. It too pressed many out and away; waves of people flowed to distant lands and inhospitable climes. Some went northwest to Europe and on to the Atlantic. Others went to the Far East, then southeast until reaching insular seas protecting Australia, or northeast to hit the Bering Sea or Beringia and its barricade of ice. Natural impediments at land's end—oceans of water and continents of ice—blocked further migration.

Technology and changing natural conditions, boats and Beringia, finally enabled mankind to breach the barriers and vault the abyss, Pangaea's seams, to Australia, the New World and more.

COMMUNITY

All species have their associated communities: predators, parasites, symbionts, commensuralists or mutualists. Humans do as well. When hominid populations were small, dispersed and disconnected, this related stream of life also was. As *Homo sapiens sapiens* became keystone, common and continuous, its biological community shared its success. Agriculture helped. Farming introduced exotic plant species, crops, to lands taken from the wild. Husbandry introduced exotic animal species, domesticated animals such as sheep, cattle, pigs, goats, chickens, dogs and cats to non-arable lands. Rodents joined the entourage. Ever since and nearly everywhere, rats and mice nest aside humans. The English sparrow and common starlings among others, hitched their genetic fortunes to the rising human star. Insects adopted similar strategies. Silverfish and roaches, fleas, lice and motley assortment of others joined the host. Those nurtured species and opportunistic others, weeds, pests and a rich microscopic world of parasites and pathogens, gathered in human-dependent biomes. Smallpox is one disease particularly important to this story.

Each human migration brought with it, in baggage and tow, these enlarging biological communities. All constellated around the emerging biological superstar, to share his destiny in suffusing the planet. The ultimate generalist and opportunist, humans migrated to and exploited nearly every habitat on Earth. The more "civilized" man became, it seems, the more biological baggage he carried with him. First Americans carried little of this baggage with them.

FIRST ALBERTANS

Possibly they were fleeing: escaping hunger, cold, natural disaster or hostilities. Along with their few physical possessions—weapons, clothing, moveable shelter and food preparation pieces—they brought tool making and survival techniques, their culture, language and religion. In all things they travelled lightly.

Or it may have been different. Not in flight, they may have followed prosperity, one that seduced them from valley to valley, or meadow to meadow with an increasing natural abundance. Following herds of grazers, flights of fowl or the ripening of berries, they came to new lands. Whichever way, with the retreat of ice, a new species advanced into the Americas. Humans certainly inhabited the subarctic Americas by 11,500 years BP, the beginning of the so-called Clovis culture and likely much earlier.[1]

Some studies suggest at least three separate migrations before the European influx.[2] The last, occurring some 4,000 to 6,000 years ago, was the Aleutian or Inuit people, the people of the north. The middle migration was of the Na-Dene or Athapaskans, a people who arrived in the Americas well after glacial retreat. Today they live in northwestern Canada and, disjunctively, in several regions of the American Southwest. It appears they originated from central Asia. The earliest migration was of the Amerinds, the probable human discoverers of America. They explored and occupied all of South and Central America, nearly all of eastern North America and most of western North America below the Canadian Shield. In their time they evolved the most diversified cultures and traditions; elaborate civilizations like those of Africa and Eurasia.

Beringia was a likely migration route for large terrestrial mammals until 15,500 years BP, when the Bering Sea breached the Beringian bridge. If satisfactory for prey, it sufficed for predators. First Americans likely crossed Beringia and, when glacial retreat permitted and corridors allowed they followed open land south onto the continental body. This corridor's narrows may have led through Alberta and opened into a commodious fan. If so, Alberta was the gateway to a paradise, swarming with magnificent creatures. Ice-weary Beringian travelers might have lurched on first seeing, feeling, touching and tasting mature, ample America. It was a wonder, a vision of plenty.

Little evidence remains of these first travellers, but about 11,500 years ago, things changed. Sophisticated methods of finishing stone spear points appeared. By fluting a spearhead's base, the stone could be made thin enough to insert into the split-end of a wooden spear shaft and bound in place. Secured, the point became a structural part of the spear and a far more effective hunting instrument. "Clovis technology," often found with mammoth kills, gave clear advantage in killing large mammals. Then Americas' archaeological record sprang to life, evidence abounding of the human presence. Shortly after, many large mammals vanished.

QUATERNARY EXTINCTIONS

After the last ice age, mega-faunal life seized those formerly glaciated lands, populating the north widely and diversely. Over the succeeding several thousand years large life collapsed and many species disappeared. Extinctions appear generally to increase after the end of any glaciation, but this event was unusual.[3] Some 35 to 40 species of large mammals went extinct while only about five species of small mammals did. The top was lopped off the trophic hierarchy. Somehow the king of beasts was toppled. Circumstances more extraordinary than a mere ice age were required to eliminate these Pleistocene behemoths.

In the "why?" debate, theories stretch from human to environmental causes. Those advocating environmental causes argue that extreme climatological, atmospheric chemistry change or cataclysmic events disrupted the fragile circumstances for large life forms.[4] Species responded by die-off. Others argue the "human hypothesis" or the "human overkill" theories—that, directly for some and indirectly for others, human beings played a determinative role.

Clearly humans witnessed the extinction event. Not only had they occupied all of the Americas by that time, their density of population was increasing. With clovis technology, humans had new and improved means for hunting large mammals. Whether for food, defence or elimination of competitors, they had motives. The introduction of a new top-level predator to any ecosystem has significant consequences; humans as the highest, have the most consequences.

Early Americans hunted mammoths and mastodons until they became extinct less than 11,000 years BP. Ground sloths and giant beaver may have been an easy kill, but for what purpose? Extinct members of the deer family were food. Undoubtedly tasty, hunting pressure by itself may not have sufficed to eliminate the savvy and prolific giant peccary. Llama, camel, horse, shrub ox and wood muskox, all extinct, were less savoury. In all, 12 genera of grazers and browsers went extinct in this end of Pleistocene event. Off to oblivion went the several species of mammoth, the mastodon, some species of deer and horses, antelope, camel and llamas, the beavers, peccary and sloths and other giant vegetarians of North America.

Predator extinctions are more complex. The largest most fearsome predators disappeared. Nature's economy dictates that large populations of prey are required to sustain her few predators. If a narrowly specialized predator's prey goes extinct, the predator soon follows. Sabretooth tigers might not have survived without mammoths or they might have died off for other reasons, whether anthropogenic, environmental or both.

Human rewards from hunting predators are more remote than hunting herbivores—elimination of competition or security enhancement rather than feast. A giant short-faced bear in one's neighbourhood would be distracting. Before long humans and bear would be stalking each other. And puny humans, with organization, numbers and weapons, were enough to dispatch the terrifying bear. Then, as it is now, humans routinely eliminated competing predators. Off to the unrelenting past went several members of

14

the cat family (the American lion, the cheetah and the sabretooth tiger), dire wolves and giant short-faced bears. Consistently, it was the larger birds, predators and scavengers that accompanied them into extinction during this period—condors, teratorns, eagles and vultures.

If first Americans arrived via Beringia at its submergence, they departed a land where animals were regularly hunted by bipeds using weapons, to arrive in a land full of unwary, unconditioned yet bizarrely rich wildlife. If, at the same time, technological improvements enabled them to better hunt and kill the largest of mammals, first New World exploitations would have been prodigiously fruitful and ridiculously easy; as easy as bludgeoning dodo birds or the great auk.

Some see parallels between human arrivals in the Americas and in other new lands. In those places that maintain mega-faunal diversity alongside evolving humans (Africa and Eurasia), humans co-evolved with large mammals and, it is reasoned, each developed survival strategies conditioned to the other. Not so for lands where humans—a new, powerful, adaptive predator—thrust themselves on unprepared and unresponsive wildlife. Shortly after man came to Australia and the large islands, many large mammals went extinct.[5] American moose, grey wolf, grizzly bear, bison, elk, caribou, deer, muskox, bighorn sheep and mountain goat, all were Eurasian emigre mammals that had co-evolutionary experience with hunting hominids. With that Old World experience (at the genetic level) appropriate predispositions for fight, flight and stealth might have enabled those species to withstand humans in the New World.

One theory is that human populations increased after the end of the ice age, perhaps reflecting the short-term surfeit from their primordial hunt. As faunal decline turned to extinction, first people's abundance ground down, perhaps convulsing into their own decline. It appears that human populations contracted at the episode's end so that a shrunken human population then shifted dependency to smaller game and gathering.

It was substantially over by the beginning of the Holocene. Some species survived for another millennium.[6] Thereafter, at least until the arrival of Europeans some 9,000 years later, few North American species went extinct. Causes of the Quaternary extinction episode may never be definitively known. While there is no smoking gun, a suspect clovis-tipped spear lies close by some casualties. With the episode over, healing and harmony began.

HARMONY AND INTERLUDE

Malinkovitch tells us the sun's power hit its cyclical high 10,000 years BP. Inertial features, cool glaciers and wet proglacial conditions, retarded the heating of the land to its maximum until about 7,500 years ago when Alberta's climate reached its warmest. Temperatures during the period from about 8,500 years BP to 5,000 years BP, the Hypsithermal, averaged several degrees higher than today. Land dried. Prairie grasses advanced to higher latitudes and altitudes, driving treelines higher up the mountainside and farther north. Populations of many creatures, including bison and humans, thinned in response to the new limiting conditions. Drought has its own destructive ways.

BISON ADAPTATION

Bison migrated from Asia to America several times. Some earlier migrants possessed great size, monstrous straight horns and slower maturation. Smaller size, curved horns and early sexual maturity mark recent bison. How did the changes occur? Some prefer the idea of rapid evolution within one species. Others claim this to be the result of competition between several species that migrated from Eurasia of which only one survived. The one-species proponents point to the archaeological record, observing that it has yet to reveal any two bison species co-resident in America at one time. If there was only one species in the Americas since the end of glaciation (the one-species thesis), its evolutionary transformation, from what was known as *Bison priscus* to *Bison bison*, was rapid. Archaeology suggests anthropogenic influences; men *most* altered the evolutionary course of bison.

Bison were at the centre of culture and economy for plains peoples. As the source of most important materials—food, clothing, shelter—the bison's welfare was theirs also. As bison moved and migrated so did the people. In the "dog days" (before the introduction of horses, when dogs pulled travois), the hunt required extreme stealth or ambush to kill the great animals. Spearing demands very close proximity. Technological evolution empowered greater kill numbers, often mass kills—drives to natural traps, constructed pounds and over jumps. Later, bow and arrows permitted killing at even greater distances.[7] Mass means of harvest created new predator benefits and new prey costs.

In buffalo jump digs, archaeologists found average ages of bison to be considerably younger than expected. That suggests high rates of mortality in the general population. The hypothesis is this: regular mass harvesting of herd animals over the long term tends to select for reproduction those who reproduce younger. The sooner the bison sexually matures and breeds, the more likely it is to reproduce. Earlier sexual maturity also tends to result in reduced adult body size. The fossil record indicates that bison of

16

recent times are significantly smaller than earlier animals and reproduce one year earlier. Long term, hunting shrank the bison.[8]

With time, predator/prey relationships change both predator and prey. The habits and practice of the buffalo shaped human culture; humans, as with all regular and consistent predators, shaped the bison's body and culture. Sometimes their relationship was nearly pastoralist. When it went well for the bison, it went well for the bison people. Generally, it went well for both for many thousands of years.

OTHER EFFECTS

Human predation affected other prey species—elk, deer, moose. Range management and modification altered wildlife species mix and numbers. Like bison people, others engaged in near pastoralist relationships with chosen game animals, enhancing habitat through use of fire or promotion of select vegetation. Fire served several purposes: to stop animal movements, to limit forest advance, to promote early successional plant species preferred by grazers and otherwise modify vegetative regimes.[9] Fire had few long-term effects.

Evidence also exists of opportunistic feeding on waterfowl and other birds in old Alberta. Gathering eggs, capturing fledglings and hunting had only local effect. Similarly, fishing played a secondary role in many early cultures so pressure was modest. Agriculture, so important to the civilizations of South and Central America, did not reach Alberta before White people. Gathering of fruits, seeds and bulbs occurred regularly but not on a large scale or with the intrusiveness of horticultural practices. Consumption was generally sustainable and the footprint left from thousands of years of aboriginal occupation was small.

Early Americans brought man's best friend, the domestic dog, from Eurasia. Dog remains were unearthed at Old Crow in the Yukon (probable date 20,000 years BP).[10] Did man adopt dog or dog adopt man, a kind of turncoat wolf? Whichever way, the dog was one of many creatures to desert the wild to team up with man. Millennia later, a profusion of exotics would descend on the Americas, following in the domestic dog's pioneering tracks.

Technological advances—changes in hunting, tools and techniques—increased the scale of the bison hunt from that of isolated individual kills for local use to more organized, mass kills (pounds, traps and jumps). Product-preservation technology—pemmican—enabled trade into distant markets, through well-established networks in which bison based trade products were exchanged for flint, chert, obsidian, sea shells and other goods. Even then, markets exerted modest but growing influence over local biology and culture, reshaping human/wildlife relationships. These influences began the bison's metamorphosis from another life form to a mere trade product. As well, these refinements in hunting and food preparation permitted increases in per capita consumption, well-being and populations.

Notions of early Americans living in "smothering ignorance, cloistered by fear to their own tribal campfires" are wrong. Aboriginal people had a growing sense of their world. They knew of lands and peoples far beyond their own. Pre-contact tourism saw plains people going to the coast and down the Mississippi. Plains people drafted maps, relied on by early White explorers, that showed the Pacific Ocean. While life had risks, it had abundance, meaning and rewards. People commonly enjoyed large, long and healthy lives strongly connected to their land, people and metaphysics.[11] And each baby had the hope for as good a future as his parents. That held true for over 400 generations. But it was not to be forever. There were distant rumblings.

DISTANT RUMBLINGS

BIFURCATION

W hen the sea swamped and resubmerged Beringia about 15,5000 years ago, the Old and New World disconnected, leaving each to their own biological, human and technological destinies. But that would not last. Over following millennia sailing and other technology progressed in the Old World enough to enable an adventurous few, begining about 1,000 years ago, to sail over the "seams of Pangaea" to the New World.

Most famous was Christopher Columbus. Queen Isabella of Castille and King Ferdinand of Aragon entered a *capitulacion* with Columbus on April 17, 1492, authorizing and financing the Columbian venture. The hope in sailing west was to find the riches of the East and, once there, to claim this unknown vastness for God and King and capital. Columbus cast off on August 3, 1492, sighting the Americas on October 12. This found-land he claimed for Ferdinand, Isabella, God and himself. By Papal Bull proclaimed May 4, 1493, mere months after Columbus' return, Pope Alexander VI of the Borgias divided those parts of Earth not yet possessed by Christian princes in two. Spain got the Americas (except undiscovered Brazil) and Portugal got the Far East (except the Philippines).

Spain and Portugal modified aspects of the Papal Bull in the Treaty of Tordesillas, 1494. Based on the flimsiest contact and the shallowest knowledge—shore landing and walkabouts—two continents, all of their life and peoples, were inserted into portfolios of one church, two countries, several kings and a number of commercial venturers.

NORTHWEST PASSAGE

England's King Henry VII declined on the Columbus prospectus, but he was not about to miss the next big opportunity to trade into the Orient. To borrow current commercial mantras, he was interested in "globalization"

and "international trade" and in doing "Pacific Rim business." Others—
English elites of the church, nobility and commerce alike—wanted to open
the Oriental door. They selected John Cabot, a Venetian, to find the way to
spices, gold, and other eastern riches.

Henry VII's patent to Cabot captured the spirit of the age and the
purpose of the endeavour in this language:

> . . . to seeke out, discover, and finde whatsoever isles, countreys,
> regions or provinces of the heathen and infidels whatsoever
> they be, and in what part of the world soever they be, which
> before this time have bene unknowen to all Christians . . .

and to:

> . . . subdue, occupy and possesse all such townes, cities, cas-
> tles and isles of them found, which they can subdue, occupy
> and possesse, as our vassals, and lieutenants, getting unto us
> the rule, title, and jurisdiction of the same villages, townes,
> castles, and firme land so found.

For this, Cabot could govern whatever lands he found and maintain its
trade as a monopoly subject to a 20% Crown tax.

On May 2, 1497 John Cabot sailed out of Bristol to the Americas,
making land on June 24, perhaps Newfoundland or Labrador. With bargain secured and lands claimed, not really that intrepid an explorer, Cabot
soon came about. Several weeks later he was celebrating in England. Cabot
felt he had neared Japan and the riches of the Orient and like Columbus,
he died believing that. Later voyages by others confirmed fears that this land-
fall to the west was not the rich Orient but a forbidding barricade—the impenetrable and hostile Americas.

Henry Hudson thought he sailed into the westerly sea in 1610. Rap-
ture flip-flopped to dismay as the bend of bay came clear. This was no
passage to the Orient. The body of water was an enormous inland sea—the
immense puddle remaining from the retreat of the Laurentide Ice Sheet.
This giant bay took Hudson's life, dying there after a mutinous crew cast him
adrift, and his name. Later the Hudson's Bay Company, the longest surviving
example of the overseas trading company, took this bay's name for its own.

Others continued sailing west, seeking the Northwest Passage and its
avenue to fortune. Some of those who landed in these parts commented on
the quality of fur-bearing animals, particularly the beaver. As fortune would
favour or curse it, the beaver possessed uniquely structured inner hair. Hatters
were mad about it as a base for the felt-like material required in the
manufacture of trendy hats. With such desirable features demand soon outran

supply, driving the European beaver to commercial extinction. Then it was on to the New World. The beaver purge passed first over the Saint Lawrence Lowlands then progressed upstream to the Great Lakes. Reports (Radisson and Groseilliers) that Hudson Bay drainages teemed with the most luxuriant beaver stirred interest among armchair aristocratic adventurers lounging about the Stuart monarchy in England. Might a New World beaver business have potential?

GRANTS, LAND AND MONOPOLY

King Charles II, Prince Rupert, the Duke of Cumberland, the Earl of Holderness and other elites in the umbra of Stuart power wished to make something of England's claims to the New World's north. The potential profit from furs, precious metals and Northwest Passages persuaded them to undertake a commercial sortie into Hudson Bay. Launched in 1668, their hired hands returned in 1669 laden with furs and experience. If suitable long-term business commitments could be arranged then a continued commercial venture into Hudson Bay might be feasible. That would involve the usual mix—a grant, a monopoly, a corporation and the participation of those closest to commercial and imperial power.

For close friends, relatives and supporters (and perhaps his personal account), on May 2, 1670 Charles II chartered a body corporate, "The Governor and Company of Adventurers of England tradeing into Hudson's Bay" (HBC) providing it with a grant of power and land of unknown but certainly gigantic proportions. The grant was of the "sole Trade and Commerce" over vast tracts of land "that are not already actually possessed by the Subjectes of any othere Christian Prince or State." Most of the grant, lands draining into Hudson Bay, well over two million square kilometres of lands, were named "Rupert's Land" after the warrior Prince, Prince Rupert— friend, relative, HBC founder and generic supporter of Charles II. With this, the company represented the "true and Absolute Lordes and Proprietors of the same territory and Lymit . . . Saving always the faith Allegiance and Soveraigne Dominion due to" the monarchy.

The Crown summarily dealt to its cronies nearly half a continent, one known, occupied and used by first Americans for over 10,000 years. For what? The only direct rent payable was "two Elkes and two Black beavers whensoever and as often as Wee our heires and successors shall happen to enter into the said Countryes Territoryes and Regions hereby granted." During the 200 years of HBC monopoly (1670 to 1870) no rent was paid because the Crown never visited the granted lands. Neither did the adventurous governors of HBC.

Straightaway the Hudson's Bay Company set to trade beaver with Native people. Aboriginal traders may have puzzled at the wondrous gullibility of Europeans. They travelled great distances under adverse conditions to exchange such useful things as iron axe heads, needles, cooking ware, guns and ammunition for the fur of the plentiful beaver. Laughter might have echoed around the bay on finding Europeans trade these for rodent hair to be pressed into strange shaped, decorative hats. Compared with the marvel and utility of Iron Age technology, furs of the plentiful beaver were as trinkets.

For its first 100 years the company sat on the bay, luring willing Native people down the rivers from lands farther and farther distant, loaded with a winter's work of furs to trade. Aboriginal ways seemed to continue as they hunted, trapped and traded—it's just that the technology had changed and they now laboured at it with higher technology, seeking the yield of international trade. Vassalage to the fur industry became the way of life, whether trapping and shooting with iron age tools for foreign markets, transporting the product down to the edge of the bay, or marketing and trading with these apparent friendly fools from Europe. Did they know the culture-shaping, potentially culture-destroying, consequences of technology and trade? Relationships with other creatures, the land, their gods, culture, economy and selves, all would change.

1730, RUMBLINGS CLOSE BY

Passed from trader to middleman to hunter, whispers from out of the south and down from the northeast told of White people, how they were coming to Alberta and of their power. Early products of their iron technology— pots, pans, trade goods made of nearly indestructible materials never before seen—obtained from Native middlemen traders, confirmed these tales, sparking the charm and intrigue. Mechanical manifestations arrived from the northeast, guns and goods. About the same time, 1730, biological émigrés, horses and smallpox, moved into Alberta from the south. It would take another 25 years for Europe's first emissary to reach Alberta and almost 150 years before White people, by direct hand and numbers, would have substantial physical impact on the land but the European envelope was now open. Escaping from it were their paradigms, powers, technology, appetites and biomes. Even before their arrival White credentials were presented: cold power, indestructible products, invisible creeping death and marvelous technology with the power of evil or benefice.

After an absence of 9,000 years, the horse returned to America, becoming a powerful, socially formative technology. Horsepower altered many things in the human camp—areas that could be exploited increased six fold;

social groups enlarged; wealth in horses promoted class differentiation; patterns of trade and theft changed; conflict over land and resources increased and with it, warfare.[1] Horses carried hunters to rich hunting grounds; they fleetly followed meandering herds of bison or quickly dispatched warriors to fight distant others. When herding bison to pounds or jumps and in the hunt itself, the hunter-horse unit enjoyed the never-before combined advantages of speed, security and endurance.

Guns came out of Hudson Bay by way of HBC inland traders. At the point of kill, the gun gave efficient, effective and remote service.[2] Guns and horses worked synergistically to multiply the powers of the hunter or warrior by a stupendous order. A large beast ridden by man, doing his bidding; the sorcery in man's hand-held stick, harder than stone, that killed distant life with thunder and smoke at the will of its holder: these combined powers—guns and horses all under a rider-man's dominion—conjured a nightmarish spectre for earlier people. How could foot bound man, woman, child or animal, defeat this ferocious apparatus?

Mysterious epidemics followed White people in the air wherever they went. Through scourges over thousands of years, Europeans developed wide immunity to these pathogens, but Americans had not. When passed to the New World, waves of disease spread through the original peoples. With immune systems unprepared, infection hit tribe-wide, ruthlessly eating individual and communal lives from within. Usually the introduction was unwitting, but not always.[3] In 1730, a plague crept up the Missouri River into Alberta. Carried by traders, this smallpox epidemic devastated nearly half those exposed to it. Raging through the Crowsnest Pass area of southern Alberta, it annihilated one clan, erasing them from being. But the envelope also held other subtler agents of construction and destruction. Some things promised advantage to Native people, some posed threat. For the land there was no good, only successions of disaster.

AND MOSES SENT THEM
TO SPY OUT THE LAND OF CANAAN[4]

Alberta's first White man slipped from the envelope a quarter of a century after these first manifestations. On September 11, 1754 near a now-place called Chauvin, Anthony Henday passed westward over a future survey line onto lands that would one day be designated Alberta. Some say he was the first white person to see it. Forces in England brought Henday to Alberta. HBC's monopoly and grant were under assault at home. Some demanded that HBC fulfil its mercantilist mandate: find the northwest trade route to the Orient; consolidate land claims; export British civilization, institutions and religion; expand the empire through exploration, conquest and exploitation; and defeat the westward-expanding French, posing competitive and imperial threats. To silence critics at home and protect its grant and monopoly, the HBC in the early 1750s cautiously authorized more western exploration. Some commercial intelligence might also help business. HBC wished to know more about the extent of other fur traders' incursions onto HBC lands; attitudes of western Native people to trade and commerce; conditions and productivity of lands and wildlife; and they wished to survey other profitable opportunities including possible overland trade routes to the Pacific and the Orient. Henday, a HBC York Factory employee and former smuggler, volunteered to undertake this reconnaissance as a paying and guided guest of a party of Assiniboines.

History talks of Henday befriending the Native people. Here "befriending" means to smile at them, assess what they have to take or trade, calculate their worth alive or dead, and smoke pipes. Native Albertans made similar calculations concerning risks and rewards in dealing with White people, but their position was one of fundamental weakness. White ambitions were unknown to them.

The honouring of Henday contains coded meanings to many recent Albertans. He marks the advent of purpose for Alberta—all before was mere nature, perhaps just a preparatory mechanical unfolding. All after was development and improvement, the beginning of civilization and the end of savagery. Henday foreshadowed civilization, enlightenment, technology, development and progress—in short, the goodness claimed in justification for the newcomers. He was the sign that these things would bless a barren land, the land and people of *terra nullius*. Some see it differently. This, they say, was the lead ripple in a sequence of waves of itinerant exploiters coming to take from the land whatever the market's appetite demanded, to export it, to enrich themselves and then move on, leaving behind a hollowing land.

ON THE WESTERN FRONT (1754-1821)

Scarcely a trickle of White people followed Henday west over the following decades. Comfortable where they were, HBC persevered in their 100-year-old credo—sit close to the bay, trade with Native people and invite no trouble. The beaver was now gone from the Hudson Bay Lowlands; extirpation ballooned out north and west. Lengthening trading and supply routes snaked up major rivers, the only effective means for inland transportation. Pressure mounted to send HBC traders where the business was, up these rivers, west and north. More White people came, some from HBC, some from elsewhere.

Delegations of deadly disease canoed up the river with traders. This companion to White trade regularly halved the numbers of Native people (1730 and 1780 were two major 18th century epidemics). As populations reached pre-plague highs, new, devastating contagions visited, leaving families parentless, or childless—stealing the heart, the soul, the mind or the future of the clan. Bearspaw oral traditions claim they fled west to escape smallpox. Ultimately they had no place to hide.

Where smallpox left off, another spirit in the envelope, alcohol, took up. Booze possessed marvellous effects for its vendor. First, it was addictive. Without cultural resistance to it (or perhaps physiological adaptation), some Native people craved it, exchanging things of great value for it. Second, it compromised the judgment of those under its influence. The intoxicated made disadvantageous deals. A third less immediate but more pervasive effect was the way it strengthened the dealer's relative position at future bargaining tables. It broke down social and family structures, respect and judgment disintegrated, connection with the past and commitment to the future evaporated with this "marvelous" trade good. Desperate people take desperate positions, easily abandoned, to the negotiating table. The level playing field fictionalized in trade theory became distinctly tipsy with drugs. The trade table wobbled unconscionably in the drug dealer's favour.[5]

Who took advantage of alcohol? Nearly everyone trading for White people. English said the French first traded liquor. In 1755 Henday records this as the French advantage. English and French agree that American free-traders were the worst. Native people say, "White people brought it." Benefits went to the newcomers and Native people suffered the burdens. Liquor brewed-in with rapid technological change, starvation, epidemics and threat by an external enemy, to concoct a blend of wicked social devastation. Some White people claimed the resulting collapse of culture as evidence that Native people could not care for themselves.

For the moment, the land fared better than the people. Fortunately, trade focused only on those few species European markets demanded. But greater competition in the fur industry lured increasing numbers of traders and trappers west. Distance made supplying westward-ranging traders out of Montreal or London too costly, so local supply strategies became necessary. Demand for bison and pemmican increased.

Metis and Native people, primarily the independent Blackfoot Confederacy, took up provisioning the fur trade. Seeing an opportunity to increase business, HBC promoted a small trade in bison robes. That appetite would grow. One trade (fur) created the demand for another (meat) that pioneered yet a third (robes). Western diversification started on the backs of the bison. Other American traders probed farther west and north, seeking new fur lands. Spanish from the south and Russians from the north claimed rights along the west coast. These Eurasian imperial competitors roused proto-Canadians from their slumber, hastening their westward expansion, driving them to grab lands and trade before others did. Increasingly, Montreal traders collaborated among themselves, trying to survive the cutthroat fur trade. During the winter of 1783-4, these Canadiens formalized a partnership called the North West Company (NWC). Scots and French, founders of the NWC, needed to settle on common strategies to compete with HBC and the freebooting American traders coming up the Missouri River.

Initially unresponsive, HBC finally fought back as business, profit and patience ebbed. By 1792 both NWC and HBC had trading posts in Alberta. HBC and NWC's war lasted more than 35 years, from before 1784 to 1821. From the near-stasis of monopoly to the dynamic change of competition, suddenly Alberta was a land of opportunity for White people. Open for business, traders paddled in. During this trade war White populations mounted from tens to hundreds, fur-bearing wildlife plunged[6] and numbers of Native people oscillated between disease-lows and prosperity highs.

Now pelt-producers enjoyed choices. Instead of the unbudging single HBC traders of earlier days, a slough of solicitous pedlar-traders scrambled to give them top dollar for their furs. Aboriginal populations and living conditions fluxed spasmodically on their economic, cultural and demographic roller coaster. Fortunately for Native people (if this sorry tale can be called fortunate) furs had value and for that White people needed them on the land.

By 1820 competition had run its course. Together, HBC, NWC (including now XY Company), Astor's American Fur Trade Co., the independents, Spain and Russia, imperialists and capitalists, had grabbed nearly all the remaining unexploited lands in the northwest. Ill effects of competition reverberated throughout the land; populations of some fur-bearing mammals teetered close to extinction. The industry suffered a classic dose of excess capacity in the face of a plummeting resource. Dividends dropped, expenses increased; the costs of competition became clear. Amalgamation was proposed to re-monopolize the fur trade on Rupert's Land—HBC with NWC under the HBC banner. In 1821 Britain's Parliament blessed this arrangement by extending the HBC monopoly for a further 21 years and expanding the grant to include lands farther northwest.

Before European trade touched the lands, Native people were self-sufficient. At first, with White trade, furs came easy. Prosperity increased, but now the people of the land depended upon trade and related technology to maintain a hybridizing lifestyle. Despite human hubris, animals underwrote it all. Dependency was a powerful tool in bending Native people to European purposes. A highly placed HBC memo of May 22, 1822 describes the strategy:

> However repugnant it may be to our feelings, I am convinced they [Native people] must be ruled with a rod of Iron to bring and keep them in a proper state of subordination, and the most certain way to effect this is by letting them feel their dependence upon us . . . In the woods and northern barren grounds this measure ought to be pursued rigidly next year if they do not improve, and no credit, not so much as a load of ammunition, given them until they exhibit an inclination to renew their habits of industry. In the plains however this system will not do, as they can live independent of us, and by withholding ammunition, tobacco and spirits, the Staple articles of Trade, for one year, they will recover the use of their Bows and spears, and lose sight of their smoking and drinking habits; it will therefore be necessary to bring those Tribes round by mild and cautious measure which may soon be effected.[7]

These gentler measures—practised with drugs, cultural nihilation, starvation, and the creation and management of dependency—seem more civilized than the direct and brutal American and Spanish strategies of guns and blood, but were they?

PLANTING THE SEED

Pioneering horticulturalists planted large gardens in Edmonton as early as 1793. As the fur industry's demand for local food sources grew, so did cultivated acres. By the early 19th century Alberta had small-scale commercial agriculture. To the north, Peter Pond (1770) confirmed earlier tales (1716, Swan or Wa-Pa-Su) of black pitch oozing out of the ground in the Athabasca region. These surface expressions of the "tar sands" hinted at gigantic subterranean riches, portending a fossil fuel industry to come. It would be another century (1880) before agriculture took firm root in Alberta and 150 years before the petroleum industry gushed to life. Until then there were other resources to capture, exploit and export.

Ships now bridged Pangaea's seams. Transportation technology joined distant continents and introduced their insulated life forms to others. Eurasian creatures took the ocean cruise to the Americas—the European envelope ripped open. Apart from White people, the vessel held a range of organisms. Some, cultivars and domesticated animals, were intended for release. Uninvited others straggled along over time—species such as the house mouse and English sparrows. Recreational animals like cats, dogs and some birds came. All manner of Eurasian plants, the so-called noxious weeds, jumped onboard in Europe and once at their New World destination, jumped out. An opportunistic community of pathogens and diseases, virtually unknown in the unsuspecting Americas, slid down the envelope's sides. Once disembarked, these exotic contents still required European-style industry, community and context to live. The mouse needed a house, the sparrow eaves, the dandelion a disturbed field. With only a few exceptions, their invasion depended on more extensive White occupation. For the diseases, they preferred Native Americans.

European technology emerged from out of the envelope to empower the hunter. If Clovis technology was enough to dispatch the giant short-faced bear, what did smoothbore gun-toting, horse-mounted hunters do for the security of the bison? The power of the individual multiplied by orders of magnitude while the prospects for the prey diminished by the same factor. Ultimately, the Americas had little or no immunity to the diseases, drugs, markets or the technology of White people and their ways.

BISON BOUNTY

efore contact, 60 million bison grazed North America. Alberta was primary range for four million, hauntingly close to its present cow population. The plains and parklands surged with boister- ous bison. They wandered in swells, where a blanket of bison might swatch a hillock, then in blots swarm a valley, only to move on up a draw in an organic mass and cascade up over the top. Spilling out onto a grassy plateau, they might spread and placidly graze, until bison wisdom told them to move on. Not much later, a time came when the plains ech- oed hollow and melancholy—no bison, no wolf, no bear.

BISON

HBC men had little need for inland food sources while located on the bay and provisioned from London. Meanwhile aggressive Canadiens, NWC and westward-advancing U.S. free traders roused HBC with an inland chal- lenge. Retreating beaver beckoned all of them ever deeper into the wilds, ever farther from supplies. To follow required inland food sources. Of their few food alternatives, one option's providence was overwhelming. This manna was pemmican.

Pemmican is a nutritious, high-energy food made of processed lean bi- son meat. Dried lean jerky was pulverized and blended with liquid marrow fat in a leather bag weighing, when full, approximately 40 kilos. Berries, other fruits or herbs were added according to custom, season or taste. A concentrated food that carried and stored easily, pemmican was the perfect mainstay for long overland trips and nasty inland winters.

Initially, pemmican demand determined the size of the organized hunt. Until the 1820s, trade required only small hunts and the Metis Red River hunt easily addressed that market. Later, Americans streamed up the Mis- souri River with bison trading on their minds, challenging HBC interests on Alberta's high plains. To thwart American expansion, particularly on Blackfoot Confederacy lands, and to obtain a more westerly local supply, HBC repaired to the plains to take up the pemmican trade with the local Native people—the Blackfoot Confederacy, (Bloods, Blackfoot, Peigan) and Sarcee. But this market proved too modest for HBC ambitions. If new bison-based products could be found, they might replace the dwindling beaver fur trade, cement relationships with the plains people and secure the land.

During the 1860s, fashion-conscious consumers on America's eastern seaboard took a fancy to bison robes. Demand increased. New tanning technology also turned bison to highly desired leather for fashion, military and industrial applications. Fast-improving production technology—involving horses, guns, transportation and organization—more efficiently turned the bison to account. After the American civil war, breech-loading and repeating rifles travelled west to help kill in what was now becoming a gorge. Prices rose, costs fell.[1] Thousands of years of hunting—jumps, pounds, drives, stalks, camouflage and traps—seemed not to affect population numbers (just phenotypes) but the new tools of hunting and killing, rendering and production, transportation and marketing, changed all that.

Bison declined, then disappeared in the nimbus of White people's westward movement. In the U.S., extinction tracked railways west, opening bison lands to White people—to their markets and technology, consumptive appetites and productive means. Equipment and hunters paid passage down the line; the stiffening carnage of their orgy chugged back up the tracks. America's first transcontinental rail line, completed in 1869, cut the west and its bison into northern and southern herds. Following that, extinction zones billowed out north and south of the railway lines.[2] Farley Mowat speculated that:

> Between 1850 and 1885, more than 75 million buffalo hides had been handled by American dealers. Most were shipped east on the railroads, which had contributed heavily to the extinction both directly and indirectly.[3]

Rail chased the disappearing bison north to Montana by 1880, just in time to aid elimination in this last stronghold. Without railways Canada's death machine did not reach the same zany heights but the bison population suffered the same precipitous plunge.

In his famous western expedition during the late 1850s, John Palliser commented on diminishing herds. The orgy climaxed in the late '60s. By the early '70s, hunters ranged farther afield to find prey. The next decade was the mop-up operation, spent reducing to nothingness the fragmented remnants of this profound life force. Impetus demanded that the last few be killed.[4] Relentlessly, they were. With nearly no bison remaining in Alberta in March 1879, Canadians negotiated with Montana to hunt their remaining few. Those were soon snuffed out.

By debacle's end, two small populations and a few scattered individuals remained from 60 million. One, the wood bison of northern Alberta's boreal forests, was so remote and inaccessible it was either overlooked or too difficult to hunt by even the most rapacious of hunters. The other, a collection of plains bison, hunkered down in Yellowstone Park's sometimes safe haven. A few remaining stragglers were captured for enclosure.

On the bison grounds Metis and Native people often did the hunting and killing, the rendering and scraping, the transporting of robes to the trading post and then down the river or rail to market, activities that were contrary to the culture and tradition of Native people. John Foster argues that the Metis were not of this tradition, claiming that:

> In their behaviour the Metis heralded the future settler society not the past. The Metis of the 1870s in Alberta were the precursors of the consumerist, single-commodity, boom and bust economy of the 20th century West, especially in Alberta.[5]

Nearly everything about the business—the scale, purpose, tools and ethic—was White, and was duplicated with agonizing conformity in other European colonies and outposts around the world.

Those involved in the bison campaign in Alberta from 1830 to 1880, lived well for a time. Several months of deadly serious killing, the fall hunt and the spring hunt, took care of material needs, while snoozing, schmoozing and boozing occupied much of the rest. Traders and top-duck hunters worried about markets, free trade, prices, production costs, costs of labour but not the bison. For a few scintillating decades the hunt brought an aura of wealth and prosperity as the bison business flared brilliantly; then that too died.

BISON PEOPLE

Before Europeans, the bison, not trade, was essential to plains peoples. Plains Native people were one member in the large community of bison-dependant life. When the bison tribe moved on, the human tribe broke camp to do the same. It was their way of life and survival. They rejoiced over the bison in song and spirit. They needed little because the bison and the land cared for them. When they wanted things from others or had a surplus, they traded, but irregularly, on a discretionary basis and among near equals. Then came a fundamental discontinuity. People from far away arrived with new beliefs and tools, new ways of doing things and new ways to compel others to do their will. Compliance promised much; resistance held defeat, perhaps death. Trade expanded rapidly. Steel pots cannot harm a Stone Age man? Cloth and beads cannot kill a wild land? Little seemed to change, but everything did.

The bison changed. Before, the bison was a fellow creature, so bountiful and useful that it forged a way of life. The bison was the keystone species; humans a dependant. Waste was limited because takings were generally small and purposes right. Direct appetite limited the hunt. One could only eat so much pemmican and layer on so many robes.

With large-scale trade the bison became something else. It became a potential—a "resource"—a thing that became better as it reduced from living mammal to pemmican, leather and robes. Hunters had only to exchange such humble things as pieces of dead bison to obtain marvellous European goods. Like the philosopher's stone, trade's elixir transmuted the base to the precious. The bison metamorphosed into knives and pots and tobacco and liquor. Fastforwarded, this is more than metamorphosis. In the commercial sacrament, it becomes a transubstantiation—bison turned to whatever money could buy.

Native people changed. Before, they were hunters. The bison was hunted for what it could provide—meat, robes, tongue or hump. Appetite for bison slaked, the hunter rested; so did the bison. After contact, the Plains people harvested the bison as a trade product, something to be traded into something else—non-bison things. No longer did the hunter/harvester ask the bison to satisfy his bison needs. He asked it to satisfy his every appetite, his globalized needs. With trade's transubstantiation, enough dead bison could provide nearly anything in the world the hunter wanted. Never having enough White goods, suddenly there were never enough dead bison. All the world's bison could not satisfy this appetite. And they didn't.

Tribal structures changed. Whether through emulation or stipulation, the new bison-business people came to reflect the White trader's structures. HBC business practices brought imperial inclinations of hierarchy to the plains. Through presents and ritualized preliminaries, trading often became elite-building and power-enhancing events. Trading chiefs elevated, the rest reduced. "Chief to chief" dealings are efficient, the one binds the many and it protects the interests of elites, whether European or Native American, from the clamour of the commoners. And if Native elites ever became too strident or principled, with modest White manipulations one chief might be deflated and another inflated, in effect the manufacture of leaders. Flat tribal structures struggled with pyramidal HBC structures and lost.

Not just tribal leadership changed. With new trade-oriented cottage industries, tribal members had new things to do. Lower-downs in stratifying Native society became the working poor—scraping hides, rendering meat, making pemmican and preparing all manner of things for trade. Polygyny (long permitted in some Native people traditions) became a tool for acquisition. Prominent traders and hunters took on many wives to perform manufacturing functions. Dickason reports what must have been wrenching cultural effects on women of this new world of businessmen:

> Where Plains Indian women had usually married in their late teens, girls as young as 12 now did so; on the other hand, rarely could a man afford to buy a wife before he was in his mid-30s. As polygyny developed, so did a hierarchy among wives, with the senior wife usually directing the others.[6]

Along with their wives, great chiefs had many horses; hundreds, sometimes even thousands.[7] Status enhancing symbols of wealth and power, horses were used not only for transportation and hunting, but as a kind of currency and medium for wealth and property accumulation. Powerful chiefs on spirited horses draped themselves in magnificent costume and elegant attire. Again Dickason observes:

> Affluence was manifested in the size of tipis, which by the 1830s could be large enough to accommodate as many 100 persons.[8]

Conspicuous consumption became part of the new, improved Native society.[9]

Around the 1840s a fundamental shift occurred in the values of Alberta's Native people.[10] Before then, status depended not on material accumulations but social, cultural and spiritual distinction. With long exposure to White priorities and institutions, European attitudes invaded Native people's traditions. A materialistic consumer mentality blended into the potent potion that would cozen Native Americans of their culture and lands.

Trade splits production from consumption. Metis and aboriginals became producers. Eastern middle classes were consumers. In this disassociative state, both producer and consumer were glorified as goodness and progress. Few paid attention to likely future consequences. All relished the present bounty; it appeared that new technology, products, markets and trade worked a cultural miracle for Native people. In contemporary terms, employment increased, incomes rose, population increased, production multiplied, per capita consumption shot up and all was well. Nicer yet, cultural ways did not appear to change except everyone had more horses in their corral, lots more beadwork, and full liquor cabinets.

Then the bison died. And so did the bison people. By 1879 the bison was gone and the people of the Blackfoot Confederacy were starving in squalor. Haughty power and independence dissolved into piteous begging for any refuse or spoilage having food value. Out of this deliquescing present, a vicious and dismal future hardened. The bargain made, trade executed, benefits enjoyed, only now were the costs levied. Faust-like, those Native people who survived could claim, "Now I die eternally."

POST-CARNAGE BLUES

After the bloody tide, scavengers swept the plains and forests to finish the job and exploit the remains. While the killing fever raged there was no time to dispose of rotting mounds of bison. Often the killers took only the hides, or tongues, or a choice cut of meat, leaving most to rot. Sportsmen took nothing except the ephemeral best, life. So the plains were leprously strewn with skeletal material, whitening skulls and ribs sloughed in decomposing flesh, a hollowing mortuary.

Scavengers did their best to dispose of the carnage, but the swift fox, coyotes, wolves, vultures, eagles and their array of small helpers, could not keep pace. White people also took to the plains, to turn whatever they could into a dollar. Bone pickers scoured the echoing plain for skulls and skeletal remains to sell as fertilizers to eastern farmers. And some turned their attention to species that had survived the slaughter.

Several subspecies of wolves lived for thousands of years alongside the bison, feeding on the young, old, sick, wounded and dead. They kept the bison herds free of disease and alert. Wolf numbers climbed during the bison slaughter. At the bison's end, White hunters heard the market say, "Now I want wolf." At this bidding, a new brand of exploiter rose up to ply his trade. This next succession in the development of the west was the wolfer.

Bullets were too expensive, hunting too difficult for these entrepreneurs. Poison—strychnine and arsenic—constituted the new production technology. The method was to leave dead bison or whatever they could kill, liberally seasoned with chemical death. Wolfers retired to their dens, to let time and poison hunt for them. Days later they would trail the prairies to find out what they had killed. Wolves died, poisoned, but so was nearly everything else—coyotes, swift fox, badgers, weasel, ferrets, eagles, hawks, and starving people. The plains wolf, dependent on the bison but able to survive its extinction, itself then collapsed to extinction. Alongside went the plains grizzly.

Some claim today that bison populations are increasing. The inference is that the species is not extinct, having survived the debacle. In a genotypic sense that is true; but it ignores other types of extinctions, ones that may be as momentous, although not, perhaps, so clear.

The plains bison was the single most important animate species in the galaxy of North American grassland ecosystems. The multiple dynamics and the complex of relationships and interactions between bison and other species framed the biology of the Great Plains. The grama grass, blue grass and wheat grasses that co-evolved in accommodation with the bison, were no longer grazed. These grasses missed the mouth, rip, step and roll of the bison. That relationship, that synergy, was lost. The wolf, coyote and swift fox, the creatures who trailed the herds, the doctors and undertakers of the herd, languished. Birds that depended on the bison to stir up insects in their foraging, amphibians that needed bison wallow and rain for reproduction—all withered in sympathy, some to extinction. That biology also involved humans in dependant ways, and those people are today extinct. There are no more bison people, only specters and romantic yearnings. Nothing was the same after; nor could it ever be.

For the bison there was another kind of extinction, that of bison culture, the herd knowledge, the experience passed on from generation to generation of migrations, ways of the rut, winter refuge and spring's first green grasses. "Bisonness" went extinct, the culture of the bison died with the last free ranging, unrestrained wild beasts. The open grasslands, sloughs, coulees and wallows, will never again know the civilization of bison.

Passing through park bison enclosures I have seen these relict lords of the plains, levelling a distant and vacant gaze through the fence off to the line of horizon. Driving by bison ranches and game farms, one sees these humbled beasts, now bent to the service of modern man. No more roving the plains searching for the most succulent greens. Now they wait for a bale of hay produced from alien grasses on lands cultured to a new regimen, provided by someone who is waiting to butcher them. They do not worry about the wolf or grizzly bear; they know no enemies except their keeper. No bison these animals! They are cows in bison robes, a phenotypic disguise. To those who say the plains bison is not extinct, yes, its genes continue, but bisonness is as extinct to nature as the prodigious flight of passenger pigeons or the seaward bounding of the great auk.

BUFFALO CHIPS, BLOOD AND BLAME

Who exterminated the bison? The triggermen are well-known. Some sought mere amusement. Wealthy tourists, sportsmen they say, arranged gala safaris to the west to display their civilization by each killing many bison. The poor emulated the elite to the extent they could afford bullets and transportation. Hewitt in *The Conservation of Wild Life* in Canada records this footnote:

> In October 1884 a Canadian Pacific tri-weekly train from Calgary to Winnipeg was boarded at way stations by passengers laden with rifles, saddles and other equipment till it was crowded to capacity. Inquiry elicited the information that *seven* buffalo had been reported in the Cypress Hills. This was undoubtedly the last remnant of the vast herds which once roved the prairies of Western Canada, and, inspired by a desire to slaughter, at least 50, and probably 100, hunters immediately started for the town of Maple Creek . . . .[11]

But amusement and bloodthirst do not create the all-consuming rapaciousness and focused discipline necessary to eliminate these millions in a few decades. Powerful forces aimed the triggermen. Who or what were the "directing minds and wills" for this debacle?[12]

Turning the millions of bison on HBC lands to account required large-scale trade and sale into international markets. Demand to do so was stimulated, enabled in part by technological innovations. Earlier, the chic men and women of Europe helped the trapper load his traps in the watery wilds of America when they demanded to wear pressed beaver felt hats. Eastern American counterparts, wearing their bison coats and using bison robes, helped load gun charges on the bison hunting grounds. Blood of the millions spattered them as much as the triggermen.

Markets reflected the ambitions of dominant institutions and elites— HBC, Canada and England will do for the minute and in a shallow way. Here lies much of the "directing mind and will" in this disaster (and many others like it ongoing at that time on Earth). Once this apparatus and driver, a machine in ways—the human cogs, physical levers, the production methods and available technology—was running at full throttle, even the market, its engine, could not stop it. When demand slowed in 1875 the killing did not. Foster describes the dynamics of the time:

The casual observer might have predicted a decline in robe production with the fall in prices. In this view Native hunters, Indian and Metis, would simply cease to hunt to produce robes in surplus amounts and return to a strategy of an earlier generation of hunting for subsistence. Such was not the case. The Metis particularly had never been subsistence producers. Rather than diminishing the production of robes the fall in prices increased production. More robes were necessary to attempt to sustain the flow of material goods from the east.[13]

This overshoot and collapse quite likely was anticipated, perhaps even intended. Some understanding of business assists us. *Beyond the Limits* explains a similar but more recent context:

Ecologist Paul Ehrlich once expressed surprise to a Japanese journalist that the Japanese whaling industry would exterminate the very source of its wealth. The journalist replied, "You are thinking of the whaling industry as an organization that is interested in maintaining whales; actually it is better viewed as a huge quantity of [financial] capital attempting to earn the highest possible return. If it can exterminate whales in 10 years and make a 15% profit, but it could only make 10% with a sustainable harvest, then it will exterminate them in 10 years. After that the money will be moved to exterminating some other resource.[14]

These principles, wielded in rougher fashion, applied to hunters and bison. Extinction has costs but it also has its rewards.

Long-term objectives might be achieved by eliminating the bison. For those who coveted Native and bison lands, Natives and bison were problems. Obstacles to cow and plough, they both had to go. One needed no excuse to shoot bison. It was good business and it might help to solve the resident people problem at the same time.[15]

That Canada intended to eliminate the bison and carried it into action is sharply underscored by a last-minute hesitation. On March 22, 1877 the Northwest Territories Council, a federally appointed body, passed an ordinance to protect the bison. Parliament and the council well knew the consequences of failing to protect the bison. Mr. Schultz told this to proceedings of the House of Commons on March 26, 1877:

It was a fact that the very existence of the plain tribes of Indians depended upon this valuable animal . . . . The same authority (Father Lacombe) . . . estimated that, at the present rate of destruction, in eight years the buffalo would be extinct . . . .[16]

Less than 16 months later, by resolution of August 2, 1878, the Northwest Territories Council repealed protection for the bison. This during the death throes of the Canadian herd. Canada, it must be noted, killed every one of its plains bison. Only American members of the subspecies survived. For Canada, empire and nation created the plan, owned the lands, had police power in place to enforce laws, set the laws and then repealed them while having clear knowledge of consequences. They proceeded notwithstanding.

The few concerned for the bison and Native people were powerless to stop the killing. Annihilation continued until there were no more. Some say extermination was unfortunate but necessary. It had to be done for development of the empire. It had to be done to civilize the northwest. It also had to be done for White people, the farmers, the trains and the nation. It had to be done to purge the plains of pests. Economic theory had it that the world was a better place for all this because the fashionable had their bevy of bison robes to pelt backs and beds. It had to be done because the market demanded it. Billfolds had to be filled and a new land of opportunity had to be seized. To do otherwise would be to stand in the way of progress, really the embracing sin.

CHAPTER 5

HUDSON'S BAY COMPANY

BC's charter, a nearly pure rendering of mercantile policy, intended not just profit for Charles II's friends but also to secure and advance his empire through conversion and settlement. That meant priests and farmers. Farmers take life at its lowest trophic level, converting habitat to tilled soil, an alien environment for nearly all wild things—a kind of clearcutting of life from the soil up. As farmers ploughed the land, preachers ploughed its people. Missionaries wanted to supplant the hunter-gatherer spirit of Native people with a shiny white new soul. This new improved Indian would throw off savage ways and take up the plough or cow for Christ and empire.

But both priest and farmer would destroy the fur business and that worried HBC. Not happy to subordinate commercial interests to imperial ambitions HBC's governors held settlers and their spiritual cheerleaders at bay as long as they could. The fur industry's exploitative ways would prove less a threat to Native ways and the land than would the coming multitudes. Preachers led the way, first arriving in Alberta in September of 1838. Cant and cadence told of healing and helping, counselling and curing, education and salvation, but their overriding objective was institutional, to expand the empires of man and God as England saw them.

HBC's monopoly irritated the church and frustrated liberals, and its failure to seize and settle the land infuriated mercantilists. All pressed to break the monopoly and settle the land. An 1849 Red River trial convicted Guillaume Sayer and others of trafficking in Rupert's Land furs, contrary to the monopoly provisions of Charles II's charter. Admonishment was their sentence.[1] With such tepid sanctions, this marked the substantial end of HBC's monopoly. But the appearance continued on, for a time. In 1859, a steamboat hooted and puffed its way down the Red River from the U.S.A., scattering bewildered canoes. The cargo on this industrial-age contraption was machines and technology from the east including a printing press for the west's first newspaper. Despite HBC efforts to fend off this new age (in a predictable monopolist response, it purchased the steamboat) mercantilism's last stronghold was fracturing.

In 1856, England's Commons appointed a Select Committee of the House to consider HBC and Rupert's Land; whether to eliminate the monopoly and open HBC lands up for exploitation and trade by others, and generally how to suffuse the western part of the empire with British civilization. Little was known of Rupert's Land then, even by HBC. The committee appointed John Palliser to lead a scientific expedition west of the Great Lakes, to assess and inventory it, and provide recommendations on its future development, settlement and usages, including an investigation into potential railway routes. Palliser's cautious 1860 report called for selective settlement as a way to bind Rupert's Land closer to the empire and thereby preclude American annexation.

Storm clouds from American Manifest Destiny swelled on the southern horizon. Imperial darkness brooded in the east. Monopoly shaken, title to grant lands under scrutiny and Americans menacing, HBC's halcyon days were over. The validity of Charles II's original grant was uncertain. Was the Crown's original claim to the lands good? Was discovery a sufficient basis to claim Rupert's Land? What about competing French discoveries? Did England and HBC's claims defeat radical or aboriginal title? Was the grant to HBC limited to certain uses? Was it revocable? What was the nature of the HBC interest? Classical liberals, Americans and Canada West all had an interest in defeating Charles II's grant. So did Native people and Metis—if they only knew.

With so much riding on the grant, HBC preferred bending to breaking. In those times when land was the key to wealth, HBC owned quite a piece of real estate, far more than it could swallow itself. HBC cast about for ways to turn this gigantic stretch of wilderness to power and profit. Changes would be required. From a traditional fur-trading mercantile corporation, with coincident obligations and duties to Crown and empire, it neatly metamorphosed into an industrial age corporation, led by power, profit and obligations to its owners.

HBC's commercial epiphany occurred in an 1862 meeting in which its future confronted its past. HBC's fur-trading tradition was represented by its governor, H. H. Berens; its future was represented by the Duke of Newcastle, who spoke for certain railway interests.[2] Peter C. Newman reports the meeting this way:

> He (the Duke) presented the promoter's idea of slashing a strip
> across the heart of the HBC territory as a patriotic gesture to tie

the Empire together. Beren's reply was as indignant as it was emotional. "What?" he blustered. "Sequester our very tap-root? Take away the fertile lands where our buffaloes feed? Let in all kinds of people to squat and settle and frighten away the fur-bearing animals they don't kill and hunt? Impossible! Destruction—extinction—of our time-honoured industry . . . .

That emphatic defence of his turf having been delivered, the Governor reverted to type and, shrewdly squinting at the Duke, queried: "If these gentlemen are so patriotic, why don't they buy us out?" "What is your price?" calmly inquired the Colonial Secretary. "Well, about a million and a half."[3]

Within months railway, banking and other interests structured the deal, arranged financing and completed it. HBC's taproot was readied for sequestration.

In this friendly takeover, original shareholders sold £100 shares for £300. Proceeds of a public offering grossed £2,000,000 to finance the purchase. About £1,500,000 of those proceeds paid out the original shareholders (a tripling of their share value), leaving an estimated £300,000 for the promoters. The Prospectus pledged that the Southern District of HBC's 1.4 million square miles (3.6 million square kilometres) of land "will be opened to European Colonization under a liberal and systematic scheme of land settlement."[4] Industrial age economic elites replaced hereditary elites at the helm of a born-again HBC.

With urging from the empire, five years later (1867), four of British North America's colonies rafted up to form the Dominion of Canada. In confederating, Canada became a satellite nation, enjoying autonomy in some things but not others. Imperial control over such matters as declarations of war, external affairs, treaties, consistency with imperial laws and constitutional change persisted long afterward.[5] Canada continued to be an instrument of imperial purposes until after World War I, and while tethered closely to empire, hobbled American expansion.

Much has been made of American Manifest Destiny, but very little of England and Canada's continental ambitions—*ad mare usque ad mare*. In 1867, the Dominion of Canada was a modest postcolonial amalgam, but its constitutional design was to expand to the world's then-largest nation. Canada's constitution dwells obsessively on the tools of empire—allocation of space, power and jurisdiction between constituted authorities. A construct of division, hierarchy, adjudication and compliance, it is nearly completely barren of life, people, rights or principles, at least until 1982. The *Constitution Act, 1867,* s.146 outlines Canada's territorial ambitions:

146. It shall be lawful for the Queen, by and with the Advice of Her Majesty's Most Honourable Privy Council, on Addresses from the Houses of the Parliament of Canada, and from the Houses of the respective Legislatures of the Colonies or Provinces of Newfoundland, Prince Edward Island and British Columbia, to admit those Colonies or Provinces, or any of them, into the Union, and *on Address from the Houses of the Parliament of Canada to admit Rupert's Land and the North-western Territory, or either of them, into the Union*, on such Terms and Conditions in each Case as are in the Addresses expressed and as the Queen thinks fit to approve, subject to the Provisions of this Act; and the Provisions of any Order in Council in that Behalf shall have effect as if they had been enacted by the Parliament of the United Kingdom of Great Britain and Ireland. (emphasis added)

With the exception of Newfoundland (demurring a coy 72 years), Canada swept all the target lands into Confederation within six years.

While Canada federated, American settlers teemed west. First by wagon, then, on completion of the first U.S. transcontinental railway in 1869, throngs steamed out by rail. Hearing of Rupert's Land, some turned north to the 49th parallel, posing yet again, another American threat to HBC interests. With the empire urging them quickly on before the Americans made a grab, Canada reluctantly bargained to purchase HBC lands.[6]

The result, signed by HBC on November 9, 1869, was a deal of modest proportions involving an immodestly large portion of Earth's surface—most of the lands once-covered by the Laurentide Ice Sheet, the several million square kilometres of Rupert's Land. Canada's payment to HBC included:

1. £300,000 cash;
2. Leaving its fur-trading business assets intact, including some 50,000 acres (20,000 ha) surrounding trading posts; and
3. The right to claim some 7,000,000 acres (2.8 million hectares) of the best agricultural lands within the fertile region of the purchase.

For Rupert's Land imperial control descended to national control; corporate control gave way to new a form of colonial control.

THE RESISTANCE

No one talked to or traded with the Native people for their lands. Far-away elites cared for their interests through gentlemanly exchange behind closed doors but the interests of those on the land were ignored. Britain's Parliament remedied HBC's title and ultimately HBC surrendered its lands to Canada. December 1, 1869 was the date proposed for transfer. In soon-to-be Manitoba none of the 558 Native people, 5,757 French-speaking Metis, 4,083 English-speaking Metis and 1,565 White people[7], not even the local governor knew particulars of this surrender:

> As late as November 1869, Governor Mactavish declared that he was still without any official instruction, either from Canada or from England, of the fact, conditions or date of the proposed transfer. It is not surprising, therefore, that the half-breeds, feeling that they had been sold "like dumb driven cattle," determined to dictate their own terms to the Dominion of Canada.[8]

To imperial elites, the residents of the Red River Valley and lands beyond were treated as no-ones and nothings in *terra nullius*. The imperial commerce was in power and space, not people and place.

HBC surrendered the lands but Canada failed properly to assume them, leaving a gap in authority even by the acquisitor's law.[9] Into that hollow flowed Louis Riel's provisional government. Riel's goal:

> . . . . was not to fight Canada, but, with the whole body of settlers, French and English, behind him, to force the Canadian government to negotiate with the half-breeds the terms of their entry into Confederation. This was Riel's constant objective from the beginning to the conclusion of the insurrection. Their own terms, embodied in a Canadian statute and confirmed by the Imperial Parliament, were regarded by the half-breeds as the only safeguard for the interests of a people soon to find themselves on the defensive.[10]

Alarmed that Natives or Metis claimed rights reserved only for White people, indignant that local wits had outfoxed imperial elites, outraged over the execution of Thomas Scott, English-speaking White people clamoured for blood. But imperial minds calculated the costs and benefits of confrontation. Badgering and buying was usually more cost-effective than battling. Assurances of fairness and justice brought these first Manitobans to the trade table. There, Canada largely had its way. Agreements were negotiated, some grievances addressed and the Red River Valley lands, now the new province of Manitoba (assented to May 12, 1870), were occupied for Canada. In this short and shallow struggle, the people of Assiniboia occupied just positions, far more than those they resisted. Even so, they surrendered upon modest concessions, some later reneged on. Riel, twice elected to the House of Commons, was refused his seat.

Perhaps service to empire is the measure that most calibrates Canadian historical figures. White heroes in the service of institutions distinguished themselves not for noble principles but for compliance in advancing the empire. These adherents contrast with the west's few people's heroes, usually Native or Metis. Riel is the Father of Confederation most distinguished for service in advancing principles of respect for resident peoples. Ultimately they hanged Riel, a "compelling rebel in a nation of cloying conformists."[11]

It was time to seize the remaining western lands. For over 350 years the intentions of England's elites were clear. Cabot, Hudson, Charles II, Prince Rupert, HBC, the Imperial Parliament, the new nation Canada and its new Prime Minister, John A. Macdonald, along with thousands of others, all followed the same path. It was the National Policy, the Imperial Policy. The fur trade continued its decline, the grant and its monopoly were memories and HBC had decided that the land itself held more lucre than fur. In the short term, the ongoing slaughter of the bison returned economic benefits. Longer term it would clear the land of a source of strength to the people of the land. But what to do then with Native people and the newly humbled Metis? Native people had become a problem to be resolved, not a resource to be exploited. Now they were the "dogs in the manger."

During Palliser's expedition, few White people lived in Alberta. About 30 acres (12 ha) were under cultivation at Edmonton House, a trading centre that boasted 150 White people. By 1870 the estimated pre-contact Native population of 10,000 had slumped to 6,000 in part because of the introduction of European weapons and diseases.[12] Monopolies and furbearers gone, the fur business thinned. The great bison massacre having now crested, "harvests" declined and the "resource" plummeted. This looked to be the cusp of boom on the turn to bust.

New business was needed—new ways of exploitation. England pioneered techniques to clear its lands of its inhabitants over the preceding centuries. The Enclosures movement purged the English countryside of its peasantry, replacing traditional land use with higher technology, machine and market driven agriculture. Might this have application in Rupert's Land? Get rid of the bison, the Native people and then bring in farmers and technology. Because this development strategy depended on international trade in agricultural products, large-scale, efficient transportation facilities would be required. Railways were the high-tech solution of the day. And so there would be a railway.

Canada's 1871 commitment to British Columbia to build the transcontinental railway meant obligations to survey, partition and parcel the west, all to tame the wild land to private and productive property, the kind that railways feed on. That began nearly immediately with the *Dominion Lands Act, 1872*. There must be the empire's law and order. Dutiful local government was desirable economically and strategically. The *North-West Territories Act, 1875* established such government. Military and police power (or a paramilitary force) was required to ensure fealty to the new law, to protect White people's private property while taking the commons from the original people. The Red Coats came west in 1874.

I n 1866, an event occurred that was the first step in a series of incidents to shatter the complacent life of Big Bear and other Cree leaders .... That summer, they learned that the Iron Stone was missing from its hill near the Battle River. Of all the monuments dedicated to Old Man Buffalo, the Iron Stone was the greatest and most venerated. It was a meteorite composed almost entirely of iron so soft it could be cut with a knife. A total of 386 pounds (176 kg) in weight, it was believed by the Indians to have been placed there after the flood by Nanebozo, the great spirit of the Ojibwa ....

"The medicine men," observed a visitor several years later, "with unbroken faith in the creed of their fathers, prophesied dire evils to follow the removal of the stone which Manitou had placed on the hill. The buffalo would disappear, there would be a pestilence and fierce war. At the time the prophesy was made, I am told, the plains were black with buffalo, 'whose ponderous tramping made the prairie quiver'; there were no indications of disease; war, though not unknown, was infrequent."

Where had the Iron Stone gone? The Indians soon discovered that Methodist missionaries had loaded it on a cart and taken it .... Missionary George McDougall knew what he had done by taking the stone, for he commented that "For ages the tribes of Blackfeet and Crees have gathered their clans to pay homage to this wonderful manitoo." He also noted that the taking of the idol had "roused the ire of the conjurors. They declared that sickness, war and decrease of buffalo would follow this sacrilege."

Hugh A. Dempsey,
Big Bear: The End of Freedom
(Vancouver: Douglas & McIntyre, 1984), 37-38.

CHAPTER 6

TAKING
NEW CANAAN

WANDER IN THE WILDERNESS

T he plunge, mastery to misery, was swift and sorry. In the 1860s plains peoples climbed their prosperity pinnacle. Two decades later they lay wounded and dying on the valley's rocks below. Brute facts tell the overriding story. Before in the Americas, Native people possessed it all and White people had none. White people had the means to take it; their purpose in coming to the Americas was nothing less. White people seized it, leaving Native people little except duty to foreign gods, kings, capitalists and the lowest stratum in a harsh social hierarchy.

But these brute facts miss the taking's subtlety and finesse. Some vouch it was done by law, but not the law of the occupiers of the land (Native Americans), or the domestic law of the taker's land (England) for that law protected prior possession. No, it was the kingly law of discovery, which required little to legitimize claims to new lands. A hired sailor need only scramble ashore, stand above high tide, plant a flag, puff his chest and crow a claim of dominion in the name of a distant king. This was discovery. Those lurking in the wood, inhabitants of the lands for millennia—knowers, lovers and users of it all; born, lived and died on it—were "nothings." Kings justified this, saying these lands languished empty until their arrival, devoid of ethically significant life, a *terra nullius*. This fillip doctrinally flicked about 100 million Americans from being.

These early claims were the pivot for the Crown's claims over Rupert's Land and, of course, HBC's derivative position. For the several centuries that the fur trade flourished, HBC had little interest in taking actual possession of much of Rupert's Land. While the west's economy centred on fur, Native people remained on the land, doing the things they had always done but in exotic new ways. Trade terms were advantageous; Native people did more on the land for less than any Europeans. The breech-loading rifle, improved transportation systems, expanding trade and markets catapulted Native people to wealth and prosperity during the mid-19th century. But the propellant for this ascent, ravenous trade and witless technology, consumed their resource. Plunging beaver and bison populations pulled down the fur trade with them, just as surely trapped and dying. European use for Native people died with the fur trade, leaving only their lands of interest to White people.

THE PROMISED LAND

But whose land was it? Perhaps Rupert's Land was not really Rupert's, the King's, the Squirearchy's or any White person's. Perhaps it belonged to Native people still; or, more heretically in this budding Christian dominion, to no man. On the other hand it might have been God-given, a new Canaan for another chosen people:

27. I will send my fear before thee, and will destroy all the people to whom thou shalt come, and I will make all thine enemies turn their backs unto thee.
28. And I will send hornets before thee, which shall drive out the Hivite, the Canaanite, and the Hittite, from before thee.
29. I will not drive them out from before thee in one year; lest the land become desolate, and the beast of the field multiply against thee.
30. By little and little I will drive them out from before thee, until thou be increased, and inherit the land.
31. And I will set thy bounds from the Red Sea even unto the sea of the Philistines, and from the desert unto the river: for I will deliver the inhabitants of the land into your hand; and thou shalt drive them out before thee.[1]

Was Alberta another promised land and its people Canaanites, perhaps part of a new Jerusalem?

Whether God's or not, it was the plan of those who thought themselves closest to him, England's elites. The beasts of the fields were driven out. The hornets of smallpox, starvation and bullets beset these Canaanites. The 300 years of clamour in the south, agonizing screams from American and Spanish blade and blasts echoed up into Alberta. Distant wailings were portentous; violence in the south might become violence in the north as White people "inherit the land."

Confederation hastened plans for Rupert's Land. Canada too, aspired to expand dominion and empire. That meant going west. It was its charge and duty; its imperial destiny.[2] A transcontinental railway would consolidate this reach of the empire. Rail would stitch the far west (British Columbia) to the east, safely enfolding the vault of land between to Canada, securing it away from American expansion and Russian probings. Here in the midfolds lay unborn Alberta. This was Sir John A. Macdonald's plan in 1871. His restatement of the imperial plan, then 200 years old, had yet to address this—when and how to winnow Native people from the land? As the market gulped the last pelts of beaver and bison, its tolerance for Native people turned finicky. In capital's calculus, when their costs exceed benefits Native people must be offloaded.

Nearly constant European wars instructed the English well on means to deal with their foes. An island-centred "military-industrial complex", its information and communication systems were leading edge, while its well-rehearsed national and military decision-making structures were efficient, unified and disciplined. Its people were compliant to command—they were civilized. Underpinning this was the world's most progressive and powerful economy, its first industrial state and its corresponding military might. A global storehouse of resource-rich colonies nurtured this mighty force's material appetites. Its unequalled transportation technology, particularly shipping and rail, carried its will wherever fear called or greed propelled.

In building empire, England learned finesse in taking. Elites found the military option generally too taxing, but military might is the hardness that stiffens softer strategies. Strategic use of military theatre and economic resources usually produced greater rewards than battle. Also, England had the advantage of knowing precisely what they wanted, to what extremes they might go to obtain it and nearly everything strategic about their opponents. One more ace lay up their sleeve.

CONDITIONS IN CANAAN

Vectors of power are one thing, factors of weakness another. A fatal debilitation might be to not know you are at war. For centuries White elites knew their New World ambitions, New World people did not. Amity-laden White signals obscured their true intent, while frequent Native attitudes of autonomy, friendship and cooperation disarmed them as to the European menace.

The effects of trade further disarmed Native people. Certainly trade provided horses and guns, but always in limited quantities, and guns were of dated technology and at White discretion. Purchasing defence from one's assailant may be risky, but trade did more. Through the specialization and interdependence wrought by trade, Native people transubstantiated from people, culture and nation into factors of production. Interdependence means the producer no longer had freedom or discretion to trade, he must trade. The transient, sometimes illusory, benefits of trade bound Native people to it, locking them inextricably to its consequences.

With the bison gone, they had no goods to trade, then no goods from trade. Having abandoned the old ways and being abandoned by the new ways, the new Native globalized free-trade, market-based economy collapsed. This shut down Native people in other non-economic and more important ways—culturally and physically. Starving on the barren landscape, their stark dependency suddenly became obvious. Independence and freedom, culture and society had been part of the trade pact. Faint hope lay with distant, faceless, ambitious men.

Disease punctuated Native people's economic, social and cultural plagues. In the winter of 1819-20 measles wiped out one-third of Blackfoot and Gros Ventres. In 1836 diphtheria rampaged through the countryside. The next June White traders coming up the Missouri River disembarked with a cargo of smallpox, killing two out of every three Native people. Six of 9000 then in the Blackfoot Confederacy died.[3] Winter 1864-65 brought scarlet fever and a return of the measles to Alberta and Saskatchewan. Another 1,200 Amerindians died and others were disabled.[4] As market hunters gunned down the few remaining bison, a new epidemic of smallpox descended. In 1870 about one-third of the Metis died of it, while for Native people, as usual, the death toll was even higher.

Riel's resistance ushered in the 1870s. At the time many treated his resistance and provisional government as the scandalous revolt of a clutch of volatile, fully crazed half-breeds against civilization's legitimate advance. Others consider the Red River Rebellion as one of few acts of integrity in a history notable for its praise of oppressors and vilification of victims. But the victorious write the story and hang the rogues.

That decade also started poorly for the Blackfoot Confederacy. Their lands straddled the international border. Just south of the border White warriors roused up:

> Early in January 1870, Colonel E. M. Baker left Fort Shaw on the Sun River, Montana, to punish the marauding Blackfoot band led by Mountain Chief, but the guide led the soldiers to the friendly village under Chief Heavy Runner, which was camped on the Marias River. At daylight on January 23, the troops surprised the village and killed 173 Indians of all ages and captured 140 women and children. The Baker massacre crushed the fighting spirit of the Blackfeet.[5]

Before 1870 on the Canadian side of the border HBC discipline seemed to restrain White people. After the HBC sale, that restraint diminished.

The White trade catalyst, alcohol, washed away the little coherence remaining to Native life. Medicine, care and compassion may have been hard to find, but where economic advantage obtained, alcohol poured forth in sufficient quantity to achieve its employer's objectives. Mounted Police inspector Denny records this bloody debauch in the Cypress Hills:

In May 1873 a band of Assiniboine were camped near Farwell's post and, as later reported, "whisky flowed like water . . . and by mid-day the tribesmen were all hopelessly drunk . . . ."

Probably nothing extraordinary would have happened but for the arrival of a party of wolfers—men who lived by poisoning wolves then selling the hides. Wolfers were disliked by the Indians because their dogs were often among the poison victims. For their part these wolfers—later described as " . . . persons of the worst class in the country"—had no concern for either the dogs or the Indians they killed.

About noon on June 1 a man named Hammond who was staying at Farwell's post discovered that his horse was missing. He accused the Assiniboine and vowed to take two of theirs in retaliation. When he asked the wolfers to help, they eagerly grabbed their rifles and six-guns.

Who fired the first shot is uncertain, as is the number of Assiniboine men, women and children killed. Best estimates are that the wolfers massacred 20 Indians, including Chief Little Soldier. He was roused from a drunken stupor by his wife who attempted to lead him to safety in the woods. He refused to go, and as he stood defenceless was murdered by one of the wolfers. Another Indian, an old man, was killed with a hatchet, his head severed then mounted on a lodgepole. Four women were taken to Solomon's post, among them Little Chief's wife. Here she and another young woman were repeatedly raped. Next morning the wolfers buried their only casualty, Ed Legrace, under the floor of Farwell's post, burned it and Solomon's, then hurriedly left.[6]

The scene in 1873 was this. The fur trade is gone; the bison is gone. With little to trade, White goods are gone. Longer gone are traditional ways. Wolfers are starting their dirty killing business. Whisky traders are selling a desperate narcotic for those who have nothing else. White people have been killing Native people with near impunity for some time and Natives live in overwhelming fear.

In 1874 the North-West Mounted Police, or Red Coats, marched west with arms but with little food, medicine or tools for the resident people.[7] No, those would be held out later as rewards for those who would sell the last item of Native commerce, their homelands. Booze was one ruse. After more than a century of dealing liquor into Alberta, on the eve of the grand caper, paramilitary forces arrive to stop that trade. Yes, managing alcohol had its purpose but they hardly came to help Native people. Primary purposes lay elsewhere.

It was the empire's order, its law, its iron will and ways that marched west with these young White men. The annunciation to Canadians and settlers was "we have secured the way"; to Americans it was "this is Anglo-Canadian soil"; to Native people "White people have charge." Red Coats told Native people not to try any Riel resistance or you will be met by superior force. This force was an essential instrument to taking possession from those in possession. If treaty negotiations or relationships turned sour, White people would be protected. Whatever was required to secure imperial interests would be done. Of particular importance they must protect and ensure proper foundations for the great western railway promised three years earlier to lure British Columbia into Confederation.

Red Coats performed their task well. White-friendly stability crawled out over the plains and up to the parklands. Small communities rooted in the shadows of trading posts. A few cattlemen drifted in. These changes unsettled Native people further. What was their place in all things? The Sioux proposed a unification of Native peoples to drive out White people but Crowfoot declined. The Canadian experience with White people had been better than in the U.S.A. Yes! The Anglo-Canadian strategy was working.

CIVILIZATION MUST GO HAND IN HAND WITH CHRISTIANITY[8]

The Black Coats of European religious institutions harmonized well with Red Coats. Religion tried to refashion Native people by crushing what little was left of them. Their message was to reject yourselves: you are bad, your culture, customs and practices are bad, your religions and gods are bad, your past and forefathers were bad and your future will be bad too, except for us. Cultural annihilation was presented in the "love" modality. We love you, we are brothers, we give you great gifts of healing and wisdom from our all-powerful God, we bring you a better way of life, we come to save your souls, we give you eternal salvation because we possess the means to heaven; but you must go through us as God's friendly neighbour-hood representative.

Cultural imperialism seemed as important as religious imperialism to the Black Coats. If only Native people would accept their suitably low place in the imperial hierarchy and act like subservient village labourers with appropriate demeanour to god, country, empire and monarch. Newman argues:

> What these opinionated parsons really meant when they railed about converting the "heathen savages" was that they were determined to make Indians not quite so outrageously un-British. "They struggled to recreate the English rural parish," wrote the historian Frits Pannekoel, describing the itinerant clerics' aspirations, "a little Britain in the wilderness, with the parson as a major landowner, teacher, custodian of charities, and law giver." They saw themselves as sharing these tasks with the other members of the elite: the squirearchy, the Company's officers and the settlement's Governor. The Anglican clergy's plans for this society placed them at the helm and made outcasts of all who did not comply.[9]

It was God's will that they go to church on Sunday and otherwise farm a section of land (if they had a family of five). Unfortunately few knew what farming was. These White fathers coaxed and cajoled, urged and seduced, promised and extolled these disease- and culture-shocked, starving, resourceless and devastated people to jump their sinking canoe for the shiny new imperial steamer.

Trade encouraged tribal structures to English attitudes of command, conformity, compliance and elitism. Cooperative, consensual and organizationally flat Native societal structures began to stratify. During trade and treaty making, men at the top, White and Native, consolidated authority and prestige, empowering chiefs and taking from tribes.[10] Chiefs sometimes failed to care for the interests of lower-downs. Compulsion inveigled its way into tribal habit.[11] During treaty negotiations White people preferred only a few chiefs, each having the power to commit their people, in effect to bargain for entire groups without their consent.[12] Buy the leader and get the tribe (and their lands), that was the art of the deal. Big Bear worried precisely for that reason.

TAKING CANAAN

Now for the prize. Canada promised British Columbia a transcontinental railway when it joined Confederation. Line commencement was assured within two years of British Columbia's July 20, 1871 entry. Completion was to be within 10 years. What implications had these covenants for those occupying Rupert's Land? White forces were powerfully aligned and Native people were weak and failing, and oblivious to the subtleties unfolding around them. They could sign or die, slow starvation or by swift battle.[13] The White strategy was to give them little, but assure them otherwise they would get less. Promise food after signing, but afterward give them what you will.

The first treaty negotiations affecting Alberta lands resulted in Treaty 4 and occurred in 1874. The establishment of the NWMP by legislation in 1873 preceded that event by a year; the Red Coats' arrival, by months. In August 1876 the Crees signed Treaty 6 turning central Alberta to White hands. In September 1877 the Blackfoot signed Treaty No 7, handing over the southern plains.

Treaties generally provided a signing bonus of $12 for each man, woman and child; reserves consisting of one square mile (2.6 km²) for each family of five; gifts to the tribe of guns, tools, clothing, food and trinkets; and annual treaty money of $15 to $25 for chiefs and $5 per individual.[14] By treaty, tools, teachers and schools would help them become farmers and ranchers and Treaty 6 promised a medicine chest. As for Treaty No. 7:

> The signatories were Crowfoot, of course, along with 34 chiefs and councillors from the Blackfoot, Blood and Piegan tribes; Commissioner Macleod and Lieutenant-Governor Laird (of Manitoba and the Northwest Territories) for the Whites. Witnesses' names provided some symbolic satisfaction: they were representatives of HBC, the NWMP and the Christian Church (John McDougall signed, but Pere Lacombe, regrettably, was ill and could not be present)—in other words, the three great spearheads of the invasion of settlers that was then in the offing.[15]

After the signing, the exotic White 1% held 99% of the land. The resident Native people, 99%, were permitted a derivative beneficial interest in the remaining 1% of the land, but even this interest would take over a century of law to establish.[16]

Treaties assumed bison extermination. Perhaps an opportunity remained for conservation of the bison and a way of life for Native people, but the Crown and capital followed the alternative. With the bison eliminated, they thought, the Blackfoot would settle on reserves and take up farming. In his *A History of Alberta* McGregor has provided this insight:

> Were they—the chiefs, not the thoughtless rank and file—
> aware of the meaning of the treaty? How could they be? They
> could understand that they would get a few dollars, some cat-
> tle and medicines, all visible items easy to comprehend. None
> of them, however, not even Crowfoot, could conceive of what
> it would be like to be cooped up on a reserve, grubbing year
> after year in a piddling field. Old Indians claim that none of
> them could comprehend giving up their hills and valleys and
> the land over which they had roamed, and have said that they
> might as well have been asked to give up the air and the blue
> sky and the sunshine.[17]

They did not comprehend, nor could they. In exchange for unbounded vastness, they received small plots of marginal land, not big enough for life, just about right for death.

By 1877, Alberta's Native populations continued in decline. Then there may have been 100 permanently resident White people. Soon too, White numbers would change. Railways have a purpose. Fill the west. Complete the taking by occupation. White ambitions at the time were focused on the plains and parklands of Alberta. With the fur trade nearly gone, the great northern boreal forest held little attraction for commercial interests. The need to negotiate treaties awaited a White use. It would take the Klondike Goldrush in 1899 to beckon Canada to negotiate Treaty 8 over northern lands. Here too, it was to ensure White control and safety.

White people claim Alberta's taking to be more civilized, less violent, than down south. And White people not Native people, they imply, de-serve the credit. American settlers flooded west long before big govern-ment, big business, and big infrastructure took over. There, ahead of "law and order," the settlers did the dirty, dangerous and vile work to wrestle the land from Native people. On the other hand, Canada's taking was cal-culated and orderly, more institutional and contrived. After "discovery" there was imperial/mercantilist big business (HBC); then colonial-national government, Canada; then their military/police occupation to enforce their law and order (NWMP); then the massive Canadian government project of surveying, assessing, chopping, dividing the land, the bait for the settlers; and then another big business engaged in preparing the infrastructure for next exploitation, the building of the Canadian Pacific Railway. Most of the dirty work was over by the time White people unloaded the train. The calculated and siren-soothing Canadian approach arguably saved more lives in the short run than the bellicose anarchic American style or the ruthless and immediate Spanish style, but the result, complete takeover, was the same.

Can the gentler atrocities of slow starving, dissipation and desiccation, out of sight, be superior to bloody defeat in battle?[18] Battle leaves no uncertainty of the resistance, the conflict and the killing. With starvation, one can blame the victim; it allows the oppressor to argue his compassion and civility.

> Take up the White Man's burden-
> The savage wars of peace-
> Fill full the mouth of Famine
> And bid the sickness cease;
> And when your goal is nearest
> The end for others sought,
> Watch Sloth and heathen Folly
> Bring all your hopes to nought.[19]

Social Darwinism made this all so reasonable. There was little doubt at the time that all of this was necessary and beneficial:

> Let us have Christianity and civilization to leaven the mass of heathenism and paganism among the Indian tribes; let us have a wise and paternal Government faithfully carrying out the provisions of our treaties, and doing its utmost to help and elevate the Indian population, who have been cast upon our care, and we will have peace, progress, and concord among them in the North-West . . . .[20]

Native people were set aside in spectral White cocoons, the reserves, threaded through with ignorance, arrogance and vile motives. Even the story of the devastation of Native people died. Unwritten, it was as if it had not been. The myth of the civilizing and selfless White people was written, and therefore it was. Native people became "ghosts of Canadian history."[21] White people shifted the burden, washed their hands and turned to enjoy the spoils.

THE AFTERMATH

After the stripping of Native people from the land, remnant autonomy and freedom oozed away into remote White hands through the *Indian Act, 1876*, reservation living and the de-programming business. The church continued its pogrom; supplanting Native gods with White males in God's clothes, gods that looked strangely like priests or pastors. Exhorted as the only hope for their children's future, education's two-edged sword sliced children from their parents and vestigial past while submitting them to a never-ending assault for assimilation. Cultural diversity was excised in the quest for the monoculture of English language, English traditions, Christian religion, high technology, Earth exploitation and materialistic accumulation. Education was not the objective so much as obedience to an alien god, people and government. Residential schools were primary weapons in this campaign.

Externally managed and isolated back on the reserves, Indianism withered, dying the agony of slow dismemberment. With lands parleyed away, they held no bargaining chips except the face of misery. Even that was hardly visible, buried as it was on reserves where the conscience of the White people was most often represented by the exploiters and managers. These dusty, dirty, littered reposes were asylums of despair. The only general rights left to Native persons were to hunt and fish on unoccupied Crown lands.[22] They lost everything except a conditional dominion over animals. Thus the hierarchy was maintained—Native people just above animals and even that imposed hierarchy was a White construct.

In only 140 years, with new and improving technology and international trade, the plains tribes had scaled high on the ladder. Their leaders were splendid, their economies vibrant, their cultures waxing. And they were ambitious, competitive, and innovative in an international economy. Then their sun set. Perhaps Native people traded beaver until it was gone, traded bison until it was gone, and then traded their lands until they were gone. Trade may have eaten Native people the same as it ate the bison. Both could profitably be exploited and both stood in the way of imperial ambitions for the west. Both were eliminated; one quickly by guns, the other by disease, alcohol, starvation and treaty. Bison ended up barely surviving in their enclosures, so did Native people.

Now, 10,000 years after the Quaternary extinctions, animal life was again in full retreat. Recently the lands lost the furbearers, bison, prairie wolves and plains grizzly bears. Remnant populations of other life hid out in isolated areas, in the high mountains, or the deep forest, in their refugia, hoping for respite. But starving people equipped with the most recent weapons prowled the land. The little bit of remaining life would soon be in the pot. Neither Native people nor White people had much disturbed the soil or the vegetation, and only a few exotics had arrived to displace nature's long work. Despite a denuded and depopulated surface—a vast silence— the land beneath remained sound. The next assault would be on the land itself. 🐂

CHAPTER 7

TROJAN, IRON, WAR AND OTHER HORSES

IRON HORSES

T he first commercial train chugged into history in 1825, steaming from Stockton to Darlington, England. By the 1840s, the "decade of the train," all Europe clamoured to get on track. Snorting, smoking, chugging, charging steam engines terrorized the quiet countrysides of Europe's newly industrializing northwest. None had more iron will about iron horses than England. Folk of the heath and moor cringed when first they saw these smoke-billowing, whistling and wailing mechanical monsters, railing determinedly on to the next factory or town. At the dawn of the Industrial Revolution, country folk might have marvelled at how the future was becoming "now." Everything about them and many things within them were changing.

Trains chugged through Palliser's mind as he surveyed the "Great Lone Land" from 1857 to 1860. As imperial emissary to probe the western reaches of Rupert's Land, he concentrated on the land's riches and ways to exploit them. His party assayed Earth's surface as a medium for agriculture; the rocks, a bed of valuable minerals; the forests, lumber; and all of it for sources of energy. While Palliser's expedition rejected the idea of rail from Canada to the Pacific, a shadowing Canadian expedition led by Hind and Dawson did not. Hind promoted the west's "fertile belt" as abundant and rich. Rail, he said, provided the means to settle and exploit it. Others agreed.

Just as new sailing technology had opened high seas and distant shores to European voyages of discovery, railway technology opened up remote heartlands to European capital and exploitation. Whether by sail or rail the rule remained the same—the first to seize, grabs the rights to exclusive pluck and plunder. American ambitions and resentments (Manifest Destiny, the Monroe Doctrine, the residue of anti-British sentiment from the American Revolution and the Fenian antipathy) wanted British influence out of the Americas, firmly supplanted by Uncle Sam's neighbourly persuasion. They saw Rupert's Land as a nice fit in their holdings. Once they stopped fighting each other in their Civil War (1861-65) their ambitions would likely again turn north. For that reason British and Canadian interests hastened to bind Rupert's Land closer.

Binding west to east, permanently securing the remainder of British North America to the empire, capturing a capacious land with enormous resources and gigantic opportunities, all required a railway. Despite great distance and daunting geophysical barriers, with scarce regard to low population, and hardly a glance at cost-benefits, Canada induced the west coast colony of British Columbia to enter Confederation in 1871. To secure this deal and cement a nation, Canada promised to build a railway from Canada to British Columbia within 10 years, joining sea to sea. Rail would channel across Canada's newest province, Manitoba (1870). From there it would track over an ocean of plains to the Cordillera, then over breakers of shining mountains and on down to the Pacific. This aggrandizing stroke bound British Columbia to the Canadian packet, catching and containing all between them in the sandwich.[1]

As beaver and bison perished in pelts and profit and with no new beasts to plunder, new resource ventures were required. With Native people effectively eliminated, new people were needed. Most would come in by rail. According to the plan, immigrants would pay passage and flood the prairies. The inputs required for a world-scale agricultural industry and all the material needs of a burgeoning population would be carried in by rail. On the way out, cars would be filled with the grain and cows of the prairies. Rail would farm the farmers. Trains would train the land.

RANGE COWS

Between the time of committing to the railway and its construction, ranching briefly blossomed in Alberta. Just after the 1877 signing of Treaty 7, about 1,000 head of Montana cattle were herded into Alberta to test its suitability for overwintering. Would not the long, nutritious and ungrazed western grass fatten cows as well as the bison? The cattle thrived and so would ranching, Canada informed its friends and supporters. The demand for cattle was increasing at the time with the general prosperity that followed the end of the American Civil War. With wallets peacefully bulging, expanding populations of Yankees and eastern Canadians ordered more beef. The *Dominion Lands Act, 1872*, as amended in 1881, permitted 21-year leases of up to 100,000 acres (40,500 ha) per applicant for a penny per acre per annum. With security of leasehold estate and extremely modest costs for such vast lands, interest buzzed among eastern politicians and lawyers, many of whom came to be owners and directors of first Alberta cattle companies.

In 1881 and the years following, droves of cattle flowed into Alberta. During 1882 Canada granted leases covering more than 4,000,000 acres (1,620,000 ha), most of it in southwestern Alberta. In what was fast becoming its habitual *modus vivendi* government actively involved itself in transportation, product quality, marketing and the general promotion of the beef industry. But open-range ranching was only fine for the moment. It, like the bison, stood in the way of grand, more intense plans for the west. Even as Canada got into it, the cattle business was fast changing. New breeds and breeding practices, need for predictable feed, intensive land use practices, and the desire for fee simple land ownership, all encouraged the slicing, fencing and boxing of the west. But first the railroad must be built.

DERAILED

In 1871, immediately upon British Columbia joining Canada, John A. Macdonald started groundwork for this great railway. But what railroader would commit to such a colossal venture, the world's longest railway project to date? Inducements to undertake the continent-spanning project were commensurate with its scope—vast and uncertain. Government had construction money, a huge inventory of land, monopolies, subsidies and just about anything else required to get the job done short of a general increase in taxation. As further incentive, profits from running the railway were potentially enormous. If part of the railway went through the United States, American railroaders would gladly commit to such a project; but that might leave Canada open to American exploitation, perhaps extortion, and ultimately annexation (that seems no longer a concern). No, it must be built on Canadian lands by Canadian or British railroaders. Macdonald quickly offered the project to Canada's preeminent businessman, Hugh Allan. Macdonald hoped to have a satisfactory agreement to build the Pacific railway in place before going into the 1872 general election.

Despite rumours, Canada's second national election seemed fair and proper. In appearance the enfranchised citizens (few that they were) re-elected Macdonald's Conservative government by a thin margin after a tight race. It looked as if Macdonald's railway would be laid. Later, rustling behind the veils of power spilled out for all to see. Macdonald's Conservatives, it seems, may not have won the election as much as purchased it. And the money source was American funds laundered through Hugh Allan. For this it was agreed that Allan would lead the new Pacific Railway consortium.

He would also draw Americans into the venture. As the Pacific Scandal regurgitated, people wondered whether the new nation's "directing mind and will" was its publicly elected officials, the business community, Americans or the highest bidder. Perhaps it was all of them? None of payoffs, collusion, delay or the appointment of a Royal Commission populated by compliant judges could erase the worst political evil of all—getting caught. For that, a scarcely repentant Macdonald resigned and the great railway derailed for the moment. The collapse of his government in 1873 and the election of the Liberals in 1874 put Macdonald in opposition.

Meanwhile, the *Dominion Lands Act*, 1872 authorized the division of the western lands. Over the next decade surveyors pegged, chained and carved the large portions of the western plains and parklands into quarters, sections and townships in preparation for the free land feast to follow. The NWMP were created by legislation in 1873 and trooped west in 1874. In 1875, the *North-West Territories Act* provided government for matters of a local or private nature. Authorities cleansed the lands of Native people in the following years, so that little remained to derail the great Pacific Railway escapade.

BACK ON TRACK

Re-election in 1878 revived Macdonald's National Policy, his national dream and his succubus, the railway. The Canadian Pacific Railway Company (CPR) would construct it. The founders included an American railroader, an HBC official, a Member of Parliament, and a banker of national reputation. This Anglo-Canadian-American syndicate of businessmen and railroaders sublimated the National Dream into the great Canadian road. The Canadian Pacific Railway steamed from dream to reality, off the plans and onto the land. A railroad to build, a land to conquer and money to be made. The CPR raced to do it all.

In railway construction, the end-of-line is an assault on the senses: a melee of machines, hardware, smoke, noise, rails and engines, with dirty, rough, busy people herding clamorous teams of animals, all frenetically rushing about in myriad tasks. Its vulgar mechanical way is nearly organic. The resources required to move the end-of-line forward flowed up the line, as if through a vascular system, to the linear thrust at its lead edge. Its meristem, the growing tip of the Industrial Revolution, pressed onward, penetrating further and further into the virgin land.

Up and around, down and through, across bison lands, Native lands, hour by hour, mile upon mile, this gigantic rhizome probed westward. It thrust through the last outpost of the empire established yesterday, onto the new last outpost of the empire, christened today. Nodules on the rhizome became villages on the line. Rail placement generally, and sidings, storage or stations specifically, germinated the locations of future cities and towns, and determined the first lands for farming. A decision of CPR management created a new settlement or assured the survival of an old one, sometimes changing its alignment or layout and always changing the land's future.

The rail line came to Alberta from out of the east in the spring of 1883, on its westward thrust toward the mountains. June found it in the tent city of Medicine Hat and by August it had driven past the little ramshackle village that had sprung up around Fort Calgary. With cunning, the CPR directors placed their new station a mile west of the fort, apparently handing the largesse in land to their friends. Justice J. C. Major of the Supreme Court of Canada commented on the arrival of the railway in 1883 and its effect on James Lougheed, grandfather of former Alberta Premier Peter Lougheed:

> From the time of his arrival, Lougheed commenced speculation in Calgary real estate. The CPR owned the section of land on which Calgary was located. Public records show that five lots purchased by him in 1883 for $300 were, within a few years, worth $50,000. As solicitor for CPR, it has been alleged that he had inside information on where the CPR planned to build its station and thus determined the direction of expansion. The railway eventually built its station one block away from his lots and his fortune was assured at age 29.[2]

The next succession of exploiters understood how railways worked. Railways were the philosopher's stone that turned the base to precious, wilderness to wealth. From then on things would be done in the new ways. In that summer the die was cast and the game played—"The game is done! I've won! I've won!"[3]

Like Native people, fur traders disappeared from sight, supplanted by railwaymen and real estate speculators, the first succession of new-age exploiters. Not far behind were settlers and their attendants, the rural merchants, to share in taking the land. Waterborne transportation, the way of the west for hundreds of years, dried up. The canoe sank into obscurity. Fort Benton on the Missouri in Montana, formerly cheap and convenient, now obsolete, became a supply connection of an obscure bygone era.

Even time changed with rail's advent. Sanford Fleming, CPR's chief engineer, fathered the Universal Time system, dividing planet earth into 24 hours. Regular schedules required standardized times; trains would run on time in the new West. Nature's smooth continuity was displaced by the jumps in time that machines favour, time-slicing seconds, minutes and hours. The jerky new discipline of industrial time came into effect on November 18, 1883.

Rail's design and technology gave the humanscape in the west its skeletal infrastructure. Auxiliary lines would be laid to enable remote exploitation, all radiating out from the central rhizome, the axis of the attack. The vascular system branching and spreading out from the line would pump and suck until all about it was transformed. That summer, Alberta joined the agricultural and industrial revolutions. It pledged its future to primary industry and international trade. Its role was to be a supplicant, a provisioner for the empire and the east. With fur, game and Native people effectively gone, its purpose now was to be a breadbox for imperial appetites; it would feed their multitudes.

One last spasm racked the land. A deeply troubled Riel returned from exile to lead a protest over Canada's handling of the North-West territories and its resident peoples, the Native and Metis remnant. As in 1869-70, failure of pleas, petition and protests lead to the declaration of a provisional government. But things had changed since the Red River Rebellion in 1870, including Riel himself. Stanley describes Riel's most significant error:

> Riel, in his weakness, made one great mistake; the situation in 1885 was vastly different from that of 1869. In 1869 the North-West had not belonged to Canada, there were no military forces in the country, and Red River was effectively isolated from Canada by the formidable barrier of geography. In 1885 everything had changed. The North-West had been transferred to Canada and was now Canadian territory, there was a strong force of Mounted Police in the country, and the barrier of geography, which had made the North-West the "Great Lone Land," had been penetrated by the Canadian Pacific Railway.[4]

With the signal of Major Crozier, "Fire away, boys,"[5] at Duck Lake on March 26, 1885, the ill-fated North-West Rebellion ignited. Those shots ensured that there would be funding to complete construction for the financially troubled CPR. The CPR carried the military resources necessary to overwhelm Riel's provisional government. Later, some irreverently suggested CPR should erect a statue to Riel.

Immediately on hearing of the Duck Lake bloodshed White people coalesced to oneness. With scant regard for the issues and less for the principles, White people lined up with their tribal colour. Nearly a thousand Alberta Whites, virtually everyone able, joined militias to fight the uprising. Almost all were recent arrivals having come with or after the rail 18 months earlier. But off they went, as if defending homelands held from time immemorial against an evil new invader.

Rail put down this rebellion. CPR carried the 5,000 volunteer troops over thousands of miles and transported marvellous new weapons, including the machine gun, to overwhelm the several hundred insurgents. With Big Bear's final surrender on July 2, 1885, the rebellion was over. White militiamen obtained their reward in lands. For assisting Canada in defeating Metis and Native people, White warriors received 320 acres (130 ha) of land or $80 in land scrip, the same things for which the Metis and Native people had themselves been struggling.

Later, at Eagle Pass in British Columbia's Monashee Mountains, CPR drove the last spike finishing the railway, November 7, 1885. Days later, November 16, Canada hanged Louis Riel and eight Native people, driving deep and deadly another last spike. With a last shudder and sigh the collective ghost went up. It was done.

LANDLORDS

The Canadian Crown was now the greatest landlord; it held most of Alberta's lands under the Rupert's Land purchase. It also suffered the greatest obligations and burdens. It must settle with Native people and Metis, establish military and government control, police, survey and allot lands. Its staggering immediate obligation was paying for the railway. It would be a long time before the west would produce sufficient tax or tariff revenues to pay for that even under the most aggressive development scenarios. For government it was essential to sooner turn the land to profit, to develop the west as rapidly as possible.

CPR was the next great lord of the land. When Donald A. Smith drove the last spike on November 7, 1885, CPR earned its 25 million dollars and 25 million acres (10 million hectares) of western lands "fairly fit for settlement."[6] Those lands would be selected from the odd-numbered sections in a 24-mile-wide (39 km) belt on either side of the railway lines. These lands were the best by stipulation and design. CPR selected lands most likely to be enhanced by the layout of their railway. CPR received much more than statute provided. Newman in *Merchant Princes* claims:

> The syndicate was granted an eventual $206 million in cash, subsidies and stock guarantees in addition to 25 million acres in land grants . . . . According to John Gallagher, a historical researcher, when all the tax benefits and value of the land

exchanges are taken into account, the CPR received gifts from the country worth $106,300,000.[7]

CPR also owned the railway. Whoever and whatever came and went, arrived and departed through them. If reputation is right, neither their lands nor their services came cheap.

One other great laird of the land was the more retiring HBC. It continued its declining fur and merchandising business, focused on the far north, while passively awaiting fruits of CPR and Canadian efforts in enhancing the value of its southern lands. Their one-twentieth of the fertile belt (lands south of the North Saskatchewan River)[8] and a combined 4,000 acres (1,600 ha) surrounding each of their posts, would be held scrooge-like with a flinty eye, and a close accounting, patiently waiting for the efforts of others to deliver them bonanzas. Business as usual for the "Bay."

Joined to these several huge landlords were the colossal institutions of empire, government and church. Otherwise the land was bare. The institutions taking root in the west wanted more of their foundation stock—White Christian Europeans. Churches wanted more souls, empire and nation wanted more soldiers and workers, business wanted more resources, producers and consumers. For racist reasons among others, they would not rely on the land's Native residents to exploit the west. They demanded a different race of people. That meant immigration from Europe. Languishing without serfs, the local lords had the lure—land, land, land—and now a railroad to get them to it.

CHAPTER 8

WHITEOUT

DEMOGRAPHIC DEVELOPMENT

D emographers think that the state of technological development in a people generally determines their maximum potential population, the upper limits. The power of the loins regularly presses those boundaries. Each technological advance—first tool-making technology, then agriculture, finally the "scientific-industrial revolution"—surged populations logarithmically higher. The last colossal bulge of human population, particularly European peoples, began about 300 years ago with the start of the "scientific-industrial revolution."[1]

Numbers multiplied rapidly during the Industrial Revolution, enlarging cities and states. By 1845 Earth held over one billion people. Europe's population was 250 million and Britain had about 18 million. From there, Europeans spilled out and over the world, seeding the planet with new Europes. Between 1845 and 1932, 60 million people left Europe, nearly a third of those—18 million—were from the British Isles. These radical demographic and technological changes convulsed England's countryside. Romantic poets lamented the end of the bucolic life.

SQUIREARCHY

In the years following the Hudson's Bay Company Charter (1670) England and its colonies underwent great changes, changes that would affect the world in many ways. The Glorious Revolution of 1688 placed parliament at the pinnacle of formal power in England, leaving the monarchy itself in a state of compliance. But parliament itself was held in servitude, firmly dominated as it was by a few big landowners, the so-called Squires. These new absolutists got down to taking care of their interests, private interests—securing and exploiting property. Too long, they felt, the land suffered under feudal inefficiencies. Too many ineffective, unproductive peoples populated the lands. Agricultural technology was archaic. The commons were wasted or improperly used. To the Squires, land was not a home for people and place for nature; it was a resource to be exploited with its product sold into cash markets in ways to maximize profits.

The Squires instructed parliament to erase feudal obligations. Using legislation's might, the Squires overthrew feudal tenure systems, replacing them with an early, land-focused form of capitalism. From the late 17th century to the early 19th century, the Squirearchy passed thousands of laws now known as the *Enclosures Acts*.[2] Feudal interests were extinguished, peasants ejected, yeomen coerced into sale, commons were appropriated and everywhere the English countryside was stripped of people and wild places, then laced with fences. Domestic pogroms uprooted the rural subsistence peasants and drove them into urban squalor and ghettos. According to economist Robert L. Heilbroner:

> In a single century, the greater part of the yeomanry was converted into a demoralized mob of paupers who would haunt Britain for 200 years. Riots broke out: in a single uprising in the middle of the 16th century 500 rioters were killed and their leader, Robert Kett, hanged. In another instance a certain Duchess of Sutherland dispossessed 15,000 tenants from 794,000 acres of land, replaced them with 131,000 sheep, and by way of compensation rented her evicted families an average of two acres of submarginal land apiece. And this happened in 1820, at the tail end of the enclosure movement, nearly 50 years after the American Revolution![3]

In the century following England's 1746 victory over the Scots at Culloden, Scotland's crofters were ejected from the land in "clearances." Similar purges occurred in Ireland, but there other disasters exacerbated the exodus. In 1845 the potato blight arrived to help drive the subsistence peasants from the land.

Now with uncluttered titles and unfettered possession of their lands, the Squires turned to commercial agriculture. Landlords ejected old customs along with the peasants and introduced new cultivation, fertilization and seeding practices. Through selective breeding of domestic animals, bloodlines with greater productivity or superior market fitness replaced the old. Fresh capital, recently developed equipment and tight management skills were injected into operations. Farming shifted from a way of life to a way of business.

With the enclosures, sheep, not people, occupied the land. Wool production increased and the woolen industry expanded. Colonies shipped cotton to England, in part because of the nurturing mercantilist protection afforded by the *Navigation Acts*. Technology and capital developed ingenious mechanical devices to fabricate materials, then marvellous power-generating devices to drive these machines, expanding production prodigiously. The landless peasantry resorted to cottage-scale manufacturing or employment as wage labourers in expanding mills and factories. England industrialized using its new abundance of idle humans, the vast capital amassed by the gentry, a globe-girding empire of both resources and markets, its mastery of the seas, railways and the most advanced productive technology of the time. Industrial age itinerancy replaced agriculture's permanence. Entire populations left the land for industrial jobs in the booming cities or left the continent looking for new land. Like Native Americans, they were social, economic and environmental refugees. Unlike them, they had new lands to go to.

Most emigrated to the new Europes, imperial colonies of like people located in friendly temperate climates with a sympathetic Home Office if things got troublesome.

> The great wave of European emigration did not begin until the 1820s when the combined pressures of rapidly rising population in Europe, poor food supplies and a low standard of living (plus better transport) all encouraged emigration. Between 1820 and 1930 about 50 million people emigrated from Europe. Apart from the White Highlands of Kenya, and Costa Rica, few settled in the tropics; most went to the United States and the white colonies of Canada, Australia and New Zealand together with South America.[4]

Europe's poor loaded on boats casting off for the New World, transferring to trains and wagons, some shifting to foot, to go to their new lands; there to make their fortune. The massive diaspora continued until after the Great War, by which time population growth slowed almost to a replacement level, one in which birth and death rates were nearly in balance.

DEMOGRAPHIC STRATEGY

If, as Will Rogers observed, no more land is being made, then population increase results in relative per capita land decrease. David Ricardo knew that scarcity of man's most critical resource drives up prices and rents.[5] So did speculators. One path to wealth for landholders is simple and powerful. Lift not a finger to exploit your land, just increase the numbers of those who wish to do so. Each population increment ratchets up the relative value of your limited resource. Population growth tends to make the rich richer. Technological innovation also ratchets rewards higher by increasing the potential production from a fixed resource base. In this context Galbraith comments on the works of Henry George (1839-1897):

> George's attention was attracted originally to the wonderful increase in western land values (and the accompanying specu-lation) that came with increasing population, the railroads and economic development in general. Little, often none, of this largesse could be attributed to any effort of the owner. Since social factors brought the increase, society had a right to that increase.[6]

It was this phenomenon that England, Canada, HBC and CPR were inter-ested in recreating in the old Rupert's Land. Many of the rewards would gravitate to them. With this demographic strategy (or population policy) in mind, government and capital set to re-peopling the west. Population and technological advance would bless Rupert's Land's well-positioned land-lords with a bountiful harvest. The federal government, with the biggest stake and upfront expenditures, felt most pressure to fill the west. Then the question was, "By whom would they be best served on these lands?"

Elites would not let Native people back on the land. Non-Whites had no place on the new land. Blacks, recently liberated from the Confederacy, were not wanted, at least not as free men to own and till the soil.[7] Orientals and East Indian people fell into the same category despite their abundance and their thousands of years of agricultural traditions.[8]

> Calgarians' hostility toward Chinese laundrymen culminated in an anti-Chinese riot in Calgary in 1892 at a time when the town had a population of approximately 4,000. The riot was triggered by the outbreak of smallpox among a few of the city's Chinese residents. The public mood turned ugly after a few Whites also came down with the disease and three died. After the release of the Chinese from a police medical quaran-tine on the evening of August 2, 300 men, subsequent to a "cricket match between two local clubs followed by a dinner at which some of the participants got drunk," attacked the Chinese laundries, hoping to run the Chinese out of town. They badly wrecked one of the laundries and 'visited' three others where they 'roughed up' the Chinese proprietors and cut off their pigtails. The town police did not appear during

the early stages of the riot, perhaps because the mayor was in sympathy with the rioters. Only after the eventual appearance of the Mounted Police, who began making arrests, did the crowd disperse.[9]

With the railway built, White tolerance for Chinese diminished. Now that White people not Native people possessed the land, tolerance for smallpox also diminished.

Whitedom had its gradations. Those from Europe's southeast were different from those of the northwest. Italians, Greeks, Jews or Arabs were unacceptable.[10] That a few came was testimony to their chutzpa, not the official welcome. In his book *Patterns of Prejudice*, under headings "Immigration Policy", "Promiscuous Foreign Immigration" and the "Ethnic Pecking Order," Howard Palmer opined on the perspectives of the political elites just after the turn of the century:

> They gloried in the exploits of the British Empire and believed in loyalty to God, King, and country. They had been taught to believe that the Anglo-Saxon peoples and British principles of government were the apex of both biological evolution and human achievement . . . . The desirability to Canada of particular immigrant groups varied almost directly with their physical and cultural distance from London, England, and the degree to which their skin pigmentation conformed to Anglo-Saxon white.[11]

Experience modified the rule, excluding London's intellectuals, criminals, leftists, and urban poor because they did not know how to farm. Settlers had a particular purpose, to turn this vast land to account, to farm it, not to make trouble. Canada needed people to do dirty and risky work, to produce the wheat, cows, and pigs to support eastern business and feed the empire. Immigrants must be compliant, concerned most with farming and accumulating material wealth. They must be motivated to part with their homeland and cultures—they must be nearly desperate or very adaptable.

Trade-offs were required between race and function. Some, like Clifford Sifton, the Minister in charge of immigration from 1896 to 1905, preferred farmers over Anglo-Saxon purity. Slavic people sufficed for Sifton. Others, like his successor Frank Oliver, were not so prepared to dilute racial purity in favour of farming capability. Permitting Slav or Galician immigration, he claimed, was to accept "a servile and shiftless people . . . the scum of other lands."[12] Only British or, at least, the near-British of northwestern Europe would do for him. For the right kinds of immigrant, land was free, a giveaway often seductively promoted as new Shangri-Las with the added lure of government promotions. Commerce in three great imperial commodities—European people, capital and land—met and mingled at the end of the railway. But for the land and Native people, this demographic strategy might have been a wonderful solution.

At the time the last spike was driven in the Canadian Pacific's continental line, only days from the hanging of the Metis rebel, Louis Riel, in the fall of 1885, Alberta held about 6,800 White people and Metis. Most of the White people had arrived in the preceding two years during the construction of the railway, a dribble of railwaymen, realtors, promoters and some early settlers. A pervasive economic depression had held the world in its grip off and on since 1873 and free lands elsewhere had yet to be taken up. Better locations closer to civilization's amenities blunted enthusiasm for Alberta's free lands. Despite widespread massively funded emigration campaigns and stellar infrastructure in the railway, the White flood did not come. By 1891 Alberta held only 17,593 White and Metis people. But the European demographic machine was still pumping out people and when the deluge turned, it would be massive.

FILL 'ER UP, CHECK THE OIL

Dribbles turned to streams of people so that by 1895 Alberta's population had increased to some 30,000 White people and Metis. Not fast enough! In 1896 Sir Wilfred Laurier's Liberal government appointed Clifford Sifton as Minister of the Interior, to take charge of lands and immigration. This demographic rainmaker, a modern Moses, started working his miracle in 1896, pelting down God's chosen people, itinerant agri-Whites, on the "promised land." He took to filling the west as his sacred duty. A turned-around economy, the end of pernicious drought, adoption of some new technology, a ballooning European population, aided his mission. And at his urging the masses came.

Most wanted in on the real estate bonanza. One could claim homestead over a quarter section of land by paying a $10 filing fee and undertaking three years of improvements. A secondary market in lands blossomed, including colonization companies, HBC and CPR, but also earlier homesteaders and government. An exuberant Peter C. Newman describes how new railways branched out from the mainline, each nurtured on land grants:

> By the time the prairie land boom reached its peak, the West
> had gone railway mad. Two new transcontinental lines were

snaking across the prairies and piercing the wall of the Rockies to do battle with the CPR.

Branch lines wriggled over the West, crossing and criss-crossing the plains, turning the land into a vast spider's web of steel. Every community, no matter how small, felt itself entitled to at least one railway. Almost every community got one, and some got several.[13]

Railway madness also sponsored another fever. Each new railway shipped infections of land speculation up and down the line.

In urban areas, such as they were, real estate was the big business. It directly employed 10% of Albertans. Others were mere speculators. With a constant influx of new naive buyers, towns and cities rapidly expanded without apparent thought, plan, or direction. Developers surveyed subdivisions far out onto the empty prairie, anticipating runaway urban populations and the rewards of selling to them. At each stride on the expanding urbanscape, there was a real estate promoter with a mouth full of promises, hands full of paper representations and, usually, a folio fat with the money of dupes.

Municipal governments often cloaked a gallery of promoters, architects of blue-sky scenarios and other get-rich-quick schemes. Greed cemented a transcendent urban unity. In their zeal to promote endless growth, "bigger is better" and "this will never end," civic boosters failed to properly attend to the real problems that civic government ought to address—the provision of services, land use planning, care for present-day citizens and sane development for a sane future.

From 1910 to 1913 Alberta ascended the roller coaster of a boom, when property prices and the promise of profit soared above the Rockies. Nothing like it had been seen since the boom and bust of Calgary in 1883 when the railroad went through town. Everyone rode up on the hype. It peaked in 1914 before the war. Then land values plunged to Earth with a crumpling thud. The facade of growth and prosperity toppled, leaving exposed the ramshackle slums. Blue-sky promises turned dark. History tells of the rich chaps who made it in the booms, buying status and respectability. White or Native, the story of the squalor and deceit is rarely told. What noble purpose dwelt within this land-feeding frenzy? What high aspiration, what civilization?

From 1881, when Alberta held 1,500 White people and Metis, to 1901, the population bulged to 73,022. Then it was on to 185,412 by 1906 and swollen to 374,295 by census time in 1911. The army of White people continued to march onward to their promised land so that by war's outbreak in 1914 there were 470,000 people. Growth slowed as mobilization for the next European bloodbath began. Great Britain took comfort entering the Great War (a war in which Europe engaged the rest of the planet) knowing that Rupert's Land was dutifully growing grain to feed it.

Of Alberta's 1914 population of 470,000, some 300,000 farmed, cultivating around 2,500,000 (one million hectares) acres. In 33 years, one-third of a century, population increased by 300 times. Native populations decreased from 10,000 or more in the 1860s, to 6,000 by 1914.[14] Whisky, smallpox and war, it appears, were less murderous than treaties, trusteeship and development. The former inhabitants were dead and dying. The occupation was complete and Laurentia subsided under a new dominion. Something profound had happened.

A photograph shows the log cabin Marshall Copithorne's grandfather built in 1867 [sic] to stake out his future in Southwestern Alberta; beside it, a larger cabin where the first child was born; and on a hill behind, the newly constructed frame house where the third generation grew up in a little more comfort but in the same rugged tradition with freedom as its theme.

Dwarfed in his weather-toughened hand, another photo shows an upstart three-year-old in cowboy boots up past his knees and, beside him, the bowlegged hired man in his stockinged feet, shyly proud of being worshipped by the boss's son.

Grown up and now boss of the ranch himself, Copithorne grins again.

"You'd work for two weeks straight just to get a compliment out of one of those guys. They were real cowboys. We don't have them nowadays, or dang few of them. Anything could happen out in the open range and they'd be able to cope with it somehow or other. You'd get bucked off and your horse would run off on you and you'd be left to walk 10 miles on a thirty-below day . . . . It was just a different era from what we're in now."

He gets up, tall and loose of limb, walks to the window and looks out—past the windsock beside his landing strip, past the sleek van used for transporting the exotic cattle he imports from Italy, past the four-wheel-drive truck used for modern-day round-ups. His gaze sweeps the bowl of the valley, 10,000 tawny acres dotted with cattle, and up the other side of the shadow-dark lee of the Rocky Mountains.

Even the language had changed. "Genetics is my business really. We treat cattle now as a machine to harvest what we grow on the ranch. And genetics is just a mechanical way to produce a better machine, a more efficient machine . . . ."

"You know the term 'tied to the land'? I sure am tied to the soil—me and the cows . . . . Respect for the land. Respect for our greatest resource, which is our land, eh? I guess you could say that my whole life is dedicated to preserving this land for future generations."

Heather Menzies *The Railroad's Not Enough*: *Canada Now* (Toronto: Clark Irwin, 1978) 73-75.

CHAPTER 9

SODBUSTING

HOMESTEAD DAYS

B
efore contact there was no agriculture in Alberta. Conditions were too extreme for available technology. Temperatures ranged widely, precipitation was modest; neither were predictable, making agriculture too risky. After contact, agriculture was not encouraged. HBC preferred profits to farmers. Agriculture awaited appropriate technology—trains, ploughs and early maturing grains—and with no markets, there was little point. In Alberta's south the Blackfoot Confederacy, herds of bison, capricious but common drought, and nearly impenetrable sod further stood in the way of farming.

Reportedly Peter Pond tended a garden in the lower Athabasca region as early as 1787. By 1810 homegrown barley supplemented trader's diets in Fort Edmonton. A few cows came to Peace River country by 1833 and Reverend McDougall trailed cattle south to Morley (west of Calgary) in 1873. Some 200 years after the HBC grant of Rupert's Land, Alberta's largest agricultural enterprise was 12 hectares (30 acres) of sown barley. From first ranches about 1879, to Billy Cust in 1881 with his green thumb sowing 130 acres (50 ha) to wheat, 36 (15 ha) to barley and 12 (five hectares) to oats, Alberta warmed to agriculture. In the summer of 1883, the railway cut the industrial age's first channel into Alberta: this was the breach and along it would come homesteaders.

Under the Dominion Lands Policy a prospective homesteader paid a $10 application fee for a quarter section of land (160 acres or 65 ha). If, after three years occupation, sufficient improvements and cultivation were done, the homesteader became owner. Additional Dominion lands could be purchased for $1 per acre. This early Alberta Advantage undercut the Americans where homestead periods were five years and land prices ranged from $1.25 to $2.50 per acre.[1] Few came in response to these first promises of free land. Then Clifford Sifton, Minister of the Interior (1896 to 1905), plenipotentiary of Rupert's Land, spurred the pace from trudge to

REEDING THE ENTRAILS • AN ALBERTA ECOHISTORY

trot, then whipped it into a headlong gallop. Alberta's population hyperinflated, from 30,000 in 1895 to nearly half a million in 1914. In 1905 about 2,000 km² were under the plough and even with this influx, tilled acreage merely redoubled by war's outbreak.

During the Great War prices boomed; $.91 per bushel of wheat in 1914 climbed to $2.30 in 1920.[2] Rains came, shooting crop yields and profits higher again. Seeded acreages tripled, net incomes multiplied and then multiplied again. Wheat was king and prosperity settled over rural Alberta. Free land could still be had.

From war's end in 1918 through much of the '20s, drought baked Alberta's southeast. Fierce spring and fall winds or hot dry summer gusts lifted topsoil off, wafting them away toward Saskatchewan. Settlers' dreams dried and blew away with them. In the late '20s, money and rains again wetted settlers' dreams but prosperity was only too brief, turning to a nightmare at decade's end. Commodity prices halved, then rehalved as world recession became the Great Depression (1930-1939). Net revenues plunged into the deep red.[3] When that could hurt no more, grasshoppers came. When only stubs remained, drought assailed the land once more.

Prairie sod knew how to resist recurring drought, farmers did not. Ploughing flayed the sod skin from the land, permitting sun and wind to strip the moisture deep within. Winds eroded light soil areas, claiming the fertility of over two million hectares of land, depositing them downwind in sheltered areas as shifting dunes and sandhills, badlands. Alberta's tilled lands may now have lost nearly 50% of their humus content, most by Depression's end.[4] Despite difficult conditions, the agricultural land base grew. Tilled land jumped to 62,500 km² by 1929, much broken by team and plough.

During the '30s Robert England commented on the imperial strategy for the west:

> There have been few more significant movements of capital and men than that from Great Britain to the Dominions, by which, in the generation prior to the war, Great Britain assured herself of her food supply. Railways in Western Canada were therefore as essential a part of the machinery for war purposes as shipbuilding yards or the equipment of heavy industries.[5]

Wars and rains bestowed their double benediction on farmers at the end of the '30s as yet another European engagement spilled over to engulf the world. Tractors and threshers became the swords and spears for Alberta's farmers during this next Great War, World War II.[6] Postwar years brought the rains again, prices steadied and profits rose as the nation managed to dismantle and reintegrate its war machine better than it had after 1918.

AGRICULTURAL TECHNOLOGY
PLOUGH

The fibrous, dense and resilient sod-mat of grass covering the North American prairies protected them from wind, rain, fire and ploughs until John Deere's steel mouldboard plough, developed in 1846, penetrated this tough tangle.[7] The shovel's inclined steel blade cut into the lower roots, lifting the mat up and flipping it over. Deep soils turned up while surface grasses and herbs—the cactus, sagebrush, soapwood, bunchgrass, blue grama and buffalo grass—were ploughed under as green manure. With this blade the hard dry soils of America's plains might be ripped deep enough to permit grains to sprout and root down to moisture. Western lands now had value.

First sodbusters talked of an eerie moan coming from the earth when the plough's steel blades sheared open the tight primeval mat. Over millennia, forces of grass, forb and nematode laboured with micro-powers of bacteria, fungus and algae to endow the mineral media with structure and fertility. In each gram of soil a billion microorganisms, diverse and fragile, toil to recompose and sustain soil. With a pass of the plough, the building stops, the process turns and bio-entropy begins. Plough in hand and oxen out front, teamsters might have sensed what a truly deep cut they took of the prairie wool.

Introduced crops relate differently to the soil than native plant communities. Where once the soil was a sustaining element in an interdependent dynamic system, now it becomes a degenerating resource. Turned skyward, unprepared and unprotected, tilled earth faced a hostile environment of whipping winds, beating rain and rapid temperature changes. Each crop extracted more from the land, leaving less for next year. New techniques, like summerfallowing and more recently zero tillage, slowed the decline, but did not stop it.[8]

WHEAT

Wheat generated from an unusual hybridization of wild grasses. Its seed was so large that it had no means of dispersal. About 8,000 years ago, Hittite agriculturists collected its germ because of the food value of that extraordinarily plump seed, saving it and dispersing it wherever it could be grown. Wheats now are among the planet's most numerous plants. Settlers ploughed up the prairie wool to plant this helpless, fat, tasty imposter.

Alberta's short, dry growing season demanded a special wheat. Red Fife wheat had relatively early maturation, hardness and quality, so settlers packed it west with them. Later in 1909, farmers tried Marquis, a new cultivar developed by the Crown at its Dominion Experimental Farm. This quality hard red spring wheat matured several critical days earlier than Red Fife. The precocious Marquis made those wildlands with shorter growing seasons economical to farm.

WATER

Starting in 1876 local farmers constructed small-scale irrigation structures to combat the always-threatening drought in Palliser's Triangle.[9] Later CPR felt irrigation might help develop and sell some of its 25-million-acre land grant (10,125,000 ha). In 1903 it:

> . . . accepted a three-million-acre (1,215,000 ha), 48-mile-wide (77-km-wide) block of land between Calgary and Medicine Hat, along with 800,000 acres (324,000 ha) in the Northern Reserve, as the final installment of the many millions of acres awarded it for the building of the main line of its railroad.[10]

There the CPR dammed and diverted the mighty Bow River to these arid lands, as if "the Bow River were flowing out onto it."

Irrigation's thirst is quenched by Alberta's wild rivers. It consumes 80 to 90% of their diverted waters, distorting riverine and hydrological systems and cycles. Spring flows are captured in reservoirs to store water for mid-summer, when irrigators need the water. On-stream reservoirs disconnect upstream aquatic life from downstream with miles of deep stagnant waters. The cottonwoods, guardians of riverbank and floodplain, require flooding to set their seed. Dams stop the flood. Without over-the-bank spring freshets, cottonwoods below the dams and reservoirs do not regenerate. These groves are foundation, column and dome to riverine ecology.[11] Whether for water and food, shelter and wintering grounds or hibernaculum, nesting and cover, prairie river valleys host and nourish nearly all plain's life in critical ways. Wild native fish populations, in poor condition in the province as it is, suffer and decline with their river. Terrestrial wildlife, upstream separated from downstream by miles of exposed reservoir mudbank, inevitably disconnects and declines.[12]

Irrigated farming uses energy, chemicals, fertilizers, pesticides and of course, water very intensively. This water appears nearly free but is not.[13] Irrigation products, mostly grains and hay, feed Alberta's heavily subsidized, sacred cow. Irrigation systems are wasteful and sloppy; about 50% of the diverted river's flow reaches the crop zone and 25% returns to the river.[14] The remainder, with loads of agricultural fertilizers and chemicals, seeps elsewhere percolating through the ground to new drainages or evaporating back into the hydrological cycle, leaving its distillates behind. Irrigation adds to groundwater, raising water tables and sometimes inundating surface lowlands with dissolved salts, minerals and chemicals, choking them by soil salinization.

About 6,000 km² of Alberta's lands are irrigated, 5,000 km² in irrigation districts. Gathering and distribution systems take up more land, degradation consumes still more. Irrigation dammed the south's major river systems. Government argues that dams prevent downstream flooding in populated areas, a greater concern now that government has authorized the clearcutting of headwaters forests. Some speculate Alberta's rivers will be the water source not just for irrigation but for Alberta's next natural resource industry, water export.

MECHANICAL

Internal combustion power and new mechanical devices overran the farm between the wars. Mechanical monsters—tractors, swathers, thrashers, then combines, each able to do the work of hundreds of animals and tens of men—drove dray animals and teamsters from the field. Farm size grew and farmer numbers shrank. Horse populations fell from 800,000 to 100,000. Earlier technological innovations lured people to the land and drove nature off, now technology's efficiencies, product of military and industrial processes, drove people from the land. Many homesteaders, scarcely one generation on the land, left for the city. Pioneer days were over in Alberta.

FERTILIZERS

Fertility diminishes when nature's recycling systems are ousted and replaced by unidirectional flows of nutrients and the energy required for ploughing, harrowing, seeding, weeding and reaping—from the ground, to the bin, to the rail, to international markets, to the gut, to the sewer. Each ploughing turns the field up to sun and wind. Tractors and heavy equipment excrete fumes and smoke, not cow pies or horse apples, they do not fertilize the land but acidify and compact it, squeezing and burning the soil. Under the drawbar of industrial-age agriculture, soil structures deteriorate.

By the 1950s, much of the land's natural fertility was lost. Alberta's natural gas reserves provided a ready feedstock to fill this nutrient void. This natural capital from millions of years past could be converted to fertilizers, providing additional years of productivity from slumping soils.

But the resultant crop yields came at a cost. By themselves and in combination with other chemicals and uses, fertilizers have altered the soil's chemistry, condition and content.

CHEMICAL

Agriculture is a war with the wild kingdom. Untamed nature is the enemy. Concerned that the "beast of the field multiply against thee," farmers must purge other life.[15] In the early days this meant killing the blond-pelted prairie wolves, massive plains grizzly bear, herds of bison and wapiti. That progressed on to smaller life—Richardson's ground squirrels, chestnut-collared longspurs and Melissa blues. Today it includes the microscopic.

The battle begins with ploughing, by preparation of the field for cropping, by elimination of all other life forms. This provides a suitable host medium for the chosen life form, wheat and such. After seeding and sprouting a defensive battle begins. Nature counterattacks with battalions of weeds and pests. "The cutworm cutteth, the rust rusteth an' the 'hopper hoppeth!"[16] Monocropping fields provide a blanket banquet of some creature's favourite food. Its predators having been eliminated by the farmer's earlier purgings, an orgy of reproduction follows. Horizon to horizon ravenous insects set upon the homesteader's crops. World War II armed the farmer for this. In finding new ways to kill people, scientists devised tempting means to mass-manufacture selective poisons to eliminate other pests.[17] Rachel Carson's 1962 classic critique *Silent Spring* traces the chemical industry's parentage:

> This industry is a child of the Second World War. In the course of developing agents for chemical warfare, some of the chemicals created in the laboratory were found to be lethal to insects. The discovery did not come by chance: insects were widely used to test chemicals as agents of death for man.[18]

Warriors themselves, and quite liking the biocidal effects of these new chemicals, prairie farmers took to them like sawflies to a wheat stem.[19] Nearly any vexation that might be chemically disposed of, was.

What do these chemical cocktails do to the soil's micro-organic community, the land, the Biosphere? Today, in this arms race, humans seek virtual elimination of local nature. Chemical engineers now construct poisons of such broad spectrum that they kill everything on the land—systemic biocides. Genetic engineers fabricate crops, genetically engineered plants, that are resistant to these biocides. Finally a true monoculture is possible—everything dead but one. And that one species—the crop—is not natural but genetically engineered. Not that the intent is any different from technology of old; it is just the awesome mastery over the death of life. A few wonder, and fewer question, this civilizing of the land.

DOMESTIC ANIMALS

Horses, cows, pigs, sheep, goats, chickens, turkeys, ducks, geese, dogs, cats and others unloaded from off the ark or out of the European "envelope" along with the homesteaders. Others disembarked with this familiar menagerie—the plant, animal and human pathogens, and the weeds and pests, both big and small. All came to homestead the land. Each brought its community of effects along.

Climate, fertility or topographical features forbid some lands to the plough. Domestic animals were the intermediate machine, the tool, to exploit the non-arable or wildlands. The cow's ruminant stomach is the indefatigable factory that turns wild grass to meat or milk or leather. Continuously we seek new methods to make these factories more effective. Genetics increase the meat or milk productivity of these biological machines. Horticulture changes the land's productivity and carrying capacity. Some land might be broken and seeded to exotic grasses. Others are left unploughed but cleared, scarified or altered through introduction of exotic high-yielding species of plants, and chemical suppression of others. Fire, herbicides or other management technology provide more auspicious circumstances for grazing cattle. As a result native flora is eliminated.

Native fauna is also eliminated, displaced by domestic animals. Cows became surrogates for bison, not synergistically but degeneratively. Unlike the bison, they are a keystone species only, perhaps, for starlings, sparrows, clover and White people. Cows displace the wapiti, antelope, mule deer, moose and mouse. Formerly ubiquitous, the ground squirrel provided plains predators their main course; killing it eliminates those trophic levels above it. When done-in by strychnine, their predators—the hawk, fox and ferret—die fast. When erased by other means, predators die more slowly. Today some talk of ground squirrels as Alberta's next export commodity—pets, apparently, for the Japanese.[20]

The cow's top predator, humans, displaced all others. Cougar, wolf and bear were resolutely eliminated to keep the cow safe, happy, productive and available exclusively for market appetites. While bison's grazing habits maintained diversity in native vegetation on the plains and parklands, the cow's preferences and practices collapse diversity. They graze favourite or nutritious native grasses to elimination. When overgrazed, pastures degrade to thickets of sage, shrubby cinquefoil and weeds.

Never the adventurers, cows overgraze near their favourite watering places, trampling their banks, eroding them. They foul streambeds, silting them up, suffocating aquatic life and water quality. Populations and diversity among avian and fish species plunge. Waterways occupy only a small portion of grazing lands but they are the most critical to other life. Effects of the destruction of them ripple widely.

The cow provides an efficient dispersal mechanism for exotic species. Weed seed came on their hides, in their feed and deep in their complex gut. These clever passengers of the ruminant stomach sprouted, rooted and grew in cow pies. Wherever cows wander so do venturesome clovers, thistles and other Eurasian plants. Weeds adore a disturbance so they love the plough.[21] Wild mustards, wild oats, thistles and dandelions and hundreds of others, came west. Wherever the settler set foot—plantain is aptly called "Englishmen's foot"—weeds sprouted. Today's traveller sees little native vegetation in settled areas. Most is Eurasian. Even on Alberta's highest mountains or most deserted valleys, rarely is one beyond sight of exotic plants. In mountain meadows, up to 40% of the grasses may be exotic. For every exotic, there is one less native plant and, perhaps, one less native insect, fungi or other dependant.

Invertebrates changed too, although less is known of this. Common earthworms were introduced. Today concern increases over their ecological effects.[22] Like the weeds, any number of insect pests came overseas with their favourite food source. Houseflies followed man out of Africa through Europe to the New World. Cabbage moths and lice chummed along with their respective hosts. Native insects were eliminated, some by design, others unintentionally. The Rocky Mountain locust loved agriculture; it was extinct by 1902.[23] Where now is the giant carrion beetle? In the war on pests, many helpful creatures, from birds and bats to spiders and nematodes, died in friendly chemical crossfire. Postwar pesticide exuberance did incalculable damage, but crops looked good.

Vertebrate wildlife leapt out of the European ship—starlings, English sparrows, pigeons, rats and the house mouse. Some native American species developed exotic-like affinities for human habits and habitations. The white-tailed deer was an eastern species that liked White people and moved west with them—Manitoba by the 1820s and Alberta by the turn of the century. Wherever there was cover and farmers, the white-tailed deer presented itself, displacing the mule deer. Introduced eastern greys may displace some indigenous red squirrels.

More obscure are diseases introduced by exotic species, usually domestic animals, to wild native species and, possibly, inter-species with humans:

The domestication of animals, which involved close contacts between humans and animals (with animals often living in the same buildings as humans), exposed people to a range of diseases which already affected animals. Some of these were able to adapt to humans as new hosts and flourish in their new environment, others slightly changed their characteristics and became specifically human diseases. Many of the common human diseases are close relatives of animal diseases. Smallpox, for example, is very similar to cowpox and measles is related to rinderpest (another cattle disease) and canine distemper. Tuberculosis also originated in cattle as did diphtheria. Influenza is common to humans and hogs and the common cold certainly came from the horse. Leprosy came from water buffalo. After living for some 10,000 years in close proximity to animals, humans now share 65 diseases with dogs, 50 with cattle, 46 with sheep and goats and 42 with pigs.[24]

As surely as smallpox devastated Native people, introduced diseases ravaged wildlife. What effects had canine and feline distemper on the wolf and mountain lion?[25] What effects might whirling disease have on native trout? What did blue-tongue and lungworm do to the bighorn sheep? And what of anthrax, bangs and rabies?

The politics of interspecies disease transmission play out today in Wood Buffalo National Park bison. Its plains bison herd descended from survivors of last century's bison campaign. In the '20s domestic cattle infected this bison herd with brucellosis and tuberculosis. When these diseases were eliminated from the Canadian cattle herd (1984 and 1992 respectively), government agriculturists and the cattle industry determined to eliminate the Wood Buffalo herd ("depopulate" is the brave new word) and thereby eliminate these diseases. Their plan was to later reintroduce disease-free and pure wood bison. A federal Environmental Assessment Review Panel recommended depopulation, but it has yet to be acted on.[26]

With Frankensteinian zeal, science and technology work hard and long to create new monsters. Genetic engineering and manipulations increasingly strip nature from these sorry creatures, replacing it with attributes having economic advantage. The milk cow becomes less a cow, more a biological support system for the udder. With bovine somatotropin (BST) these udders become prodigious drug-charged milk machines for humanity. Modern habitat for these inert creatures is intense factory environments, more crowded and brutal than the factories of Dickens' day. Specialized breeds come to slaughter with production line efficiencies and mass kill techniques. Force-fed, narrowly constrained, drug-driven, hormone-stimulated creatures, like veal calves and broiler chickens, never see day's light before slaughter's darkness. Relentless pressure accelerates the speed and efficiency of this. Designer geneticists toil to manufacture the perfectly replicable genotypes to produce the homogenous phenotypes industry demands to efficiently feed or clothe the consumer. With cloning technology these too will become perfect monocultures.

Today agriculture searches the wild kingdom for new species it can turn into consumer goods. Most bison are now cattle. Wapiti were noble animals. They too, are becoming an aggregation of products. The wapiti's efficient stomach turns herbs too wild for cows into wapiti meat—taking up those wildlands that cows will not touch. Agribusinessmen cut and grind proud wapiti antlers to dust to export to the Orient as aphrodisiacs while universities research ways to use these same horns to bulk up athletes, just about the same activity—phony hardness. Bear's bladders do the same. Today people farm ostrich, llamas, deer, trout and anything that somebody may crave. Most claim love of nature as their motive.

ALBERTA'S LAND BASE

The federal Crown holds about 10% of Alberta's lands: national parks (9%), First Nations lands (less than 1%), and other federal works and responsibilities. Provincial authority divided the remaining lands into two areas. The Green Area is approximately 350,000 km² or 53% of the province and contains those stretches considered appropriate for forestry and other resource or extractive industries, but not "settlement." The remainder, the White Area, is approximately 245,000 km² or 37% of Alberta. It hosts agricultural and other intensive humans uses, much under the regimen of private property ownership. Farming and ranching claims over 32% of Alberta's lands, that is some 208,110 km² of the 638,235 km² total.[27] Lands under cultivation or "improved lands," crops or summerfallow, occupy over 110,000 km²; unimproved pasture or other less intensive agricultural uses occupy just less than 100,000 km².

Agricultural lands were among the most productive wildlands. They supported the greatest populations and species diversity of fauna and flora. Formerly the range of the bison and the great bears, now they are host to wheat, oilcrops, feedcrops, cows and pickup trucks. Neoteric Alberta contains some 5.6 million head of cattle, 1.85 million pigs, 255,000 sheep, 100,000 horses, nine million chickens, 815,000 turkeys, countless dogs, cats and other domestic animals in addition to its three million people. By weight approximately 99% of Alberta non-human mega-faunal mammalian life is domestic animals, while 1% or so is wildlife. That 1% is radically altered through a century of abuse. In 1729, Native people had 100% of the land, now they have less than 1%. They were 100% of the people, now they are 2%. In 1729, wildlife was 100% of the mega-faunal biomass, now it has plunged to 1%. The displacement is nearly perfect.

OTHER AGRICULTURAL EFFECTS

The bison debacle ended large scale "market hunting" in Alberta. There was little else to kill and Alberta was far from markets. Migratory fowl "market hunting" had its largest effect at the southern end of migratory routes in America. On wintering grounds, that market bludgeoned and blasted birds in the millions. Local demand for waterfowl eggs and swan skins may have contributed to the stoop in prairie populations of trumpeter swans and whooping crane.[28] Habitat destruction certainly did as well.

Some wildlife—caribou, sheep, bears and whooping cranes—do not tolerate humans well. They survive only by retreat to wilderness. But wilderness itself retreated and shrank, so that by 1941 whoopers had a wild population of 15.[29] Their recovery, if such it is, testifies to their attractiveness as a symbol and to massive interventions, but has nothing to do with a more hospitable wild world. Even in Wood Buffalo National Park, their last refuge and part of the last refuge of the wood bison, *Bison athabascae*, giant dams threaten their summer home.[30] The plains grizzly and the plains wolf survived the bison's passing, only to die with the wolfers and first settlers. Pinnated grouse or prairie chicken were ploughed and "pot shot" to death. The land suffered a succession of purges, strips.

These days agrarians claim to be true environmentalists. They care for the field and nurture the range, but their purpose is to take not to save, to exploit not nurture. A few species eke out fleeting existences on agriculture's margins, in the ditches and rock piles aside from the vast monocultures; but they do not live in nature, they exist in refugia awaiting this ice age's end and a better day. The future will bring more of the same—more technology, more production. Every slough, pothole, border and borrow pit must produce. The throbbing drumbeat "more production," the ubiquitous mantra "more technology" and the numbing ululation for "more trade" turns residents into automatons, vacantly following orders for more and more, received from farther and farther away. The Promised Land is nearly deserted now. Birds fly through on migration. They fly over amorphous furrowed seas populated by occasional giant machines, a furtive worker or two on a monoculture checkerboard, but otherwise the land is funereal.

RECOLLECTIONS OF GROWING UP IN LODGEPOLE, ALBERTA IN THE PEMBINA OIL FIELD

eteran "rig pig" Harry says he remembers the early '60s like yesterday. "I was young and perfect. Everybody remembers their perfect years.

We were all in a hurry. Those oilfields took a zillion years to fill but everybody wanted them drained now, or sooner.

"We lived on Pan Am F Lease, drove lease roads out, lease roads back, company truck of course, lived in a company skid shack, 'Mobile home parks,' some were called.

"It wasn't bad money if you could hold it. Trouble is, there was nothing to do but rough-neck, play cards, and drink— drink at the Frontier, drink in tin trailers, steal a nip in the cab of a pickup.

"Myself, I was always saving for a Parisienne, but roads in them days, rrrgh. Built 'em fast, with tons of heavy rock cuz everything kept sinking, eh, boggy and all. No place for a car.

"But those Parisiennes, I tell you, low? Wide? Long? They was it!

"Wanted a red car cuz everything else was black.

"I stayed 10 years, if I'm counting right. Longer than most. But nobody goes in there with a one-way ticket.

Excerpt from *Today is the Frontier* by Lorne Daniels
Calgary Herald, December 30, 1995, D 11.

CHAPTER 10

OIL MOIL

THE WAY IT WAS

hat to do with it—perhaps caulk and seal canoes? A Cree named Wa-Pa-Su (also known as Swan) noted a strange black pitch, bitumen, in his reports to the HBC. Might it have value one day? For two centuries little would come of this mention of a northern Alberta riverbank seeping black guck, but Wa-Pa-Su's 1719 notes on the Athabasca Tar sands is Alberta's first written record of fossil fuels.

Palliser noticed coal exposed by cutbanks in Alberta river valleys. In 1870 an American, Nicholas Sheran, spied coal seams along the Oldman River near present-day Lethbridge. By 1872 he had bored his coal mine deep into the bank. Knowing better than anyone that the CPR was coming and it needed coal, Alexander Galt (father of Confederation, railwayman, entrepreneur and insider with the highest imperial contacts) arranged the 1882 takeover of the Sheran Mine through a company headed by one William Lethbridge. This coal would fuel the westward-probing CPR.

Just when Palliser ended his sortie into the western wilds, 1859, the first North American oil wells were dug and drilled. Many produced light gravity oils that transported safely and easily, making them splendid fuels for an automated and mobile age. In 1876 Otto cranked up his internal combustion engine, a prototype for a next generation of power plants. This engine required safe portable fuels like petroleum-based gasolines for its mobile applications. With automotive civilization welling up, any place promising oil held promise.

Around that time, 1874, Stoney people told bison hunter, wolfer, trader and first White resident of Waterton Lakes, Kootenai Brown, of extrudes seeping into Cameron Creek above Upper Waterton Lake. The Stoneys used this viscous liquid as a lubricant, ointment and unction—so did Brown. Years following, after hearing Brown's stories, a string of promoters and would-be oilmen (1889-91 and then from 1902-1907) tried their luck with "black gold" at a drilling settlement called Oil City in what is now

Waterton Lakes National Park. A few wells produced and one, the Western Oil Company well, blew wild, oozing slick into Waterton Lakes. "There it spread out, killing thousands of ducks and fish," according to Ed Gould's book *Oil*.[1] For good and for bad Alberta had oil. In time it would be found in abundance.

Oil City cameoed Alberta's conventional oil development, a life cycle now only half played out. Itinerant explorers strike oil. They capture and produce this non-renewable resource. Others circle in, clamouring for their piece. The field is produced to depletion. Oilmen lower their derrick and tent poles to move on, taking what still has value and leaving behind roadways, disturbances, castoffs, pollution and introduced exotics. The Oil City play dried up by 1910 and the buildings started their long decay.

While laying the railway line near Medicine Hat in 1883, CPR poked under the parched prairies seeking water. It hit ubiquitous natural gas. By 1890, with "all hell for a basement" as Rudyard Kipling said, Medicine Hat harnessed this fiery devil to their purposes. Neighbours warmed to natural gas. Promoters did too, hustling deals up and down the railway line—some went so far as to drill wells. In 1909, near Bow Island, an 8 million cubic feet per day gas well came in.[2] This well, Old Glory, and others from nearby CPR lands produced enough gas to pipeline it to Calgary, Lethbridge and other consumer points along the way.

Near present-day Turner Valley, a rancher noticed strange substances bubbling up along the creek bank. Sensing opportunity, William Herron leased the surrounding lands. He and others, including a surge of lawyers (later to form a core group of Alberta's elite and one, R. B. Bennett, a future Prime Minister of Canada), drilled the Dingman Discovery well, hitting a rich production zone of naphtha on May 14, 1914. A brief orgy of petroleum field flim-flams followed this first boom in what was then known as Turner's Valley.[3] Within months of Dingman No. 1, a young Bosnian assassinated the Austro-Hungarian Archduke Francis Ferdinand (June 28, 1914). Europe ignited in war, inflaming the world with them. Canada joined in August 4, 1914 and Turner Valley turned to fuelling the war effort.

Turner Valley did not gush again until October 14, 1924 when Royalite No.4 blew in, out, and, later, up. Catching fire on November 9, this rogue well incandesced night skies kilometres distant. The drama of the event and the magnitude of the discovery reignited speculation. Hucksters and hustlers once again hit the streets of Calgary. This time the puff turned to reality. Significant oil and gas reserves lay beneath Turner Valley.

In 1936 drillers finally tapped into Turner Valley's deeper basins of crude oil and again the valley went development wild. Gould recounts:

Pumping stations, absorption plants, tank farms and derricks dotted the foothills. But the most noticeable feature was the flares, hundreds of them, all over the Valley, making so much light that the glow could easily be seen from Calgary, 40 miles, (64 km) to the northeast.

The author . . . could count as many as 14 huge flares from the front door of one family home near Longview. Dubbed Hell's Half Acre, the flares caused unnatural flower and grass growth in the areas around them and farmers swore they could read their newspapers from a long distance away and go hunting rabbits at night without further illumination.[4]

A glorious foothills valley deliquesced into a sickly industrial site. Pollution settled over Little Chicago and Little Philadelphia, names pretentious boosters pinned on the valley's precocious clapboard towns. Over a trillion cubic feet of gas was flared, hazing the atmosphere with shades of sickly browns and sulphurous yellows. Underlying streams bubbled viscously with kindred colours.

Later the field lost pressure, production declined and the boom fizzled. Transient exploiters drifted off but the mess stayed behind. The puffy towns of Little Chicago, Little New York and Little Philadelphia lost their boom and bluster. The only survivors, Little New York, now known as Longview, and Turner Valley itself, still have people, the others only weeds and ghosts.

Alberta's "eureka!" was February 13, 1947, its world oil debut. That day Imperial Oil's Leduc No. 1 blew in, the discovery well to a field containing over 200 million barrels of recoverable oil. Here was a land with oil and a government with ambition to exploit it. The remainder of the Seven Sisters[5] and lesser multinational oil companies followed Exxon (Imperial Oil's American Parent) to Alberta. The industry quickly found Alberta's elephants, including the expansive Pembina field southwest of Edmonton and Rainbow Lake-Zama. From Texas and Oklahoma, wherever local prospects paled, seekers journeyed to this new Promised Land to drill for black gold, to strike it big, to cash in, and to move on.

Gould claims, with merit, that the big oil discoveries multiplied local growth:

This increase in oil and gas production affected every person on the Prairies by widening the job opportunities through new industries and increasing construction and strengthening of public finances. Farm mechanization was speeded up, provincial debt was lowered and cities like Regina, Calgary and Edmonton doubled their populations.[6]

Unlike the settlers detraining from the CPR decades earlier, the new settlers came by car, bus, and plane and shared one overwhelming focus—to
enrich on black gold. Gould also described the early oilfield worker's circumstances:

> "You could always tell an oil worker's house," the man said.
> "It may have been only a tarpaper skid shack, but there was
> always a brand new car sitting outside it." "And an outside
> toilet too," his wife added.[7]

RECENT HISTORY

With Leduc No. 1, Interprovincial Pipeline started to lay pipe east, penetrating Manitoba in 1949, Sarnia by 1953, and then on to Toronto. But
Alberta's expensive oil could not compete in the eastern market with more
inexpensive offshore oils. Oft-forgotten out west these days was Canada's
accommodations to Alberta and its newest industry. Based on recommendations of the Royal Commission on Energy, the Borden Commission,
struck in 1957 to inquire into energy issues, the federal government of
John Diefenbaker implemented its National Oil Policy (NOP) on February 1, 1961. Industry obtained a monopoly over markets west of the Que-
bec-Ontario border, all under the nurturing regulatory eye of the new
National Energy Board (NEB). Ontario energy consumers paid significantly
higher prices to support Alberta's petroleum producers and government.
Protected from world prices, marketplace competition, and free trade, the
mostly American multinationals got down to the business of finding and
selling pricey Alberta oil.

These mercantilist policies were not potent enough for some in the
industry. In his *The Blue-Eyed Sheiks* Peter Foster recalls the Independent
Producers Association of Canada (IPAC) pithy plea to Ottawa in 1969:

> Canada is the only nation capable of self-sufficiency which
> gives only limited priority to domestic oil; permits a drain of
> hundreds of millions of dollars for overseas oil; leaves half the
> nation totally dependent on overseas supplies, thus ignoring
> the problem of security in emergencies; and leaves it to an-
> other nation—the United States—to provide the lion's share
> of market growth for a Canadian resource.[8]

Entreaties for government intervention turned to "butt out" when world
prices headed higher several years later.

In 1971 the Organization of Petroleum Exporting Countries (OPEC) cartel constricted oil supply, driving world oil prices up. By the mid-'70s world oil prices quadrupled and after 1979, virtually quadrupled again—all told from US$2 to US$40. With the OPEC epiphany, the oilpatch gospel now praised free markets and "world oil prices." Suspicious of provincialists and fair-weather free-enterprisers, Pierre Trudeau's federal government imposed its National Energy Plan (NEP), a plan that required the industry, producing and consuming provinces (east and west), and the federal government to share benefits and burdens of OPEC's manipulations. IPAC got some of the measures (now thoroughly despised) so eagerly prayed for in its 1969 submission. Alberta's premier, Peter Lougheed, fought the NEP by threatening to twist closed his fossil fuel tap to the east. Suddenly sharing, security and nation building were the devil's work. About then the epithet "Freeze in the dark, you eastern bastards" circulated.

Brian Mulroney's federal government eliminated Trudeau's hated NEP. Through the Western Accord, entered with the producing provinces in March 1985, oil moved to world prices; gas would follow shortly. To ensure that the public interest not interfere with business, Mulroney's people equated the public interest to the private interests of those buying and selling the resource. This doctrinal prestidigitation they called Market-Based Procedures for gas. It is "founded on the premise that the marketplace would generally operate in such a way that Canadian requirements for natural gas would be met at fair market prices."[9] Similar principles applied to oil. Mulroney's market magic gutted the public and national interest.

Mr. Mulroney did not rest there. With daring he moved Canada into a sovereignty netherworld with Article 9.04 of the Canada/United States Free Trade Agreement (FTA):

> Either party may maintain or introduce a restriction . . . with respect to the export of an energy good . . . only if:
> a. The restriction does not reduce the proportion of the total export shipments . . . relative to the total supply of that good . . . as compared to the proportion prevailing in the most recent 36-month period . . . measure.

FTA's super-sovereign covenants provided the Americans rights to that proportion of Canadian production they enjoyed over the previous three years. Cold Canada pen-stroked away rights to 55% of its natural gas and 45% of its oil (in today's proportions). Trade metamorphosed from discretionary to mandatory.[10] Now national interest was not just an irrelevant interest, but an excluded interest. Like the *Enclosures Acts* centuries earlier in England and the Indian treaties of last century, people were excluded from the benefits of the land.

INDUSTRY PRACTICES

Finding and capturing substances enfolded in formations thousands of metres and millions of years below Earth's surface is no facile quest. For Oil City, Old Glory and Turner Valley, discoveries seemed as much luck as method. The rustic ways of finding oil—surface observations, intuition and divining techniques—gave way so that after Leduc the majors pursued petroleum with scientific precision, technological power and businesslike discipline, all applied with hound-dog determination.

Seismics, a favoured geophysical information gathering tool in fossil fuel prospecting, involves the detonation of small explosive devices, set at certain distances along surveyed, cleared lines. Deep-earth echoes rebound and are recorded by sensitive devices placed in matrix across the targeted area. Seismic records indicate critical features to subterranean geological formations and their potential for hydrocarbons. Seismic's millions of kilometres of cut and cleared rights-of-way (five million kilometres by one estimate) criss-cross the province.

Desirable lands are obtained from government and private interests, often through "farm-in" arrangements. Roads are rammed to a drilling location, sometimes miles distant over challenging terrain, up mountains, across scree slopes or through muskeg or swamp in the Green Area. Over 500,000 km of petroleum access roads slice Alberta.[11] At roadend contractors clear and level a hectare or larger drilling site and excavate a sump as repository for perhaps 25,000 barrels of drilling wastes, and a flare pit to dispose of bad gas and other pollutants into the atmospheric commons.

A drilling tower, mobile buildings and large equipment are deployed to the lease site with military precision, transforming it into an industrial site. The tower structure and platform enable the bit-tipped steel stem to drill ever deeper into the earth. Crews sheath the hole with metal casings to protect it from cave-ins and prevent the entry or escape of materials. Mudmen circulate various materials throughout the hole, to lubricate drilling, regulate temperature and downhole chemistry, and suspend out solids. Periodic pressure, mechanical and chemical tests indicate characteristics downhole and productivity potential of zones. If successful, the well is completed as a producing well. If not, it is cased, cemented and abandoned.

Secondary and tertiary recovery methods increase a well or field's total recovery. Techniques include water floods where injectors pressure-drive large volumes of water through the production zone in a subterranean flood, driving oil to capture wells. Other treatments include carbon dioxide injection, acid treatments, hydraulics, steam and subsurface explosives. To date about 200,000 fossil fuel wells have been drilled in Alberta.

Production flows up the well bore, then through the field gathering system to the battery installation. A battery is a central collection, processing, stripping and measuring plant that prepares the hydrocarbons for further processing and pipelining. About 13,000 oil batteries, 3,200 gas batteries and 1,300 gas plants are out there.[12] An estimated 400,000 km of power lines have been strung in the upstream oil effort. Pipelines are laid in trenches excavated in a right of way, a 5-metre width cleared of vegetation. Fences, gates, bridges, tunnels and special facilities such as compressor and pumping stations are required along the line. Alberta's interconnected grid comprises over 260,000 km of pipelines, all dedicated to taking oil and gas off to processing plants, refining and market.

BITUMEN

Over millions of years, long subterranean migrations brought heavy oils called "bitumen" to or near the surface in great pools in Alberta's north and east, pools such as the Athabasca Tar Sands (the largest), Cold Lake, Wabasca and Peace River. Together these comprise some 4 or 5,000 km² or 6.5% of Alberta.[13] Estimated recoverable resources are colossal. Wa-Pa-Su spotted these bituminous deposits in his 1719 travels.

Science and technology have examined everything from chemical baths, hot water immersions through to subterranean nuclear bombs as means to separate bitumen from its associated sands.[14] Large-scale commercial exploitation began in 1967 with the Great Canadian Oil Sands (now Suncor) plant. In 1978 a consortium of government and large oil companies opened a larger plant (Syncrude). Both employ processes that strip the overburden, sometimes many metres thick, from above the tar sands. The underlying medium is excavated using large-scale strip mining techniques; the severed ore is slurried and run through a multistage heat, water and chemical separation process. Residual hydrocarbons are refined, fractured, or synthesized and processed for market. Expansions and new projects costing billions of dollars are proposed or under way—$5 billion for the present but swelling to $25 billion by 2020.[15]

INDUSTRY EFFECTS

If it were as simple as gasoline coming from the pump and oil from the can, the industry might be nearly benign. But oil and gas lie deep in the earth, broadcast widely, and it is a long and tortuous path from their discovery bed until their ultimate conversion into entropic energy, atmospheric pollution and garbage.

Well boreholes penetrate many strata, some carrying salt water, others fresh, a few coal, gas or oil. Despite efforts, interstrata movement of water or other material occurs, polluting some formations and draining others. Chemicals, some toxic or radioactive, may be introduced downhole to move through formation, often assisted by induced massive fracturing of the strata. Downhole casing and cementing minimize effects but have a finite lifespan. After depletion the well is abandoned. Abandonment and reclamation costs are estimated by some to average $60,000 per well, motivating others to avoid proper procedures. Even when done by the rules abandonment only postpones problems. Depending on the downhole chemistry and physics, steel casing's integrity may last a century or more, but they will finally corrode and rupture. Then downhole problems will percolate about, posing groundwater and surface problems. Alberta's oil fields will ultimately become a subsurface Swiss cheese menacing future Albertans and the land.

In the White Area, the 37% of the province that is settled, industry's surface effects are difficult to separate from agriculture's. Producing and abandoned well-sites, batteries and plants stand out prominently but other developments are more subtle, hidden by the plough. Oil and gas roads are nearly indistinguishable from others; seismic and pipeline right-of-ways submerge beneath a sea of summerfallow or monoculture crops.

White Area lands are often privately owned so that oil and gas operators negotiate surface use agreements directly with farmers. Accommodations result to fit agricultural practices, well-site location and road design. In this rude symbiosis farmers receive rents, damages, and other monetary considerations and the land receives mounting exploitation and cumulating impacts. Surface activities destroy topsoil, sometimes polluting it with toxic waste but also resulting in groundwater contamination.[16] Neither farmer nor oilman wants to interfere with cropped areas, so the little margin land left, refugia for plant and beast, become access roads and lease sites. This ad hoc multiple-use planning ensures the fullest, fastest extraction of value from the land, but oil's intrusions pump its "fair" from the land and leaves its "foul"—deep wells, deep soil disruption, more intense pollutants and new exotics.

Alberta's 200,000 wells each have their one hectare or larger well-site. Small industrial sites, they are often noisy and malodorous. They clearly belong in the Noosphere. By themselves, these wells occupy over 2,000 km² of Alberta's surface. Connecting them are hundreds of thousands of kilometres of roads, pipelines, and powerlines linked into almost 20,000 processing facilities, all crosshatched by millions of kilometres of seismic.

Industry's pitch is that it creates energy and, once beneficially used, it ceases to be. That is not so. They do not create, but merely transport and transform. Nature created the organic materials pooling in Earth's depths. Industry takes it to the surface, then transfers it to applications usually thousands of kilometres distant. Nor do hydrocarbons cease to be when consumed. Whether for energy, lubrication, plastics or other materials, hydrocarbons metamorphose in use from the beneficent to maleficent. Slave to thermodynamics' first law (energy-matter cannot be created or destroyed), every barrel of oil or bin of coal ever burned is still with us, diffuse but active—and menacing. Our air, the atmosphere, is a convenient garbage can for much of it. Out of sight, out of mind, but not out of the loop or out of play.

With about 0.5% of the world's population, Canada "contributes about 2% of the world total of CO_2, is the eleventh-largest CO_2 producer in the world and the third-largest on a per capita basis."[17] Alberta leads Canada by a stellar margin in per capita greenhouse gas emissions. With less than 10% of the population, it produces 27% of Canada's emissions or more.[18]

It will worsen in the future. As the economic efficiency of Alberta's conventional fossil fuel industry dwindles, more and more energy and resources are required to extract each additional barrel of oil. Progressive exploitation of lower-grade, higher-cost oils, results in proportionately larger surface impacts, dissipated energy, wasted resources, and greenhouse gas emissions.

In 1992 Canada signed the Framework Convention on Climate Change and committed to holding greenhouse gas emissions to their 1990 levels by the year 2000. Canada and Alberta's partial response, called the Voluntary Challenge and Registry, uncaged rather than restrained emissions. By 2000, Canada's greenhouse gas emissions will be 12 to 14% higher than 1990. Alberta's "Advantage" will be to greatly exceed that. Now Canada has conditionally targeted a new standard. Its December 10, 1997 Kyoto reduction target is to reduce emissions to 6% below its 1990 level for the period spanning 2008 to 2012. Most of Alberta's commitments go the other way.

As Alberta's fossil fuel mix shifts from conventional oils to heavy oils, bitumen and synthetics, average contributions to greenhouse gas emissions increase. By 2010, non-conventional sources will provide most of Alberta's production. Inefficient and terribly polluting, contributions from their upstream production result, some argue, in roughly 10 times the carbon dioxide and methane emissions of conventional oil.[19] When government subsidizes and promotes exploitation of these resources it is also subsidizing and promoting smothering increases in greenhouse gases.

Since Leduc No. 1, Alberta has liberated 50 years of fossil fuel production to the atmosphere. Millions of years of carbon fixing have been "defixed" in decades. Atmospheric carbon dioxide levels have increased to "some 25 to 30% higher than they have been at any time within the last 160,000 years."[20] That will continue to increase while the resource lasts or until nature violently rebels. The penultimate product of the hydrocarbons industry is pollution; its ultimate product is not energy but entropy.

RESOURCE ISSUES

Industry encourages the idea of nearly infinite reserves of oil and gas. That was the strategy in the early '70s:

> At the beginning of the decade, big oil was telling the government, and the government, in turn, was telling the Canadian people, that Canada had virtually limitless reserves of oil and gas.
>
> In June of 1971, in what rates as one of the most misinformed statements ever to emerge from the lips of a cabinet minister, Energy Minister Joe Greene announced that "at 1970 rates of production, (Canada's) reserves represent 923 years supply for oil and 392 years for gas."[21]

More subtly, this wrongheaded strategy continues today. Worry over future supplies encourages resource conservation. Resource conservation defeats sales and cash flow, thus it is the industry's enemy. But few seem to care. In the past a 50-year supply was required before oil could be exported. That was lowered in stages. When it reached 25 years in 1987, the Mulroney government dropped the concern, lowering the bar to a frigid zero years supply.

Any production diminishes Alberta's ultimate conventional oil resource because it is a non-renewable, depleting resource. Drilling adds to proven reserves but not to ultimate reserves. When production removes more than drilling adds, proven reserves decline. Since 1969 drilling has consistently failed to replace production. The *Daily Oil Bulletin* June 17, 1997 headlined recent declines: "Alberta's Reserve Additions Replace 41% of 1996 Oil Production." With Alberta's conventional oil production of 54.8 million cubic metres (345 million barrels) and additions to reserves of only 22.6 million cubic metres (142 million barrels), reserves diminished to 341.8

million cubic metres (2,151 million barrels). At current rates of production (345 million barrels per year), Alberta has less than 6.3 years of conventional reserves, this despite the oil patch's most feverish activity ever in raising and spending money. Licensed wells increased from just over 4,000 in both 1991 and 1992 to record breaking levels in 1997 when 13,212 wells were drilled.

Why focus on conventional oil and gas? They are Alberta's most valuable fossil fuels. The highest quality, easiest to find, exploit, produce, sell and transport, conventional reserves profit industry the most. The least expensive monetarily and environmentally,[22] they earn the giant's share of land fees and royalty income for the Crown and the public purse.

Then, when conventional oil is gone, the tar sands remain. The bitumen or oil sand resource of Alberta is titanic. Alberta Energy and Utilities Board (EUB) estimates that Alberta has in place some 400 billion cubic metres of oil sand or bitumen "of which 49 billion cubic metres (about 12%) are estimated to be ultimately recoverable." Only 269 million cubic metres or 0.5% of it has been produced.[23] Qualitatively this resource is not so grand.

Bitumen's limiting factors are not resource size but economic and environmental consequences. So wasteful is the process that some estimate it takes two to make one—two barrels of oil equivalent (BOE) produce only one barrel of oil. High-cost heavy oils and synthetic crudes are produced while offloading enormous byproducts: expanses of sterile excavated lands; hills of overburden and processed sands; lakes of toxic water and winds laden with gaseous and precipitate wastes. And the giant mechanical moles, tar sands-throughput machines, burrow on, turning life in front to sterile mounds behind, and some oil.

Alberta's nominal 1% royalty on tar sands production fails to cover associated public capital costs, expenses and subsidies.[24] Tar sands production exploits effectively "free land" without recognizing its public and natural burdens. Even if economic, the planet's tolerance of fossil fuels may be crossed long before the resource is consumed. In other words, supplies may last more than a century, but Earth's absorption capacity thresholds may be crossed much earlier.

As for natural gas, until recently the frenzy was to sell it under nearly any circumstance. In Turner Valley days, there was little demand for natural gas, so it was vented into the atmosphere. Provincial regulators slowed that waste by making industry conserve gas until it could be marketed. This ultimately resulted in gas accumulations. To pass this "gas bubble," industry sent salesmen south with dumping on their mind. Since FTA's birth in 1989, Canadian producers pitted their gas against every other energy resource and said "we will not be undersold!" One commentator claims:

> Simply stated, too much gas supply has been trying to sell into much lower available markets. Price has been sacrified [sic] for volume – BIG TIME! In 1996, Alberta gas producers collectively, in effect, "left on the table" over Cdn$3.5 billion in gross revenue by driving up the U.S./Alberta price spread with excess supply.[26]

It seems they were not undersold.

Exports took off. In 1987 the U.S. received 38% of Alberta's gas or 25 billion out of 67 billion cubic metres. Seven years later in 1994 they got 57% of production or about 65 billion of the 114 billion cubic metres sold. Over 55% of Alberta's gas is exported to the U.S.A. in this inventory clearance. FTA guarantees the clearance sale's continuation. Industry is captured not only economically, legally and in its developed infrastructures, but by its export market. Its heart and soul is elsewhere. Non-Canadian interests largely own and control it. Land ownership (primarily by international major oil companies), debt ownership (often by foreign parent companies), technology ownership and marketplace power, are all strings on the puppet industry, pulled from beyond the borders.

Until 1983, additions to reserves from drilling generally exceeded production, so that the "gas bubble" grew. Since then, lavish drilling expenditures have failed to find sufficient gas to replace reserves. Large pools were found long ago. Finds now are smaller, lower quality and located in disconnected pools. Reserves to production ratios reveal a steep dive from 75 years to 9.1 years.[27]

THE LAST BISON HUNT

But it does not end there. In some ways it has just begun. Over 250,000 new wells must be drilled; 500,000 km of all-weather roads built; millions of kilometres of seismic shot; 200,000 km of pipeline must be laid to get the last economic conventional fossil fuels out of the ground and down the pipeline. Government will be called on to provide incentives to ensure that happens, to sustain the industry and to protect jobs. The public will dig deep in their pockets to subsidize these last takings. Most activity will happen in the Green Area, the land not yet fully exploited. It is off now to the Eastern Slopes and the boreal forest.

High-grading—taking the easiest, most accessible, fastest and highest-quality resources—seems only natural but it leads to higher-cost reserves. Flush production turns to marginal production, elephants turn to mice. Fat royalties thin, revealing a past dependency on easy money,[28] and every time government cuts another social program for the people, citizens glower.

Like the Metis bison hunters of 125 years ago, each winter the industry goes out onto the land to hunt their resource, and every spring they come back with less. Finding rates shrink while finding costs swell; reserves fall. But hey, there are still a few bison out there. Someone said there was a herd in the Cypress Hills. And when they are gone, we will move on. Oil's permanence is in moving on.

This describes production's half of the story. Consumption is the other half. While hill and valley were ravaged to find oil, valley and hill are devoured in consuming it. From Bill Cochrane's first Alberta automobile, cranked up on August 8, 1903 at High River, to the end of World War II, the great automobile culture overran the province. Petroleum, internal combustion engines and autos replaced the beast of burden and the leg of man. In doing so it also ran amok over nature, its first big roadkill.

CHAPTER 11

BUSHWHACKING

HEWING A HOME

F orests returned with glacial retreat. Early Americans followed them north, making their demands: firewood, tools and shelter; their plants and animals for food and clothing. When Europeans came, their first hunger was not for the forests but its residents. After the fur trade collapsed and Native people went out of business, Europeans reconsidered the forests.

Railway construction lured loggers and lumbermen west, to supply the materials to construct the railway and the clapboard boomtowns springing up along the track. After the last spike, trains would drop off an expanding market of homesteaders and townies demanding stores, houses, barns, sheds, machinery, fences and wooden sidewalks. Loggers journeyed deep into the winter woods with cross-cut saws to fell, trim and buck logs. Horse teams pulled and carted these logs to the road, rail, river's edge and on to newly opened sawmills, springing up to feed the new appetites. Towns grew and neighbouring forests shrank, but few worried then. Forests went on forever.

More than wood, wheat was the imperial pleasure out west; farmers were preferred over foresters. *The Dominion Lands Act, 1872* chopped the arable stretches of Rupert's Land into farm-sized plots, leaving the vast treed expanses, Europe-sized chunks of forests, for a later day. The Dominion Forestry Branch, established in 1899, oversaw Alberta's forests. Federal control over natural resources was necessary for Canada to attain its National Policy objectives—rapid settlement and exploitation of the west—so it held back natural resources when it brought Manitoba, Saskatchewan and Alberta into Confederation. Other provinces controlled their resources from first joining Confederation and so a clamour rose up that never went away—second-class provinces populated by second-class citizens crying for equal treatment. After the settlement period, Great Britain and Ottawa relented, constitutionally devolving control over natural resources to the prairie provinces in 1930 with the *Natural Resources Transfer Agreements*.

In 1948 Alberta divided its lands into zones.[1] The area of homesteaders, farming, wide occupation and urban development, more like settled Europe than native American, it called the White Area. Firmly in the Noosphere, it required one kind of administration. The other, the wood, marsh and mountain not yet settled and more difficult to exploit, was the Green Area. That contained just over 350,000 km² or 53% of the province. Assayers calculated 54.2% of that to be productive forest, 5.8% potentially productive, 36.4% non-productive, while 3.6% was water. This clung tenuously to the Biosphere, dreading the day when technology and markets would make its subduction worthwhile.

The majority of Alberta's 661,190 km² were forested. Originally Alberta's forested ecoregions were:[2]

	Area (km²)	% of Alberta
Aspen Parkland	52,148	7.9
Boreal Forest		
Lower Boreal Cordilleran	93,061	14.1
Upper Boreal Cordilleran	33,029	5.0
Low Boreal Mixedwood	76,900	11.6
Mid Boreal Mixedwood	210,143	31.8
High Boreal Mixedwood	39,856	6.0
Boreal Subarctic	20,104	3.0
Total Boreal Forest	473,093	71.6
Cordilleran related		
Montane	5,714	0.9
Subalpine	26,060	3.9
Alpine	14,656	2.2
Total Cordilleran	46,430	7.0

Nonforested regions occupied the other 13.5% or 89,514 km². But settlement changed all this. Homesteaders cut and ploughed most of the Aspen Parkland ecoregion, leaving only tattered remnants. For large animal life, every Alberta forest today is a crumbling mausoleum, a ghost of what it once was.

Remoteness insulated the woods for a time but rapid technological advancements thinned that protection. The highly mobile armaments that set World War II's strategy, tempo and culture contributed to those advances—gas-powered internal-combustion horsepower retired grass-powered horses by war's end. Chain saws replaced the slow and sweaty man-powered cross-cut saws. Steel and gasoline ruled the green.

The postwar and Leduc booms fed the human influx, all wanting homes, offices and cities. The world wanted more paper and lumber, so the market wanted the forest. Roads provided access, the way. In 1957 the north-south Forestry Trunk Road sliced through Alberta's foothills. This sheared open the Rocky Mountain's east slopes forests from Coleman, near the international border, north through nearly all of the foothills, montane and subalpine forests to Grande Prairie. From this trunk, other roads branched up the east slope of the Rocky Mountains and into the apron forests of the foothills and parklands.

If the forests were to be intensively and extensively exploited, large and long-term management tools were required: by 1954 Forest Management Agreements (FMA) provided companies exploitation rights over discrete forested lands and by 1966 Timber Quotas provided users committed quantities of the Annual Allowable Cut (AAC) established by the Crown for each forest. The same year the Forestry Trunk Road went in, the Hinton mill launched Alberta's pulp and paper industry. Its feedstock was a mixture of montane and subalpine forests composed of softwood mostly, a narrow resource base in Alberta but one easily and profitably exploited. Procter & Gamble's Grande Prairie bleached kraft pulp mill belched to life in 1973, fed on its rich outlying coniferous forests.

By area approximately 70% of the province is wreathed by the great boreal forest. Part of the world's largest forest—the taiga—this forest crowns the Northern Hemisphere from Norway over the Chukotski Peninsula, on through Alaska and Canada to Newfoundland's Avalon Peninsula. Formed on the decay of glacial retreat, stoic through thousands of cold winters, surging in short mild summers with low to moderate moisture, the boreal forest marks one of life's spectacular triumphs over ice and stone. Pine, spruce, tamarack and fir, blend with balsam poplar and the dominant tree species, aspen poplar, to compose the taiga, the circumpolar giant.

Enormity of size hints at enormity of profit, but what technology could best exploit it and for what markets? Technology for pulping hardwoods developed during World War II but aspen had troubling aspects. As with the tantalizing but niggardly tar sands underlying Alberta's taiga, government and industry turned their creativity and capital to research and development, seeking technological keys to unlock the northern forest to exploitation.

WORLD CLASS
FORESTRY!

When OPEC lost command of petroleum prices in the early '80s and Alberta's fortunes fell alongside, the Crown cast about for new bounty. Its gaze settled on the northern forest. The usual formula (known today as the Alberta Advantage) would be employed—mega-deals with foreign ownership, foreign capital, foreign technology, publicly contributed infrastructure, public subsidies, low resource prices, low taxes and low environmental standards. Alberta hit the market in 1984 with its world-class, second-to-none forest promotion. Solicitous videos, glossy documents and alluring assurances criss-crossed the planet seeking someone to turn the forest to cash flow.

This search ended in Japan. In February 1988 Alberta and Daishowa announced a pact involving an FMA covering about 40,000 km² of Alberta lands (25,000 up front, 15,000 later, on expansion), or about six percent of the province. Near the town of Peace River Daishowa would build and operate "Canada's Largest Hardwood Pulp Mill" using bleached kraft processes. The mighty Peace River, rising in British Columbia's high northern Rockies, would provide its water to Daishowa and carry away the mill's discharge. Alberta Wilderness Association describes Alberta's generous tribute to Daishowa:

> The Daishowa FMA provides the cheapest royalty rates in the world for raw pulp (28 cents/air-dried tonne of aspen pulp). Alberta provides some of the cheapest fuel costs in the world (natural gas). The public pays the entire cost of fighting forest fires in the FMAs, and of raising nursery trees for attempts at planting back a cleared forest . . . . Daishowa was given an initial direct government grant of $75 million, and the public has funded an enormously expensive bridge across the Peace River to the mill, and maintained costly repairs to the rail line that continues to slough along the sandy banks of the Peace River.[3]

The mill began operations in 1990.

LUBICON LAKE

The news media told Albertans about this *fait accompli*. As in Riel's day, the Crown disposed of kingdom-sized chunks of land without openly consulting the people. Residents' lives would change forever. Some Lubicon Lake Cree, living so remote from White people that they were "discovered" in the 1930s, heard of losing their homelands only when Daishowa's sub-contractors began clearcutting.

Earlier, the oil industry had announced its arrival in much the same way. In 1979 Alberta completed the first all-weather road into Lubicon lands. In the next five years the oil industry motored in, drilling about 400 wells within a 25-km radius of the Lubicon's community. Some estimate the oil companies' revenue to be $500 million annually. With this came the usual interventions—seismic lines, roads, lease sites, traffic, pollution and noise. For the Lubicon unemployment, welfare, alcohol and anomie replaced hunting, trapping and gathering. There was small mercy. Oil did not clearcut the land.

Then foresters drove the road, first for pieces, and then in 1988, for it all. Even now, Native people seem to be non-entities in *terra nullius*. Little has changed from the time of the HBC charter or the Red River Rebellion of 1869-70. The Lubicon have yet to obtain settlement of land claims despite global efforts at intervention. The Lubicon and their unbowed chief, Bernard Ominayak, testify again to White usurpations.

Months after Daishowa's project announcement, the Crown broadcast that it had yet a bigger and better forestry project, one to consume much of Alberta's northeast. It involved higher technology, greater capital and more land. Its mill would be constructed on the Athabasca River by Alberta-Pacific Forest Industries Inc. (Al-Pac), owned in part by Mitsubishi Corp. Alberta's Texas-talkers claimed it would be the world's largest single-line pulp mill. Its projected land base covered "roughly 100,000 km²,"[4] more than 12% of Alberta, about 73,000 km² from the Green Area in FMA, and the remainder from forested White Area lands. Again in the manner of Charles II, Alberta's Crown dealt away another colossal slice of land, not to Prince Rupert but to the first prince of capital, Mitsubishi.[5]

Later, Premier Don Getty promised yet another forest to a group of investors huddled under the veil of Grande Alberta Project (GAP). GAP was announced on December 1, 1992, Getty's last week as premier. Questions of the sufficiency of the Annual Allowable Cut (AAC) circled the GAP. Before GAP it had been announced that:

> The coniferous and deciduous AAC in the province stands at about 14.3 million cubic metres and 10.4 million cubic metres respectively. Approximately 96% of the coniferous AAC and 81% of the deciduous AAC is either allocated or provisionally committed as of April 1990.[6]

The last inventory of Alberta Forests, the Phase III inventory, had been completed in 1985. Alberta's next comprehensive inventory, the Alberta

Vegetation Inventory (AVI), announced in 1991, was only one-third done by November 1995. Undaunted, on September 9, 1996, the Crown announced an agreement in principle to persevere on the GAP, relying on a second timber supply report that confirmed the adequacy of the forest for the GAP Project and its other user, Manning Diversified Industries. Together the two FMAs require approximately five percent of Alberta's AAC, another net 15,000 km^2.[7]

GAP would build Alberta its first paper machine, one to produce lightweight coated paper. When announcing GAP the Economic Development and Tourism Minister, Dr. Stephen C. West, claimed:

> This project . . . . provides a critical building block in establishing northwestern Alberta as a major manufacturing region. It's another clear example of the success of Alberta's economic strategy in upgrading forest products in the province and keeping the jobs and investment at home. This project uses advanced technology to create a high-quality product that will sell in global markets and create jobs for Albertans.

Environment Protection Minister, Ty Lund, closed the Press Release with a little eco-bilge, "Our stringent reforestation laws combined with second-to-none insect, disease and fire control programs are essential in ensuring a sustainable timber supply and a sustainable forestry industry in Alberta."[8] GAP's mill—but not its natural resource, the forest—would be submitted to the Natural Resources Conservation Board (NRCB) for review. Shortly after announcing the continuance of GAP, October 1, 1996, Alberta released a Request for Proposals to exploit another northwestern forest, the Footner Timber Development Area, having an area of about 28,000 km^2, another four or five percent chunk of the province, perhaps to sponsor another pulp and paper mill.

GOOD INTENTIONS

The Crown's intention in a FMA is to take a vast expanse of land and life, commit it to one industry, reduce it to one commodity and transform it to one value. Daishowa's FMA contains this recital:

> WHEREAS the Minister desires to provide for the fullest possible economic utilization of forest stands and stable employment in local communities, and to ensure a perpetual supply of benefits and products while maintaining a forest

environment of high quality by maximizing the value of the timber resource base and ensuring that it yields an uninterrupted flow of timber over time.[9]

In this transubstantiation, a forest becomes a "perpetual supply of benefits and products." While FMA's are issued in 20-year renewable terms, they tend to endure as long as the trees remain harvestable.[10] At least two reasons suggest this. First, when committing the forest to forestry, private capital, public expenditures, infrastructure and human resources all combine to perpetuate the commitment. Ending a forestry project chops more than the mill. It terminates employees, closes down service industries, collapses dependent or one-industry towns, areas, economies and political constituencies. Second, land exploited for forestry has little utility for other things. An exploited forest, even with adequate reforestation, is no longer a forest but an input farm for a mill.

It happens like this. Alberta trees generally take about a century to grow to cut-size. AAC reflects that in annual incremental cuts of about 1/100th of the commercially harvestable trees. But only about half the land area is commercially harvestable, the rest being grass, scrub, scree, swamp or stream; so it is that each year AAC approximates one-half of one percent of the entire forest. Reflecting this, government and industry claim that they take less than one-half of one percent of the forest each year. To resist such modest sharing, the wealthy and powerful ones intone, is selfish of nature lovers, future generations and other forest users.[11] Of course, this modest sharing insures the forest's ecological fragmentation within 30 years, gutting within 50 and elimination within the century. On tolling the century, it is a plantation.

TRAGEDY OF THE PRIVATES

North American forestry supplies were particularly tight from 1993 to 1995. To keep mills going, businesses scoured the wooded regions of America, looking for trees, prepared to pay top dollar. Prices climbed. This temptation was too troubling for most. As the *Calgary Herald* reported:

> Garry Leithhead, executive-director of the Alberta Forest Products Association said about half the province's land base lies within provincial forested lands, and private forested lands amount to 2.3% of Alberta.
> "In two years, the available coniferous timber on private land will be liquidated," Leithhead said.[12]

Logging trucks daily removed hundreds of loads of logs off private lands and reserves in Alberta in what has been referred to as "liquidation logging."[13]

Attempts to regulate logging on private lands failed. Government subverted attempts to moderate avaricious private land owners. The Municipal District of Pincher Creek rescinded its forestry bylaw in 1995 because, as its Reeve disclosed:

> Both the minister (Alberta's Minister of Environmental Protection) [Ty Lund] and Pincher Creek-Macleod MLA Dave Coutts told him the entire provincial caucus believes property rights should have priority over environmental protection.[14]

Just three months earlier the Oldman River flooded threatening life and property. Clearcutting of private and public lands higher up in the Pincher Creek, Castle, Crowsnest and Oldman River watersheds contributed to the flood.

Observers of liquidation logging wondered how "private property" promoted resource conservation, ecological integrity or pride of ownership. Landowners stripped their land and reduced it to money with alarming speed. Forests fell, wildlife fled, watersheds bled and erosion mounted while landowner's banked the green in this "tragedy of the privates."

HERBAGE TO GARBAGE

Railways dominated the 19th century and motor vehicles triumphed in the 20th century. Whether in Brazil or Alberta, roads provide the axis for access to, information about, communication with and exploitation of the wilds. Alberta's Forestry Trunk Road wormed deep into the heartwood of the eastern slopes in the late '50s, opening it to invasion by anyone and anything that might motor through. Caterpillar tractors roared out from it, gouging logging roads across hillsides, down drainages and across flats. Screaming feller-bunchers, a 35-tonne, deadly efficient, tracked machine that cuts and piles logs, invaded with the skidders that grapple or cable logs out of the woods, and delimbers that strip branches and stack logs.

Industry declares that "in some respects, timber harvesting simply began to take over a role formerly played by fire,"[15] so that after clearcutting the forest is as good or better than a natural forest—a shallow but soothing idea. Forests suffer fewer natural fires now, but more human-caused fires, plus the effects of surge logging and clearcutting.[16]

Fires do not produce roads. They do not take massive machines onto the land to cut and remove its product, and in doing so to rut, gouge, rip and tear apart top- and subsoil. They do not disturb by scarification, leaving soils exposed to desiccation by the sun and erosion by wind and water. They do not displace nature's dominion with alien technology and exotic life. Fires do not strip the land's product and haul it on a one-way path to distant garbage dumps and land fills. Fires do not clearcut and remove logs, processing them into dimension lumber, veneer, plywood, oriented strandboard, and pulp and paper.

Pulp and paper production requires powerful reducers to separate fibres from the natural wood glues (lignin) in preparation for the bleaching stages. In the kraft pulp bleaching process, chlorines whiten the fibre but they also interact with the organic materials to produce organo-chlorines. Some of these chemicals, including dioxins and furans, may be carcinogenic. These are dumped into the atmosphere, flushed into the water or deposited terrestrially where vectors for distribution carry their polluting and poisoning effects, in Alberta and far beyond. Ten pulp mills (seven from Alberta) drain chemical cocktails into Lake Athabasca. From there the brew streams on to the Arctic Ocean through the MacKenzie drainage. Greatly persistent, some bio-accumulating and magnifying, this toxic concoction flows into perhaps the least resilient and most fragile marine and terrestrial ecosystems on the planet, in the Arctic.[17]

Alberta Advantages

Forests are scrubbers. Plants capture atmospheric pollutants, mostly carbons, and photosynthesize them to carbohydrates and other benign or beneficial substances. Deforestation reverses this process, turning the beneficent to the maleficent, destroying the scrubber all the while polluting, ultimately releasing the forest's carbon sink into the atmosphere, creating even more adverse effects such as global warming. What we most urgently need, we increasingly destroy. Energy production and consumption have given Alberta a big lead over Canada generally, which in turn is a world leader in CO_2 emissions. Alberta exacerbates the problem by being a world leader in destroying solutions. Few other places have set upon their forests with the cutthroat glee of Alberta. Here Alberta is globally competitive—the Alberta Advantage.

The advantage is born of ignorance. Alberta approved pulp mills before properly examining their effects, as, for example, on northern rivers.[18] In its closed door decision making, industry promotes its self-monitoring and public-denying model, saying in effect, "trust us to perform the watchdog obligations and to report ourselves to government and the people if we breach the FMA, plan or government regulations." In an era of vast forestry expansion, Crown scrutiny over public lands and forests is in severe contraction.[19]

The advantage is also born of forbearance. When mills are running, regulators have little resolve to interfere unless there is a clear and immediate threat to public health with a magnitude sufficient to make it a political event. One mill in particular, Procter & Gamble in Grande Prairie, was charged with some 167 pollution offences under the *Clean Water Act* on the eve of selling-out to Weyerhauser. They left Alberta with sale proceeds of $400 million and a few convictions. Some considered the timing auspicious for politicians, but suspicious for the people and land.

The advantage is also found in public sector giveaways. Crown revenues from stumpage do not cover costs of managing forests, resource degradation, any fair allowance for environmental damage and opportunity costs.[20] On the expenditure side, government has been most generous with loans, guarantees and financial inducements to forestry companies, while building at no or low cost the roads, bridges and rail systems that forestry needs to exploit the resource. One estimate is that government loaned, guaranteed, granted or spent for industry $1.35 billion as part of an aggregate $5 billion investment in pulp mills.[21] Now its largesse takes the form of forgiveness. In 1997 the Crown forgave about $244.2 million of Millar Western's accumulated debt and in 1998 about $155 million of Al-Pac's.[22]

Alberta contributes its forests, subsidies and manpower while foreign capital and technology take net returns. Alberta's raw materials are transported to foreign processing installations where value is added. The *Globe and Mail* in the article the "Great Alberta Give-Away" put a dollar value on the loss to the province in 1989:

> Natural resources are dirt cheap compared to the profits generated by their end products. A stand of 16 aspen 16 m high fetches tree royalties (stumpage) of about $1.40 for Alberta. That same aspen, converted to bleached kraft pulp, is worth $950 in the hands of a company like Mitsubishi. The paper refined from that pulp is worth between $1,300 and $2,000.[23]

Through the '90s Alberta has argued that it must compete in the global marketplace where prices are set. That sort-of-true assertion obscures a more fundamental truth: aggressive suppliers, who dispose of their commodity at nearly any price, drive market prices down. With stumpage near the lowest on the planet, the "Alberta Advantage" aims to provide abundantly for capital at the cost of its land and people.[24] In doing so it fouls its own and its neighbours' nests.[25]

Export-led forestry's large-scale clearcutting reduces forestry diversity and forecloses other uses, which reduces the human community that lives with the forests. It eliminates local, small-scale, value-added forestry and other forest use options.[26] With forests committed by grant and monopoly, plants built, communities rendered forestry-dependent, governments conditioned and disciplined by free trade agreements, no retreat is likely. Now that 70% of the industry is foreign-owned and 80% of its product goes to external markets (92% of pulp), Alberta's forests belong to others.

A DEEP CUT

Nature's ambition is to go beyond Earth's thin surface. Fish swim to take the sea. Birds fly to possess the sky. Trees finger higher, elevating life—diversifying, thickening and enriching the Biosphere. The forest's 20-m-high structure hosts many communities. Some live below the floor, others possess the lower levels and some climb upward through to the canopy, the communities of epiphytes, insects, birds and bats. It is nature's high-rise, dense strata-title condo living. When the forest falls, its communities collapse into a chaotic plane of debris.

An old-growth "climax" forest is the ultimate in long, complex successions. Industry and government newspeak calls it "overmature," and claims that the solution to this problem, overmaturity, is to chop the forest down and not allow that maturity again. Yet the fate of "overmature" trees in the old-growth forests is shared with their dependants—the pileated woodpecker, the nearly extirpated woodland caribou and the neotropical migrants. So it goes for the grizzly bear in the west, the owls in the dark forest, the bay breasted warblers in the canopy and the people of the wood. Clearcuts cut flesh as well as fibre.

After the forest is trucked away, the floor wizens and shrivels. Without vegetation's insulation, it heats and cools to extremes. Without the tree's cushioning effect, rain pelts and wind scours its face, carrying away the soil's minerals, dropping them to Earth in distant places, not as a medium to support life but, in eroded material's way, to stifle it. Siltation and wind deposits smother neighbouring lands. Only a temporary, shallow confused layer remains behind. Scarification rips that up, tossing it about. The forest's cycle is broken. The blunt takeover of natural systems creates a new *terra nullius*.

Nature provides the first cut free. The next cut costs. In forestry's long crop cycle a tree regrows (doubles) in about 100 years but money doubles in nine (at eight percent per annum). In the inflating world of economics, nature has no inherent value and money grows exponentially faster than trees.[27] This provides no economic incentive to reforest. Capital and Crown's begrudging purpose in "reforesting" is not to reforest but to crop the land, to

117

reestablish ("replicate or exceed") yields of primary product, lumber or fibre. Most of the stock for this crop is seeds or seedlings from provincial sources.[28] Exotics are the way. Researchers are developing fast-maturing cultivars, new kinds to deeply reduce the 100 years from planting to harvest.

After planting, managers ensure the land remains denatured. A "free to grow" policy weeds out economically undesirable species, eliminating the diversity forests demand but plantations eschew. Mechanical means, chemicals, fertilizers, pesticides, herbicides and broad-spectrum biocides are applied to ensure the crop, denying the forest's return. Crops are selected for commercial characteristics—uniformity, growth, product quality and market appeal. Monoculture plantations have little genetic, species, age and ecosystem diversity. The second cut, one century later, is lower in quantity and quality because reforestation has leakage and higher costs.[29] Unlike the first cut, this is a cut of culture, not nature.

FOREST'S FUTURES

Earth is running out of forests and capital celebrates. Is abundance a curse and scarcity a blessing? The MacDonald Commission talked of the bright future brought on by diminishing forests:

> For the years to 2000, world demand is projected to expand, at most, about half as rapidly as demand for paper products: that is, at an annual rate of 1 to 1.5%. However, some intervenors at our hearings argued that the outlook beyond 2000 is brighter:
>
> > As the population of the world increases, you are going to see a tremendous increase in the demand for forest products . . . They say that nobody will be able to meet the world demand for forest products after the year 2000.[30]

This "bright" future means people having to do without, elimination of last forests and rocketing profits for the companies. "We need everything out there . . . we log to infinity."[31] Its biocidal implications are staggering.

Alberta's immense FMA grants to multinational corporations rival the Hudson's Bay Grant. As the Dominion Land Survey in the late 19th century chopped and divided the land in the White Area, so the Timber Quotas and FMAs are now chopping the Green. As the railway brought the occupying forces and machinery of exploitation into the heart of the White Area, roads open up the heart of the Green to new exotic exploiters. As international markets clamoured for fur, bison, wheat, then oil, now the world bellows for pulp and lumber. Alberta's forest plan is world class and globally competitive with any plan of natural destruction on the planet.

Forests turn to tree farms; the highways of the fur traders, our rivers, turn to sewer outlets for pulpers; trees turn to garbage and landfill. Monetary elation is decay's momentary companion. Folks enjoy a rush of economic activity, jobs and unsustainable lifestyle as they cruise Main Street in the north in big pickup trucks with chrome moose-lights. The deals are done, commitments made, plants built and forests fall. Each spring for the next century, less forest will bud and green. Finally it will be the great northern tree farm. The forest will be dead. While politicians prance and praise, entropy is at work, securing Alberta's future.

CHAPTER 12

WHITE MAN'S CARESS

SUBDUE AND REPLENISH

I n *A History of Alberta*, James G. MacGregor describes White incursions into Alberta by 1870 as:

> Outside Edmonton the only evidences of the white man's caress were some missions and 10 fur trade posts . . . . In 1870, then, except for one or two whisky traders' shacks in the extreme southern fringe of the province, Edmonton House, four isolated mission stations and 10 outlying fur posts more or less tributary to Edmonton were all that the White man had to show for a century of residence in Alberta.[1]

MacGregor's panglossian metaphor "White man's caress" ignored much. Horses; guns; smallpox; disappearing furbearers, bison and Native people: all betrayed the White touch. Buildings were the least of White intrusions. Those reflected small White populations, not large White ways.

In 1870—the time of *Rupert's Land Act*, the Red River Rebellion, Confederation and the solicitation of British Columbia—White people's economic activity in Alberta focused on exploitation of wildlife; developments were some wooden frame buildings; agriculture involved several acreages, introduction of horses, cows and some animal and plant exotics; and high technology was trade goods, guns and trapping equipment. Bison would last a few more years and smallpox visited again that year. With prey vanishing as the decade unfolded, the fur and meat business ground down, the bison-based boom crashing by decade's end. Then even White and Metis populations shrank, perhaps by 25%[2], as itinerant exploiters moved on to new killing grounds—but what plans White people had to "caress" the land!

With the plains wolf, bear and bison dead and gone; with Native people herded into their enclosures; the land was sterilized and safe for farmers. And the people came. They came from overseas, they came from down east and they came from the northern states, filling the trains, then the land. Alberta's population increased over fourfold from 1891 to 1901. From 73,022 in 1901, the numbers climbed to 185,412 in 1906, on to 374,000 by 1911, reaching 496,525 people in 1916 after the outbreak of war. Of those, over 300,000 were rural dwellers.

Before 1921 government reflected interests of those distant institutions intent on settling and occupying the west. Their focus was not on the land and people, but on the National Policy, developing and exploiting the west for the elites of nation and empire. Homesteaders grumbled about their humble role in this scheme, gradually struggling to political action through what has come to be called "prairie populism." Farmers thought if they could just possess elected government, they would obtain control over their destinies. People today suffer the same delusion.

A monoculture of farmers stormed the ballot box in 1921's election—voting for their landed interests, their industry and their nearly unified worldview. The United Farmers of Alberta (UFA), not a political party until that year, seized the legislature, intent on deposing the national elites—CPR, eastern capitalists, eastern markets, and centrism. Agri-politics began a 50-year reign. This revolt echoed of England's Glorious Revolution and the transcendent Squires 233 years earlier. Unlike the Squirearchy, despite winning every election until 1971, usually in landslides, and ruling with oppressive legislature majorities, agri-politics seemed never to achieve its coveted social power, just political administration.[3]

Alberta's population grew from about 615,000 in 1921 to 732,000 in 1931. Rural Alberta matured as a grain economy, nurtured by satisfactory prices, better yields, more compliant government and occasional good fortune in the weather, at least until things turned. Just as Alberta took control of its natural resources from the federal government (1930), stock markets and resource prices collapsed followed quickly by general economic depression. Values of nearly everything in the trade-dependent industrialized world plunged, including wheat.

Economic collapse precipitated it but weather exacerbated the Dirty Thirties difficulties. Biting hot summers dried crops as they sprouted, leaving soils exposed to dirt-gripping winds that eroded millions of hectares of soil, contributing to the land's despair and production's decline. Grain prices fell to one-tenth their high. With fickle civilization abandoning them, desperate men and women reverted to hunting-gathering, begging and beseeching. Nearly anything digestible might be eaten, anything of value sold, not to build tomorrow but to save today. Ground squirrels were seen in a new, more tempting light. Few Whites thought to compare their lot with that of Native people half a century earlier.

In the Depression's depths, when everything seemed to fail, Alberta's preacher/educator William Aberhart exhorted, "get back to the Bible" and took his biblical message political. Blinded by Aberhart's bright light, in 1935 voters fled the short distance from UFA to a new movement and its grand experiment—the Christian farmer "funny-money" party/movement called Social Credit (SoCred). Albertans abandoned the UFA with solidarity peculiar to their tribal politics.

Little went right for Alberta's new premier (1935 to 1943) in his first few years in office—but rains and the reassuring winds of war returned in 1939, blowing prosperity into the luffing sails of Aberhart, his wallowing crew and his heaving sea of followers. SoCreds would hold office for 35 years, during which time oil would ascend as the new resource wealth, ultimately defeating agri-politics. Primary industries still dominated Alberta but the province was changing from rural to urban, from agriculture to fossil fuel-led, from being administered by rambunctious, parochial Christian agriculturalists to management by a more worldly, focused few.

Most arable lands (and some that were not) had been broken by war's end. Technology developed between the wars and during World War II—tank-like large tractors, self-propelled equipment, fertilizers, chemical pesticides—expanded the size of farm each farmer could manage. Pressures of trade and markets compelled farmers to adopt the new technology and expand to those new techno-economic limits or suffer defeat from their neighbour's competition. Capital substituted for humans, displacing farmers so that farm sizes grew, farmer numbers shrank. After half a century of flooding into the countryside, the deluge subsided.

Nearly two-thirds of Alberta's 1930s population was rural but immediately after war's end 45% of the population, then about 800,000 people, resided in cities. This reflected the diminishing relative importance of agriculture, the increasing importance of oil, and less so, secondary and tertiary economic activities. Although changing in form, the economy still remained dependent on what was taken from the ground. Until 1947 and Leduc, it was farming. Leduc then yielded up new horizons for exploitation leading to a next sweep of itinerant exploiters.

The quarter century following Leduc saw the Alberta economy metamorphose from one cast in an agricultural techno-morphology, to a dynamically growing one cast in a fossil fuel morphology. Founded more now on non-renewable fossil fuel, the province's flame would burn bright for as long as its flush oil flowed. The immediate postwar population had doubled by 1971 to about 1.6 million people, earning on average eight times the incomes of those from just before the war. Another million would be added over the next 20 years and per capita income would double again.

URBANIA AND AUTOTOPIA

Before World War II urban areas were scattered, modest congregations, dedicated primarily to serving surrounding agriculture. Agro-industrialization changed people's relationships to the land, driving many to the towns and cities. Oil accelerated this tendency, and, by 1970 only 30% of Albertans were rural.

For the oil patch, with its hunt-find-exploit-deplete-move-hunt wanderings, land becomes a transient, disposable resource. Peregrination is inherent to fossil fuels. Once out of the ground, oil becomes the fuel to power internal combustion engines, bitumen to pave networks of roads, and feedstocks for plastics to build modern vehicles. Its galaxy of related technology constructs the powerful, highly mobile means necessary to extract and exploit resources from remote lands—the mechanical/industrial apparatus required by global-scale agriculture, forestry, and petroleum (including heavy oil) projects. Residency was no longer required for exploitation. Information Age computer and telecommunications technology heaped on to increase people's severance from the land.

Automobile culture motored oilmen into the province and farmers into the city. Alberta's first auto in 1903 multiplied to 3,400 by 1913. Numbers jammed upward to 34,000 by 1919. Cars, buses and trucks, 890,000 by 1971, number two million today. Akin to the introduction of horses, guns and smallpox in 1730, the introduction of automobiles revolutionized Alberta, converting it to a new land inhabited by a new people doing strange new things.

The auto bloom layered roads across the land. Before the war more miles of railway cut Alberta than secondary roads. By 1946 over 800 km (500 miles) of bitumen roads and 14,000 km (9,000 miles) of gravelled roads crossed the province. That swelled to 137,000 km (86,000 miles) of public roadways in 1970 of which some 8,000 km (5,000 miles) were paved. More recently, Alberta has 14,000 km of primary, 15,000 km of secondary and 129,000 km of local roadways. These roads do not include the hundreds of thousands of kilometres of private roads and pathways whether for the oil industry, logging, farming, ranching, rural development or recreation. And where roads do not go, weekend 4x4ers, all-terrain vehicle and snowmobiles rut and wind their ways through the dying wilds. Track and tire mark nearly every square mile of the province.

Roads link Alberta's 15 cities, 117 towns and 175 villages, and surround all in radiating matrix, deep into the forests, high into the mountains, chopping and tiling the plains. They lead to every place that is any place. About 65% of Alberta's three million people live in larger cities, more than 15% reside in smaller centres. Nearly 20% live in rural contexts, nestled next to the city or out encroaching the wilds, and now, from city shadows to shade of the woods, farms host a mere 7% of Albertans, only about a third of all rural dwellers.

Autos dictate the "way" in auto-culture. Its facilities—the complex of highways, streets and lanes—are the asphalt and concrete circulatory system that flows traffic to distance-sequestered components of human life. Automobiles permit home, work, store and play to be separate, specialized and distant. Thus they germinated strip malls, shopping malls, drive-in movies, fast-food outlets, service stations, freeways, parkades and suburban developments, allowing growth to expand outward rather than upward. An automotive template shapes city morphology—size, shape, structure, layout, dispersal, separation of functions and interconnections.

With automobile culture came other corridors of convenience. Electrical and telephone lines webbed the air. Water, sewer and gas line grids netted Earth carrying their commodities downstream for use and disposal. Dams interrupted rivers, diverting fresh water to some use, replenishing the waterway downstream with discharge.

To most drivers, Earth becomes a linear sterile gallery—lines of pavement and power, low-scale buildings and flashing signs, noise, and pollution. Neighbours are those at work, recreation or market, but not likely those living down the street. Home becomes residence, a location for sleeping and, sometimes, eating. Spilled flat and far, margins sprawl. Rapid growth starved the heart of the old railway town to feed the periphery of the new auto city. The inner city decays. Out of that blight, a nipple of skyscrapers marks city centre—the nexus for control—and nurses the Noosphere.

WILD TIMES IN THE BIG CITY

City development eliminates most native life forms. Structures occupy approximately one-third of city topography. Another third is dedicated to automobile infrastructure—roads, lanes, parking and garages. Only the remaining third, transitional and landscaped areas, has potential for non-human biological activity. Landscaping is geo- and bio-cosmetics. Static design replaces natural dynamics; the exotic displaces the native. Garden fashions and greenhouse genetics determine biological successions in landscape in ways calculated to enhance the image of owners not the function of the land. "Scape" triumphs over "land." A frustrating chorus of disturbance-loving exotics, the weeds, join the larger "lawn and dandelion" habitat characteristic of cities.

Animal species similarly suffer in the city. There is the usual screech and splat of exotic birds. English sparrows, starlings and rock doves (pigeons)

compete for slop-overs with native opportunists—ring-billed gulls, magpies and crows. Robins, the common remnant native songbird, enjoys treed
residential areas. The Canada goose, now wildly abundant on urban golf
courses and riverine parks, distinguishes itself as being particularly synanthropic, having increased its local population by about 40 times in the last
15 years. Perhaps 10 pairs of mostly hand-reared and released peregrine
falcons nest on Alberta's downtown high-rises. Developers claim this as
evidence that the wild kingdom survives happily in the Noosphere and
industry helps nature. Few other birds linger long in the cities.

Small native mammals sometimes persevere as opportunists or scavengers in the urban context. Coyotes seem to have found a new niche. The
odd skunk, raccoon and rabbit hide out in urban ravines. A few garter
snakes survive the tires and tots of the city, but it is difficult. The lower
trophic rungs or steps in the ladder of life—nature's grocery stores—are
systematically stripped away. Insectivores starve because insects are discom-
forting, except for a butterfly or two. Anathema to civilization, insects are
eradicated in chemical fogging. Swallows and bats go when the mosquitoes
go; voles die with the native grasses. Most frogs have croaked, disappearing
globally at rates faster than nearly any other orders. An Alberta Environmental Protection Press Release of April 10, 1997 advised that, "only 10
breeding populations of [the northern leopard frog] once distributed widely
across Alberta, are now known in the province."[4] It will be a lucky little
boy who will pocket a pet frog in the future.

The trend is toward exotic. Only the most resilient or opportunistic
native species survive. Magpies loot the northern oriole's nest for ome-
lettes and the crow devours the yellow-rumped warbler's fledglings. They
compete with the introduced eastern grey (black) squirrel and the neighbour's cat. Even parks, with their manicured lawns and dog-walking people, do little for wildlife while nurturing illusions of naturalness. Cities are
sterile, but more than that, they represent sterility with ambition, one that
leaps out, far beyond the city's bounds.

SUB-URBAN

Automobiles love the suburbs. Speed shrinks space, sponsoring sprawl. Baby
boomers, with smaller families but bigger houses on even larger lots, drive
this outward dispersal. Each front-drive-in garage has its attached house
and each parking lot has its attached factory or office. Between them stretch
lengthening, multi-lane highways and freeways constructed to embrace
home, work, shopping and recreation venues. Postwar Albertans overswelled
their city into the country, transforming the city's margins into acreages,

hobby farms, satellite communities and other lavish land uses. Outskirts integrated with the city through multiplying connective tissue—roadways, electrical-ways, communication-ways, waterways and sewage ways. Except holidays and weekends, sprawl became the suburbanite's natural context, the habitat of man in auto-culture.

Areas girding the city—outskirts, acreagedom and conurbation—have their successions as they blend into the rural. As the city grows, land suffers increasingly intense uses. More construction, development and landscaping displace the farms as land succeeds to urban. Satellite and bedroom communities intensify linear disturbances for utilities, roadways and other suburban connections with the city. The city periphery is alive with introduced species, exotics, life forms associated with agriculture and landscaping. Man's introduced predators, dogs and cats, free range the apron, but there is a new exotic thrust these days. Alongside horses and cows are now fallow deer, ranch elk, paddock bison, caged ostrich and penned llamas, as the butcher mind-set wildly leaps from species to species. Some native vegetation persists despite the constant threat of exotic displacement. Happily also some insects persevere and in so doing feed the few songbirds.

City Shadow and Gravity

City shadows fall farther than the acreages. Utilities, primary and service industries, tourism and recreation—all finger-out deep into the country. Each creates unique pressures on the land. City sourced, they consume the hinterlands. In 1911 Calgary Power started production of hydroelectric power from water captured in dams upstream of Calgary on the Bow River. Now in over 10 sites the Bow River is dammed to store potential energy, regulate flow, protect settlements from flood and ensure water supplies. Each use has its upstream and downstream consequences. When taken together, these transform a wild river into a public utility of dams, reservoirs, diversions, recreational outlets, effluent receptacles and pollution transmitters—tap and toilet for society.

Riverine habitat is the critical component of most biomes and also the most threatened. People like it as much as critters do, so river valleys suffer overwhelming development, intervention and interruption. Sometimes the development becomes so intense and congested that it corks the river valley. It corked the Canmore Corridor west of Calgary. In that conurbation, natural processes are dammed terrestrially as surely as dams cork the waterway.

Urbanites use wildlands as commercial playgrounds on grand scales—"all season, world-class destination resorts." The pecuniary potential of Banff's hot springs whetted commercial appetites in 1883 when the train

127

opened them to the genteel world. After an initial flurry of claims, frauds and patronage, Banff grew to be a world-class destination resort. The use of wild land as in situ consumer goods, items of commerce and resource for exploitation, is the foundation of Alberta's tourist industry. Nature is a product that can be pieced, priced, packaged and sold but the consumer must be taken to the feast, not the feast to the consumer. Automobiles, buses and planes now feed the national parks to the people. As centrepiece to Alberta's fourth-largest industry, Waterton, Banff and Jasper provide tourism the backdrop splendour of the Rockies, the old west and wilderness recreation.

Cities avalanche out into the wilderness on weekends and holidays, democratizing the wilds, populating the forests with a new transient exploiter. Most want the theatre of wilderness but not the fact. A luxury item, only certain kinds of wilderness have value. Parks must be aesthetically pleasing; they must have opportunity for recreation use; they must be accessible and non-threatening; and they often must have amenities the affluent expect. Around the campfire phoney history can be sold, of brave cowboys and bloodthirsty Indians, of noble pioneers, respect for the land and love of the wild. This might be presented to a well-heeled voyageur from afar, prepared to pay for a suitable yarn with a pleasant ending, spun in rustic theatre with modern conveniences.

Some of the least productive habitat on Earth—mountain arête and boreal bogs—are the last refuges for beasts, for no other reason than they have kept man at bay. Tourism's new capital idea is that places formerly accessible only to mountain goats and marmots have also become items of commerce. The arete and the bog now suffer periodic infections of consumers. Whether hunting, fishing, ATVs, cross-country or downhill skiing, hiking, golfing, camping, orienteering, mountain biking or mountain climbing, urbanites swarm the wilds.

Some defend the wilderness by promoting the love of it, arguing that love motivates protection. Ironically, love lures people to it. When they love it they want to touch it. Consumer demand for wilderness is increasing and every touch has a cost. Few are immune to the need to take. An instinct to kleptomania demands they grab something when in nature—a memento, a totem, an object of natural beauty or curio; a flower, rock, leaf or berry. Often they leave something else, unwanted, behind: a dog, a cat, a disease, human waste, garbage, pitons, a disturbed site, frightened and fleeing animals, or a smouldering ember. While individual impacts appear negligible, they are cumulative. One footstep may not crush the rock jasmine, calypso orchid or alpine poppy, but 100 will.

Staging areas like the towns of Banff and Canmore develop on wilderness's margins, acting as Noosphere base-camps to provision the modern assault on the wilds. They nurture sources for outward migration of exotic life into the wilds. They host and encourage the tourist/adventurer advance. They also lure in the wild. Nearly any development and any linear interruption act as deathtraps or sinks for native life: garbage-kills, roadkills, conservation officer-kills and train track-kills. City shadows fall deep, dark and far over the wilds.

LICENCE TO KILL

Areas unsatisfactory for destination tourist resorts are used for hunting and fishing and whatever appetite seizes the new age explorer, 4X4ing up the seismic cutline. Recreational fishing hooks many. Long ago settlers fished out east slope drainages of most native trout and then stocked these lakes and streams with exotic species of trout, their favourite species from down east or Europe. Native trout are vanishing—few having survived the plunder or pollution—so Alberta's aggressive game fish-rearing industry plants some 4 million trout (primarily non-native) in its lakes and streams every year, flushing out the last few wild trout.[5] Then people with rod, tackle and all manner of outrageous but alluring contraptions, head out to this drive-in wilderness to reel back to nature.

Brookies, browns, rainbows and golden replace native bull and cutthroat trout. Waterways become enhanced media for the sport of hooking introduced fish, the toy of the recreational fisherman. The economics of it are compelling. The expensive and bizarre array of high-technology fisherman toys lure in businessmen who, in turn, hook and fillet the wallets of round-eyed fishermen with these gadgets. These wizardly props include fish finders, depth finders, sonic lures, echo-locators, carbon fibre fishing rods, all of which well-equipped, well-nourished, big-brained modern fishermen need to catch tiny-brained cold-blooded animals that evolved millions of years earlier.

Hunting continues to be an important business. Duck and goose hunting thins fall populations of migratory birds on course to wintering grounds. Hunting upland game birds, like trout fishing, usually involves shooting introduced species on or near disturbed lands. Bird hunters chase pheasants and partridges of Eurasia, many hatchery-reared, recently released and coop-stupid, for their reconnecting experience. Few native upland populations survived the plough, the cow and the potshot-hunting of an earlier generation. Big game hunters struggle more than other wilderness consumers for their reconnection, but with automotive equipment to take the pain from their legs, high-technology guns, bullets and hunting gear to aid in taking their allotted game, telescopes to sharpen book-tired eyes, guides to compensate for their ignorance, the thrills are maximized while effort and risk are minimized.

By the turn of the century, nearly every animal having market value was slaughtered by "market hunting." Whales, auks, bison, passenger pigeons; whatever could be turned to account, was. Demand collapsed when the supply died. Hunting ordinances were enacted earlier, but they had little effect in the face of more fundamental laws. In time government provided budgets, enforcement and effect to hunting ordinances but it was too late for many. The mega-faunal erasure neared completion. Perhaps 100 wood bison survived in forbidding parts of the northern forest and several hundred wapiti avoided extirpation by retreat to the wildest of the wild. Faint few antelopes survived the killing. Muleys waned. Remoteness better protected the woodland caribou and moose.

Later wapiti were reintroduced. Several national parks were established on the southern plains specifically to protect the slim remainder of the antelope—those parks later were decommissioned. Mule deer stoically defended their turf against the alien white-tailed deer and moose persevered, even advancing from time to time with their favourite browse, first successions after clearcuts. Today woodland caribou retreat to extirpation.[6] Intact old-growth forests are essential to Alberta's caribou and economically desirable to Japan's pulp companies. Without room for both, the caribou appears scheduled for clearcut, too. Capital and the Crown, both possessing nearly certain knowledge of the consequences, cut on.

Gone now are nearly all predators, replaced by the human predator. Government maintains "management plans" for the remaining wolves, bears and cougar. Usually numbers are managed down. That way holiday warriors feel little competition or threat from natural predators in their heavily armed wilderness quest. Hunter selection replaces natural selection. With emphasis on the "big buck" or the "royal rack" or the "full curl," best herd genetics are killed, stuffed and mounted. Wolves take the worst; man kills the best. Oldtimers lament the genetic decadence of today's smaller and abnormal game animals.

In the businesslike '90s all things must earn their way. Hunting, fishing, tourism and recreation generate revenue from wilderness in ways that surely compromise. Each use has its effects, most negative. As wilderness business continues to encroach the wild, truly wild animals retreat to the few remaining higher, colder, less productive but more secure grounds. Love might save the wilds if it were the right kind of love. But of the many kinds of love the one that nature needs most is the one that leaves some of it be.

CHAPTER 13

STRIPS, LAMINATES AND BIOMES

N o natural biomes remain unintruded on in Alberta and once intruded on, few survive intact. Pieces persist but disconnected remnants do not make well-functioning ecosystems. Plans are in place to eliminate even these. Our purpose now is to examine shifts in dominion from Biosphere to Noosphere; first by examining that stripped or taken away; then that anthropogenically infused or laminated on; and finally in speculating on resulting dynamics in these merged human/nature biomes. Alberta presents this family of techno-morphized biomes in stark and recent light, and, but for our entrenched ways of looking at nature and ourselves, one might be able to determine the directions of these dynamics.

DELUDED DUALISM

Alberta's popular history tells of a civilized and beneficent people (Whites) gently moving in, providently taking over management and control, and improving Alberta by civilizing its first inhabitants and developing the land. Nature still survives in this narrative and Native people, having seen the true White light of civilization, switch sides. In this progression, those Whites who most quickly seized the best became history's heroes. The theme is that in taking the most they civilized, developed and improved the most. So it goes.

Natural history maintains a similar exclusivity, avoiding human history by rarely addressing human effects on nature, leaving scarcely challenged the myth that pristine nature still exits. This history tells us that untainted wilderness lies just beyond our sight, over the horizon. Television and video offers a panorama of places where leopards lurk, wolves howl and whales blow. Academics research and publish papers discussing in detail the cycles, systems and processes of this, that or another creature in its natural context. National park wardens, ecotourist entrepreneurs and politicians avow the intact wilderness. Industry shouts, "We haven't hurt a thing." Environmentalists hoist placards fighting for this or that wild place. Coffee table books display their gorget of brilliant natural beauty, reassuringly, unquestioningly, as if it still existed. Pristine wilderness exists in books, on the screens, on promotional brochures and in the speeches of politicians and business leaders. On the land, it exists no more.

If the myth was true, and nature survives intact and unchanging, it ceases to be of historical interest. It is nearly irrelevant except as a permanent theatrical backdrop for the truly intriguing drama, that of powerful, ambitious humans in quest of progress and empire. Reducing man and nature to two solitudes creates formidable problems because it ignores this fundamental reality—humans and nature interact as part of a dynamic totality. But if we consider humans as part of nature and that human progress is, in that sense, truly natural, then, as a thinking and prudent species, and perhaps as a species with ambition and a desire to be ethical, it becomes important to see where human dominion and progress takes the human species and non-human nature. If that direction is risky or wrong, it may be that courses could be changed. It would be helpful to find ways that treat man and nature together more appropriately. One place to begin such a synthesis is by observing the effects of human progress on relatively unperturbed biomes—the effect of the Noosphere on the Biosphere—and Alberta provides a relatively clear view of those effects.

NOOSPHERE DIALECTICS

The idea that technology is transformative is fundamental to anthropology. Major technological changes demarcate the ages of humankind—Stone Age, Bronze Age, Industrial Age, to Information Age—each change synthesizing something-not- before in both the Biosphere and the Noosphere. Exploitation of Alberta followed successive technology—the horse, the gun, the train, the mould-board plough, fast-growing varieties of grain, hardwood pulping technology and heavy oil-recovery systems. This technology transformed the land and people. They changed the background conditions—negating or taking some things away, adding new things to this background, and if powerful enough in each one's aggregate effect, ultimately synthesizing something new.

In its negating or taking away from the pre-existing or background condition, technology seizes things from nature, bending, breaking or eliminating them. Sometimes this occurred by intent and design— trapping of the beaver, butchering of the bison, capturing of oil or sequestering of

Native people on reserves. At times the effects were unintended, as when technology delivered smallpox. Ploughing shortgrass prairie and draining sloughs eliminated the old. This negating or eliminating is the "strip."

Things are added. Exotic species of plant and animals invade the land or are introduced. Crops, weeds or pests come seeking niches in nature or nurture compatible with their Eurasian genesis. Noosphere adjuncts—occupation, buildings, transportation systems, production and consumption complexes, chemicals and pollution—layer on and spread out over the land. Things added on are "laminates." Laminates may replace or displace elements of what was there and, in doing so, strip something; or they may just contribute new complexities to a labyrinthine background.

In taking away from what was—the strip, in adding the new—the laminate, elements and dynamics change. Additions interact with remainders and exploit voids. The background biome changes in form and function. Changes may be to essence, enough so that the biome metamorphoses into a new biome (perhaps a techno-morph), a result of the technology applied to it and that technology's usual companions. Southern Alberta's irrigated farming regions are no longer native shortgrass prairie. They are something new, something to be considered for what it is and what it is becoming. Its successions will depend on its origins, what was stripped away (i.e., native grass) and laminated on (crops and water systems), and how they all dynamically interact. The "mature," or "climax" conditions expected in natural successions often have high diversity and low entropy, existing in a state of complex, dynamic equilibrium or homeostasis. These new anthropogenically perturbed biomes are usually characterized by high entropy and low diversity, accompanied by dynamic, degenerative disequilibrium.

BUILDING BLOCKS

Ecologists talk about an event, activity, or project having a "physical footprint" and its broader ecological effects as its "ecological footprint," "shadow," "penumbra" or its "shadow effects."[1] The metaphor indicates that intervention may result in far wider consequences merely than that within the physical footprint. When boreal forest logging destroys the springtime nesting site of a pair of magnolia warblers, it eliminates a family of overwintering warblers in Central America. Shooting one grizzly bear eliminates the dominant omnivore from up to 2,000 km² of wildlands. Introduction of a domestic sheep disease may decimate populations of bighorn sheep hundreds of kilometres distant, leaving predators to starve. Smallpox acted the same way among the Native population. Ecological footprints stomp across lands remote both in time and space.

Alberta's usual form of "development" is a large-scale resource project dedicated to international trade, a focus that demands transportation. Canoes for furs gave way to carts for robes, trains for grains and on to internal combustion engines, pipelines and telephone lines. All but canoes depend on linear incisions on the land. These are called "line" intrusions. As wide as a six-lane divided highway or as narrow as five-metre seismic lines, these lines open lands to invasion, constructing avenues for subsequent, more varied exploits. But it goes further than just the line and the physical footprint.

Line shadows cast out far beyond the right-of-way, roadway, ditch and borrow pit. In this shade, lands may be ecologically disrupted in cumulating, progressively degenerative ways. Along the fresh-cut survey line, into the wilds, comes the poacher, hunter, geologist, woodsman, 4X4er, farmer, rancher, miner, ecotourist operator, entrepreneur, tax collector and cottage developer. Perhaps the most formative event for the west was the linear incursion of the CPR, not by its physical footprint but because the Iron Horse carried the Noosphere, it provided the world transport to and from the west, for immigration of people and technology, access for market forces and means of export.

Rail, road and other linear disturbances create new habitat where some native species may be eliminated, others disadvantaged, some favoured and exotics introduced. For good reason, some mega-faunal species—grizzly bears and caribou for instance—avoid linear disturbances.[2] Less wary residents suffer whatever and whomever comes down the road—vehicles, hunters, developers, recreationists and exotics. Margin-loving native animals (e.g., robins and cowbirds) thrive in the disturbance, displacing species that rely on intact habitat—cowbirds do so by nest parasitism.[3] Omnivorous species change eating habits as readily as flipping a menu page, shifting from recycling nature to consuming human detritus. With roadside garbage increasing and nature decreasing, scavengers feast while hunters starve. Europe's shrill starlings and its English sparrows displace sweet songbirds; weasel and ferret, hawk and eagle are succeeded by dog, cat and crow, all admirably suited to scavenging garbage can entrées and the kills from marauding auto tires.

If "the medium is the message" as McLuhan claimed, and roads are a medium, they give off clear messages. A new road announces, like Charles II's 1670 Charter, that this land is claimed for the empire. The road leads to something to be taken. Then, with the road in place, everything along the way becomes available to the global appetite. The road says, "I am the way, the means of moving things about, the way to reshuffle Mother Nature by rearranging physicality." Roads are inevitably part of a larger strategy to take from one place and deposit in another—a means of strip and laminate.

Hives of activity occur at various points along lines—railway sidings, elevators, feedlots and oilfield batteries—as humble as the farmer's yard, as haughty as the city. Home to humans, synanthropic life forms and a range of uses, these centres are named "nodes." Some, like Calgary, grew; some, like Little Chicago and Little Philadelphia near Turner Valley, blossomed and then withered with their resource. Cities are nodes having such overwhelming power that they turn into Noosphere islands, sometimes defying even climate and geography.[4] And their shadows cast deep into the countryside.[5]

Agriculture, forestry and oil technology impose their own characteristic geometries on the land. The forestry industry clearcuts in blocks, resulting in an increasingly dense patchwork of cutblocks. The agricultural industry ploughs sodmat into large cultivated fields. These discrete areas of intense stripping are "blocks." As forestry or agricultural exploitation matures, blocks become so expansive as to blot out nature. Where lands are best, blocks extend over the horizon to the margins of the forest or arability.

Lines, nodes and blocks link together in increasingly dense matrices or webs. A few locations that are good for neither man nor beast—mountaintops, alkali lakebeds and badlands—remain outside the matrix but not outside its ecological footprint or shadow. They avoid physical exploitation only until a use may be found for them. There is no mountain so remote that it will not satisfy some appetite with a proper application of technology and a sufficient appetite. Then the matrix embraces them.

TECHNO-BIOMIC PROGRESSIONS/REGRESSIONS

Our baseline goes back 12,000 years ago, to glaciation's end, when a continent of ice turned to flood of water and life returned, at a time before significant human impacts. That was the time of Alberta's first big strip, the Quaternary Extinctions and its epochal human laminate. America's longest surviving native mega-faunal species—from mammoth and horse to sabretooth tiger and giant short-faced bear—went extinct within several thousand years. Those stripped from the land did not co-evolve with humans. The survivors—including grizzly bears, grey wolves and bison—were generally human acculturated newcomers, having emigrated with man over Beringia. Perhaps more than humans, they contributed to the extinctions as new predators or competitors. Perhaps not.

Eurasian humans emigrated to become the America's keystone species, laminating their kind, culture and influences on the land. Human roles in this mega-faunal decline are unknown and perhaps unknowable, but anthropogenic contributions are certain. Even if wielding only palaeolithic

135

technology, a new opportunistic adaptable top-level predator contributed to the new dynamics. Native American life retreated in the face of surging Eurasian life. Nature modified over the next ten millennia to harmonize with humans and their dominant technology (paleolithic) in what might be called paleolithic biomes. The coming of another wave of Eurasian peoples and their technology destroyed that homeostasis and biomic combinations.

Before contact, European effects spilled out over Alberta—horses, guns, disease and global appetites. A shock wave of higher hunting-gathering technology fractured the background paleolithic harmony. The fur trade, the bison debacle and then the exodus of Native people to reserves stripped the land of its last large life, marking the end of the paleolithic biome.

Appetites then turned to agriculture. Agriculture attacks the land in two general ways. One is direct, the sodbusting, soil-turning action of the plough in cultivation. This leads to the "plough biome." More indirect is the other, the mouth and gut of grazers or browsers, often the cow, to harvest the land. This leads to the "cow biome."

Ploughs capture the richest, most productive lands for agriculture, cutting this lowest trophic level from the Biosphere while eliminating vegetative, mega-faunal and much microfaunal life. Mechanical, chemical and other technology defend the species selected for culture from counterattack by nature's diversity, leaving the one cultured species, the monoculture. Biological successions on croplands are not determined by natural selection but by the farmer's estimation of what the market will demand next year. Little natural refuge remains near the ploughed field. Neighbouring sloughs, ditches or margins occasionally host fleeting small creatures. Farmers, markets, assessors and tax collectors assay these areas, calculating how to turn this "waste" to profit. In time most are purged of nature—by design, appetite, exotic displacement, shadow effect and sometimes, just because.[6] Diversity is driven from the land.

Lands too poor to cultivate, can be bent to profit by turning plants to meat to money through the cow. Cattlemen use various mechanical means, chemical regimens or exotic grass enhancements to increase meat production. Wildlife is killed, driven off or displaced by cows. Farmers tolerate little competition from bear, cougar, elk, ground squirrel or mouse. Stripped and laminated thus, the land changes, becoming the "cow biome." This biome occupies grasslands from the foothills cow-calf operation out to mixed farming and feedlot operations on the cultivated plain.

The future of the cow biome involves more range enhancement, more productive exotic grasses, more clearing of scrub, more intense management and elimination of competitors and predators. Land use intensifies as more lands are cleared, scarified or ploughed, cross-fenced, seeded, fertilized, sprayed with chemicals and cropped. While the farmer appears in charge, marketplace appetites manage the lands, continuously demanding more of them, tending toward total exploitation. Perfect exploitation will never be achieved but it is the path taken and the goal in mind. Even now, the plough and cow biomes occupy one-third of Alberta and over 80% of the White Area and their ecological shadows stretch far beyond that, to the wildest corners of the province.[7]

Oil and gas exploration pokes holes over nearly all Alberta. Lease sites, production facilities, pump stations, plants and other developments dot the map. These interconnect by lines, converging in larger and larger patterns of roads and pipelines and seismic cutlines, lacing out over the land in the "petro-biome." Nodes, patches and latticework are this industry's geometry. As the conventional resource dwindles, exploitation costs increase as do the intensity of interventions to land, air, water and life. "Drilling spacing units" will reduce in cases from 640 acres (256 ha), to 160 acres, then to 40 (16 ha), to 20 (8 ha) and to five acres (2 ha). Secondary and tertiary recovery practices will use increasingly intrusive and disruptive technology to take the last economic hydrocarbons. With oil and gas, the formerly wild biomes—plains, parklands or forest—metamorphose into petro-biomes with few intact remnants and much margin habitat that serves little ecologic function.

Petro-biome successions share some features of the plough and cow biomes. Nature's dominion is ousted as exotic species stream in, down its lines. The margins host synanthropic species—starlings, crows, robins, cowbirds and white-tailed deer—but most original residents shrink away or die off. With 95% of Alberta in the fossil-fuel prone Western Sedimentary Basin, the oil patch has probed most lands, some of it with startling intensity. Desperate to continue the flow of oil wealth, industry drills more and more, finding less and less. As oil declines, Alberta's flush population will hungrily turn on whatever remains to sustain itself. That is where forests came in.

Regions retaining good-quality forests are changing. Nearly 100% and perhaps more than 100% of Alberta's available AAC are committed to the saw. In the "forestry biome," the wilds are stripped by clear cutting and laminated with new varieties through reforestation. Its lines are the expanding complex of logging and access roads, occupying about 5% of cut areas. Its geometry expands through intensifying patchworks of clearcuts and reforestation progressions.

The market demands specific fibres and woods. New technology delivers these through intensive cultural regimes. Reforestation involves culturing the soil for a crop of selected plants. With that, the forestry biome emerges as a nearly exclusive human use zone, dedicated, like agriculture's several biomes, to holding nature at bay and otherwise producing specialized products, usually in a local monoculture. Over time the powerful diversity of native fauna and flora degenerates in the face of the usual exotics, opportunists and the intended crops. Those that dwell lower on the techno-hierarchy—Native people, trappers and small or local forestry businesses—have no place in corporate-owned industrial-age forests.

NEOTERIC BIOMES

The cow, plough, petro- and forestry biomes arise from primary production. They represent the productive efforts of some 400,000 Albertans and their associated capital. Alberta's gross employment is more than 1.7 million, therefore over 1.3 million people work daily in secondary and tertiary economic activities, producing effects not mentioned above. Many of those activities are very intrusive but, even when considered, the largest category of effects is still omitted. All of Alberta's three million people are consumers. Aggregate consumption's consequences are colossal.

About 65% of Alberta's population lives in larger cities, 15% in its towns and villages, while 20% live in rural contexts. Alberta's urban population ballooned enormously from 1939 to the present, a factor of six, and per capita income by a factor of eight. In these simple but misleading terms, aggregate urban consumption increased by a factor of approximately 50. This prodigious appetite reflects on Alberta's hinterlands in powerful and deforming ways. Acting as centrepoint or vortex, the city draws into its maw things desired from the countryside (strip). Acting as a centrifuge, the city blows out and laminates many manner of things on the hinterlands—constructing, advancing, excreting new structures, demands, pollution and residues.

Urban areas may be the home to most appetites, but satisfaction's source usually resides elsewhere. Consuming is now a long-distance affair. English appetites for fur initiated the White taking of Rupert's Land. Albertan's breakfast habit of orange juice and coffee contributes respectively to the felling of subtropical lowland forests and tropical highland forests. The physical building and maintenance of a city requires mountains of minerals and forests of fibre. City food and energy, business and resources depend on distant places. City recreation and tourism demands scenic golf courses, ski hills, hotels and roads, often in the most biologically productive of nature's retreats. Cities are not discrete or impermeable units, isolated from the surrounding lands, but depend more than ever on the lands beyond.[8] Without supporting lands, the city dies. It is on those lands that the city's shadow falls and its ecological footprint tread.

Cities most often have ambitions to grow forever, to grow numbers of people and wealth. It is good for business. It is the demographic strategy. It is the custom. It is the Noosphere's will. Talk of limits or contraction is heresy. But where does this lead?

BIOSPHERE TO NOOSPHERE

Once, an instant ago in geologic time, Alberta was pristine. The dazzling diversity of 11,000 years ago diminished to a merely magnificent abundance after the Quaternary extinctions. One hundred and fifty years ago, before Palliser spied on the land, it had 470,000 km² of boreal forest, 52,000 km² of parkland, 90,000 km² of plain and prairies, and 46,000 km² of montane, alpine and subalpine lands. On the plains, foothills, montane, mountain and parklands ranged four million bison, 400,000 mule deer, 300,000 antelope, 200,000 elk and almost 50,000 bighorn sheep. Alongside were less populous species such as mountain goats, and of course, all their predators—thousands of plains grizzly bears, cougars and 100,000 wolves. In the northern forests were 100,000 wood bison, as many woodland caribou, moose and more mule deer again. There too, were thousands of grizzly bears and tens of thousands of wolves and black bears.

Today the plains, forests and parklands are in retreat; each endangered, planned or committed to ecological obsolescence. In replacement the new biomes are 130,000 km² of plough biome, 80,000 km² of cow biome, 370,000 km² of forestry (woodlot) biome, all overlain by the blanket and matrix of petro-biome, nodal ecotones, shadows and ecological footsteps that shade, choke and crush what remains.[9] Now the wilds hold 6,000 bison, 15,000 elk, 5,000 antelope, 50,000 muleys and 500 grizzlies, no plains wolf, no black-footed ferret, no plains grizzly bears and 10 dozen reintroduced swift fox.[10] That is approximately 1% of the mega-faunal wildlife of 250 years ago.

What was, no longer is. Except for a few dogs, in 1730 there were no exotic plants or animals. Now virtually no intact natural biomes remain. Instead of wildlife, nearly five million cows, 1.8 million pigs, nine million chickens, 800,000 turkeys, 300,000 sheep and over 100,000 horses range the province. The displacement of mega-faunal wildlife by domesticated animals is proportional, pound for pound, and nearly complete. Domestic animals are well over 99% of Alberta's non-human mega-faunal biomass, while less than 1% is wild.[11] That 1% is debasing. The strip is complete, the laminate done.

SUCCESSIONS TO TORPOR

Natural systems are composed of extremely complex pieces engaged in wildly complicated dynamics, few of which are discrete. Pieces number near infinity and the full shape, features and significance of any particular piece no one yet fully understands. Parts taken away affect the entirety. Parts added also change it. The strip and laminate interact with the background natural biome to produce new dynamics and difficult new pieces. At some point in the degrading of any system it changes its essence and becomes something new; systems in relative homeostasis may be so altered that they lose resilience and dynamically transform. The immediate product of these changes may be difficult to anticipate. Longer-term products may be more apparent. That is likely in the case we are examining.

Technology and appetites determine progressions in exploiting nature. To maximize returns, best economic technology is used. Technological change enables more intense exploitation of resources, moving, as it has, from hunter-gatherer through to soil, forest and geological exploitations. Each level of exploitation has consequences. The direction—indeed the imperative with increasing population, increasing demands and an ideology of "more"'—is to intensify exploitation. Technology's potential power increases as science and economics urge the technology-formation machine on to deliver more and more ways to deliver more and more. But to what end?

"Total energy content in the universe is constant and the total entropy is continually increasing" thermodynamics tells us. Entropy is "a measure of the amount of energy no longer capable of conversion into work." Increasing entropy or diminishing capability for work is accepted physics; it is absolute. The rate at which the degradation occurs, the increase in entropy, on the other hand, is variable.

Natural ecosystems use energy available for nature's work. Natural life's complexity and efficiency slows entropy; conservation occurs in retarding entropic decay. As ecosystems lose complexity and efficiency, entropy accelerates. Modern technology takes energy capable of work, redirecting it in ways to satisfy human appetites. Usually that is sooner rather than later, so it speeds entropy. Nicholas Georgescu-Roegen described the economic process "not as a mechanical analogue, but an entropic, unidirectional transformation" or as the "entropic transformation of valuable natural resources (low entropy) into valueless waste (high entropy)."[12] Viewed this way, modern materialistic, consumer society is a swelling entropy machine.

Take a barrel of Devonian oil. Ancient life forms living on the reef captured solar energy 360 million years ago. On dying, the rocks embedded this energy. Now, through application of other energy—all the energy required to find, produce, transport, process and market oil—this oil reaches an ultimate consumer, who burns the oil. Outputs are heat and polluting chemicals, all now in entropic form, unusable and threatening in other ways. Alberta's blessed conventional oil and gas heritage from Devonian and Cretaceous times would be exploited and turned to greenhouse gases in an average human's lifetime. One genius of technology is to turn the eternal to the instantaneous.

Successions in the various anthropogenically influenced biomes lead to entropy. Although starting from different beginnings, as intensity of exploitation increases and biological systems disassemble, successions become increasingly alike. The ultimate or climax succession, entropy, holds no good for anyone or anything. The physicist's entropy is a remote, distant universal condition; local entropy is not. It slinks along, almost imperceptible in its incremental ways, just behind civilization's march.

Locally these successions involve increasing displacement of nature, a kind of biological entropy. First the large, easy and profitable pieces to the puzzle—the big animals and plants—are taken. Next successions involve the smaller, more remote and less apparent resources—the soil. The cow and plough biomes lead in one direction, the same way as forestry. Fossil fuels, because they are non-renewable, contribute prodigiously to entropy. Together these sources aggregate with those entropies resultant from secondary and tertiary activities. Each succession involves higher technology exploiting a diminishing natural base. Entropy increases, torpid amorphousness settles into a dangerous bio-entropy, perhaps abiotism.

When considering the future some look for limits. What thing is it that we will most likely run out of? Malthus talked about limits. In 1972 the authors of *The Limits to Growth* did as well.[13] In popular practice, the limits debate seems shallow, mechanistic and reductionist. The sleight of hand is to select the right problem. If the problem is running out of a resource, then technology and substitution, perhaps even economics may solve that. If the problem is running out of life or fundamental systemic decay in the Biosphere, then solutions differ.

The Laurentide Ice Sheet's takeover of Canada was nearly absolute, reigning for many thousands of years. Virtually erasing all habitat, it seemed not to devastate life. Populations survived in refugia, nunataks, Beringia or just beyond continental ice. At the end of the Pleistocene, Quaternary extinctions had great consequences for life but smaller effect on the land. But neither the ice ages nor the Quaternary extinctions altered Alberta like the most recent cataclysm, the deluge of White people, their technology and global appetites. This new flood of occupation is progressive and cumulative. Nature's subjugation threatens in its effect to be as deep, thick and cold as the glaciations. One wonders how and when its retreat will occur and the dynamics when this ice turns to meltwater.

Today there are few places for wildlife to hide. Inaccessible wilderness is now accessible. Every day it shrinks. Transient, furtive species still shadow the land like fugitives, but every year they are fewer. Zoos and parks are the refugia and nunataks, the terrestrial Arks of the 21st century. These places maintain select shallow genetics, but wild culture and dynamics are dead. Aldo Leopold's rule of intelligent tinkering, "to keep all the pieces" is difficult in practice. Zoos focus on large showy pieces. Pandas, tigers and peregrine falcons are better than frogs and fish. They are sexy and people swoon over them. Critical pieces may be small, ugly or revolting to sensitive and civilized persons. Magic lies not in the individuals but in the functioning totality. All the pieces and all the wisdom of man can never reconstruct that cosmic marvel. The public bias is away from fundamental dynamics to the shallow but acceptable emotive concerns for dewey-eyed deer and cuddly bears. This is reflected in the pattern of conservation history in Alberta.

ROADKILLS ON THE HIGHWAY TO PROGRESS

TAKING THE LAND

G od promised Canaan to Moses' people if they followed his command. Exodus 23:20-33 outlines the steps in taking Canaan—drive out the Canaanites and progressively kill its wildlife. The taking of western Canada roughly paralleled the Mosaic model. Two centuries of fur trade eliminated furbearers. In the 10 years following HBC's sale of Rupert's Land (1869) the new emperors imposed their authority, government, law and culture.[1] The Red River Rebellion of 1869/70 set the scene. The "inhabitants of the land" were driven or stripped from it. Native people ended up on reserves and most Metis found themselves, as a descriptive epithet later characterized them, "road allowance" people.

IDYLLIC ISLES – NATIONAL PARKING LOTS

But there were hesitations in the taking. It was back then that the seeds for another kind of reserve germinated. This evolved into the idea of "reserves for nature" but that was certainly not the initial conception. It had more to do with demographic, commercial and recreational ambitions of the new people:

> The year 1885 was a momentous one for Canadians. Its annals recorded the fulfilment of a long-cherished national dream—the linking of eastern Canada with the Pacific coast by a transcontinental railway. It witnessed the early settlement of the Prairies and the suppression of the armed rebellion by Indians and half-breed residents of the Northwest Territories

against the Government of Canada. The closing months of the year also chronicled the reservation for public use of mineral hot springs in the Rocky Mountains near the railway station of Banff, the first step in the development of Canada's unique and widespread system of national parks.[2]

William Cornelius Van Horne knew there was little use in building railways if you could not fill the trains. In bold strokes he solved the problem of what to do with empty trains and vacant mountainous wilderness. Tourism! It used available infrastructure, lured in international currency, made use of the otherwise useless expanses of land and looked enlightened— parks were good business. The railway mothered Canada's first national park and commercial tourism fathered it. Later a reluctant form of conservation appeared.

First settlers nearly eliminated the wildlife missed by market hunters. Lothian's *A Brief History of Canada's National Parks* comments:

> On August 15, 1903, W. H. Cooper, the Territorial Game Warden for theNorthwest Territories at Edmonton, called to the attention of his Member of Parliament, Frank Oliver, the need for preserving a small herd of elk known to exist in the Beaver Hills near Island Lake east of Edmonton. Cooper believed that these elk, numbering about 75, comprised the largest existing herd in Canada outside what he termed "the unexplored forests of the north" . . . . During the winter of 1903-04, at least 20 elk were killed by hunters in the Beaver Hills region . . . . Large hunting parties were being organized for a "shoot" during the following winter, and the complete destruction of the elk appeared probable.[3]

A National Park, Elk Island Park, was established to aid these elk (wapiti). Of these animals, 24 were saved, enclosed within the park.

Over following years more national parks were established by the federal government to reintroduce the plains bison, leading ultimately to the formation of Wood Buffalo National Park, a magnificent home for such ravaged animals as the whooping crane and wood bison. Nothing in Canadian history compares with the national parks system when it comes to maintaining the land and its native life forms. In the face of overwhelming assault on most things natural, a few precious parcels, these national parks, became retreating defensive ramparts. But even within them things were not well.

National parks are islands of refuge plucked from out of larger natural systems, in swelling seas of intensive human activity. At their biggest and best they provide some ecological buffering for a frail core, but still remain mere pieces. Outside parks, resource and commercial uses increasingly encroach their boundaries, further isolating the park as a disconnected piece of land. Islands of nature in rivers of development inevitably degrade and diminish. Traffic and development increases inside parks and internal rot grabs hold, growing with its popular success.

> And a lot happens in Banff . . . . Canada's main transcontinental railway and transcontinental highway roll side by side down the length of Banff's main valley. On the busiest weekends the road is clotted with cars, RVs, and tour buses, and a gauzy brown haze of exhaust fumes veils the celebrated vistas. Within the park lie three ski resorts and the town of Banff—home to 7,000 permanent residents. On a typical summer day the townies may see 25,000 tourists streaming through their streets.[4]

From approximately 500,000 in 1950, visitors to Banff shot to five million in 1995 and, based on current growth rates, are anticipated to reach 19 million by 2020, the Banff-Bow Valley Task Force estimated.[5] The Task Force recommended a Human Use Management Plan to stem the increasing crush.

Alberta's government owns much of the land surrounding its resident national parks. Stalking the margins closely, it looks for opportunities or waits for federal authorities to falter and transfer lands or jurisdictions to the province.[6] Conservation-minded people tremble to think what national parks would look like if operated by the province. Others shudder at the catastrophes capital might well inflict on parks as business is permitted to invade them further, despite the gentle, loving and respectful terms their commercial ambitions are invariably couched in.

Every day more people come, more exotics dig in and encroach on declining native species. Contexts change and degrade. They suffer from external rot—summer birds diminish each year because of global effects; every year more campgrounds and water slides encroach their boundaries. They suffer from internal rot—the trauma of traffic and development—in these qualitatively shrinking islands. Tourism consumes ecology in the century-old Canadian eco-tourism business. While the rot is deep, still some parks look nearly wild and almost virgin. This is ecotheatre as much as ecosystem. What remains next century will be much different.

REGULATING THE TAKING

Early on there was another hesitation in seizing the land, one that did not play out nearly so well as national parks. This one involved the plains bison and its last free and wild days. On March 22, 1877, the Northwest Territories Council passed an *Ordinance for the Protection of the Buffalo* regulating hunting of bison. For a short time the bison received some protection. Then, in what is a legislative instant, the blink of a parliamentarian's eye, on August 2, 1878 they repealed it. In these 17 months, the Crown's mind reversed from bison salvation to permitting their elimination. What altered the "directing mind and will" in such short time? This legislative reversal appears consistent with the more fundamental laws—to take and exploit, not to care for nor conserve:

> If a single lesson can be drawn from the early history of conservation, it is that states will act to prevent environmental degradation only when their economic interests are shown to be directly threatened. Philosophical ideas, science, indigenous knowledge and people and species are, unfortunately, not enough to precipitate such decisions.[7]

Years later, in 1891, the Crown amended the wildlife ordinance to again regulate the taking of bison. By then, it was too late.

Nineteenth century "market hunters" blasted and bludgeoned egret and herons into milliner's plumes. Anything the market coveted launched a biocidal business. Seas roiled bloody from the slaughter of seal, auk and otter. Whales died so that lamps might burn and corsets not burst. The prairies blotted up the blood of bison because of the want of their hides, their homes or merely their tongues. The market blasted billions of passenger pigeons to kingdom come, some in Alberta. Vendors hawked dead songbirds by the barrelful. Effective regulation came to hunting only just before large-life's end, motivated more by conservation of resources than by conservation of nature. Devastation slowed, but enforcement was rare, and the fines were small, while rewards in the breach were great. By the end of the first waves of settlement most of Alberta was barren of large wildlife.

Early sessions of the Northwest Territories Council enacted ordinances controlling use of poisons and chemicals; establishing watershed management, quarantines and pest eradication programs; and conserving certain important resources. Environmental legislation enjoyed more success than conservation or preservation legislation. The protection of property and human health and safety trumped ecology and non-human life. That was so for regulation of pioneer agriculture but later, also with hesitations, for the pioneer oil patch.

Alberta's first experiences with oil and gas were gluttonous. Hasty wells shadowing property lines were produced with open bores and greedy abandon. Operators took all they could as fast as they could, leaving their slower or more responsible neighbour as little as possible. Lascivious exploitation resulted in wells on every few acres in each oilfield's hot spots. In this lustiness, enormous quantities of gas were flared destroying reservoirs, polluting the atmosphere and leaving a needy future without. Oil's rule of capture translated to quick cash and entropy, at least until government and industry both realized their interests would be better served by more careful practices.

In 1938, Alberta established the Petroleum and Natural Gas Conservation Board to stop the flaring of Turner Valley gas and to more prudently exploit the resource. David Breen observed that the meaning of conservation changed with time:

> For early conservationists, preservation for the future was the essence of their concern, but the related idea of efficient production to eliminate waste emerged more slowly.[8]

For the board, since called the Energy Resources Conservation Board and now called the Alberta Energy and Utilities Board (EUB), conservation's new meaning seemed not to mean that at all:

> Economists have their own notion of conservation. They argue that conservation involves maximizing the present value of a resource: in other words, getting the most petroleum in the present for the least investment.

The economist's "conservation" urges depletion of the non-renewable resource in its fastest, efficient, economic way. With modest exceptions, that has been the credo of the oil patch ever since.

BACK TO THE LAND

Postwar peace, prosperity, and science gave many people greater concern for the land, even in Alberta. Responding to these concerns, in 1959 Alberta's Crown protected from development about 4,600 km² of land in the Willmore area, on the north shoulders of Jasper National Park. But there were larger problems brewing. Rachel Carsen's 1962 alarm, *Silent Spring*, accused agriculture's deadly chemicals of silencing America's songbirds. Persistent toxic chemicals that decimated faraway weeds or insects last year might poison the nearby meadowlark this year and kill humans a decade hence. Ecology claimed all things to be interconnected, all parts in a dynamic, complex whole. Unfortunately, this whole was degrading. Civilized man, long thinking himself the spider, embarrassingly found himself ensnared in the web of life, subject to all of the sticky strings, stings and poisons of the undone fly.

This "ecological awakening" rustled some Albertans to action. With his 1966 boding, *Entrusted to My Care*[9], Grant MacEwan entreated the public to better care for their land. Referring in closing to Robert Louis Stevenson's "sooner or later, everybody sits down to a banquet of consequences," MacEwan prayed his readers would find " a new dedication to stewardship of the earth and its riches, a new emphasis upon the responsibilities of good guardianship." To address this newfound grief, Alberta's Social Credit government passed several bills. Premiere among these was *The Environment Conservation Act*, assented to on April 15, 1970. It established a public body called the Environment Conservation Authority (ECA), and charged it to conduct reviews of government policies and programs to determine their environmental effects.[10] In matters other than budgets and appointments of members, ECA enjoyed some autonomy.

ECA might "inquire into any matter pertaining to environment conservation and make its recommendations and report" to the legislature.[11] Its core power was simply to publicly advise the people's representatives, the legislature. With all its limitations—government control over appointments, budgeting, limited statutory definitions and only scarce powers to report and recommend—this bill represented the zenith in Alberta's environmental protection legislation. That is so because ECA had relative independence to select which issues to address, its reports and recommendations went directly to the legislature as public reports, it could prospectively examine resource and environment issues and it had the power to require the Crown to produce information.

In 1971, a suite of environmental bills, the *Department of the Environment Act*, the *Alberta Environmental Research Trust Act* and the *Wilderness Areas Act* passed into law. These Social Credit Party deathbed pronouncements established Canada's earliest Department of the Environment, created a research trust fund and promised to protect wilderness places by preserving, "their natural beauty and primeval character and influence and safeguarding them from impairment and industrial development and from occupation by man other than as a visitor who does not remain."[12]

The late '60s and early '70s were heady times for land lovers. With a new, sexy issue, the media swarmed, academics published, public opinion swelled and politicians pronounced. The Americans took to it like the flag and Manifest Destiny. They legislated important and innovative processes and protections, initiatives that still embarrass other less patriotic lands. For a few moments in history Alberta lagged not terribly far behind.

The Club of Rome's 1972 dark predictions about man's future, *Limits to Growth*,[13] reengaged public debate on Earth's limits and human prospects. That year the United Nation's Stockholm Conference acknowledged that environmental and resource problems were not just local, but global, while proclaiming the right of all to a quality environment.[14] The people responded to these leaps to environmental quasi-consciousness in powerful new ways, ways that caught government and industry unawares. It would take time for these leaders to understand the issues and their implications for development. It would take them longer to hone the skills necessary to ensure that ecology not stand in the way of economics, growth, development, aggrandizement, power and empire. For the moment, in disarray, they confusedly went with the flow.

Peter Lougheed's Progressive Conservatives took power from the SoCreds in August 1971 just as the market price of Alberta's petroleum motherlode rose a notch. Petro-politics replaced agriculture's. His team's credo was management and control in directing Alberta's growth to a petro-dollar empire. The SoCred's environmental legislation would be harnessed appropriately for the new political-economy.

ROGUE REGULATORS

The life and death of the Environmental Conservation Authority is illuminating in this regard. ECA was best at birth, April 15, 1970. By June 2, 1972, less than a year into its new government, the Lougheed team demoted the authority from reporting to the legislature to reporting to a minister, and from considering what it wished, to considering what the Minister wished. Amendments placed ECA firmly under the control of the Minister of the Environment. Politically captured, it slid from substantial authority to reluctant underling, from duty to the public to political bidding, but it did not slip happily into subservience.

During 1973 the Crown implemented a separate, "project-based" Environmental Impact Assessment (EIA).[15] The *Land Surface Conservation and Reclamation Act*, s 8,[16] permitted the Minister of the Environment to require an EIA if an operation or activity was proposed that, in his opinion, was likely to, result in "surface disturbance." This established a basis for limited, manageable, discretionary and manipulable review on a project basis[17] and it smothered some of ECA's robustness. By 1977 legislative amendments, it was renamed the Environmental Council of Alberta (still referred to as ECA), and demoted from "authority" to "council" status, giving advice when requested, hearing appeals under specified legislation and performing such functions as the Lougheed team might find appropriate.

In its early days the ECA reviewed some projects, publicly commenting on their environmental effects. The people participated, the media reported and Albertans started to feel a larger sense of responsibility for the land. When ECA cautioned against provincial construction of the Dickson Dam in 1974 and some of Alberta's forestry practices[18], Lougheed's government fussed. By the time of the ECA's recommendation against the Oldman River Dam in 1979, they were angry.

The Conservative government's ambitions to multiply and subdue, to drill wells and build dams required the damming of the ECA if it continued to oppose. It was not that government lacked power over ECA. Government appointed its members, directed its activities and funded it. It was just that ECA persevered in doing what it was supposed to do. Few sycophants there, it told government its likes and dislikes, publicly and credibly.

Killing the ECA outright must have been politically unattractive. Clever attrition works better and the public will hardly notice a malingering death. Over time ECA's more vital members were eased or forced out, new appointments were more cautiously and slowly made, important functions disappeared, budgets were redirected, and credibility ebbed. Under Lougheed's management, environment and resource conservation issues lost their lustre, priority, and political punch. The earlier alarm had dulled. Together now, business and government managed environment and land issues to ensure that they would not interfere with growth, development and aggrandizement, commercial or political. Finally in 1995 Alberta dispatched the ECA. Euthanized, it gave up the ghost to the business-adoring Alberta Research Council.

During the time of the ECA's robustness, the Mackenzie Valley Pipeline Inquiry was commissioned to determine the need for and consequences of a multi-billion dollar pipeline proposed to carry arctic natural gas down to southern markets. Mr. Justice Thomas R. Berger of the Supreme Court of British Columbia was appointed Commissioner March 21, 1974 and held community hearings throughout the north so that all might come and have their say in their native tongue aided by simultaneous translation. Recognizing that Canadians generally had an interest and right to be heard, Berger also held meetings in the south. Native claims were considered seriously. He pioneered cumulative social, economic and environmental impact assessment in Canada.

Berger recommended against constructing the pipeline for at least 10 years and until native claims were settled. In accepting his conclusions, Canada saved both industry and the country billions of dollars because there was no market for that gas. For nearly two decades after Berger's appointment, the problem was excess gas. Only now is the gas bubble seriously deflating.[19] Government and industry recoiled from Berger's model, as if he had shone a light down an aisle that Crown and capital feared to tread—the way of the public interest. They chose a different course, capture and control of processes and regulators, the path of active inaction, a theatre for love of land.

The ecological consciousness of the '70s taught both Crown and capital that issues relating to environment and resources must be tightly managed from above. None of this direct democratic or populist stuff. Manage appearances while maintaining firm control. Independent authorities are dangerous. They might do the right thing, as the early ECA and that other rogue tribunal of the day, the Mackenzie Valley Pipeline Commission, demonstrated.

Critical to their strategy, Crown appearances of love of land must be ubiquitous and the flow of glossy misleading material never ending. Control of information is key. Suppression, misinformation and disinformation are as important as information itself. When questioned, government must boast that Alberta is the best cared for land on the planet ("second-to-none") and then pull out swollen numbers ostensibly spent to protect the environment.[20] Numbers do not lie. Albertans love their land. But a wary few looked to the land to see whether it was being loved. Each year they found more and more of it ripped, chewed, and ploughed, cut to bits by agriculture, oil and gas, forestry, industry or urban infrastructure. Less and less wilderness survived, all of it at one point of deterioration or another. Clearly, something was amiss. Could the Crown be misleading the people?

USE THE RUSE!

The late '80s revived popular concern for the land and for the future. By now Crown and capital understood how to manage the issues. Rational planning and hierarchy replaced local, democratic or popular action. International organizations played leadership roles. Government, industry and international elites crafted sophisticated plans, projects and strategies. Now salvation would come from above.

The United Nations Conference on the Human Environment held in Stockholm in 1972 led to the World Conservation Strategy in 1980.

Commissioned by the United Nations Environment Program, the global strategy was to be an aggregate of local strategies. By 1981 Canada had endorsed the idea and recommended the preparation of Provincial Conservation Strategies. Early in 1985 the Public Advisory Committees (PAC) to the ECA launched the Alberta Conservation Strategy project to prepare Alberta's local contribution for this global strategy.

Well-meaning people lined up to help devise a plan for global salvation. Later many became disillusioned with the manipulation and procrastination, coming to doubt the sincerity and conviction of the organizers. Some felt government's "conservation" strategy was similar to that Breen claimed for the Alberta Energy and Utility Board, that it "involves maximizing the present value of a resource: in other words, getting the most…in the present for the least investment."[21] When the Alberta Conservation Strategy failed to appear for its 1992 debut some thought it had died along the way. Others mused that it would miraculously appear at the millennium. Most lamented the waste of their positive efforts and good intentions.

The United Nations World Commission on Environment and Development (WCED) issued their report on the plight of the planet, *Our Common Future*, in 1987. It considered anthropogenic threats like acid rain from fossil fuel and industrial emissions, ozone depletion from chloroflourocarbons and the greenhouse effect from fossil fuel emissions. Alongside, it dwelt on the destruction of rainforests, the prospects of resource depletion and pollution devastation and, in quieter tones, the Siamese twin menace of overconsumption and overpopulation. These concerns harmonized with high-level government activities—protocols, treaties and accords—to sound an alarm and rejoice in a solution. Their report provided a panacea. The path that led the world away from disaster was "sustainable development":

> Sustainable development is development that meets the needs of the present without compromising the ability of future generations to meet their own needs. It contains within it two key concepts:
> - the concept of "needs", in particular the essential needs of the world's poor, to which overriding priority should be given; and
> - the idea of limitations imposed by the state of technology and social organization on the environment's ability to meet present and future needs.[22]

The masses pounced on this cleanly packaged, mightily proclaimed, and globally promoted bobbing lifeboat as if they were the last passengers on the Titanic.

Sustainable Development promised much and asked little. Most but not all species could be saved. Natural systems could be protected; a cap on human population (10 or 12 billion) would be wise. For all that, mankind's real salvation lay in greater consumption through higher technology, more growth in productive activities and better sharing in consumptive activities. Governments and business endorsed the scheme. The masses dammed the Jeremiads even though WCED seems to have favoured only the few. Business fervently embraced it because it gave them nearly everything they wanted. They threw themselves on the green bandwagon. Polluting companies might establish an office paper-recycling project, thereby becoming models of Sustainable Development. No matter how vile in the big things, some small thing might always be done to support a claim to green and clean, Sustainable Development. At the last moment, a happy future for all mankind had been ensured, paradise regained. Alberta joined in this crusade festooned in green.

CHAPTER 15

THE
SALVATION BAND

GUARDIANS OF EDEN

I n these enlightened times when pre-industrial ideologies guide post-industrial economies, when 17th century biology directs 20th century policy, many take from nature's abundance, but few protect it. Who saves Earth for future generations? Alberta's Crown claims to be her local guardian, but is this so?

In September 1989, a document entitled *Action on Environment*[1] slipped out from behind the veil surrounding the Crown, providing a glimpse at regal thoughts. Research in the report indicated that concern for the land might again be getting out of hand:

- 64% of Albertans believe environmental considerations should take precedence over economic development.

- Four out of five Albertans (81%) believe environmental considerations should take precedence over economic considerations when considering energy megaprojects (Environmental Monitor, Winter 1989).

- One in two Albertans (51%) is most concerned about environmental issues due to fears for human health and safety, while 32% are most concerned due to fears about the environment itself.[2]

The green dervish who bedeviled the last Social Credit and the first Lougheed governments seemed ready to blow free again. If the people love the land, can government do other than love it itself?

Action on Environment unveiled government's concern that it might lose its starring role. It implied that if Premier Don Getty's gang acted quickly, they could seize and control the green fiend, and perform the illusionist's trick of appearing to do something while doing nothing. Their words were:

> In the absence of a coordinated government approach to environmental communications and with largely reactive strategies in individual departments the government is slowly losing control of the environmental communications agenda. Instead, it is being set by environmental activists; special interest groups such as the Alberta Wilderness Association; the opposition parties; and even other levels of government. Their strategies usually are to criticize and oppose provincial policies, forcing the government even further into a reactive stance.
>
> Fortunately, the Alberta government has an opportunity to seize the initiative in environmental communications and effectively position itself as a leader in environmental protection before environmental issues reach the same level of importance in Alberta as they have in other areas of Canada. Oftentimes, it is not so much "new" policies or programs which lead to effective positioning, but proper packaging and promotion of existing programs and initiatives. An excellent example is Ronald Reagan's Strategic Defence Initiative, or Star Wars. Much of the research and development into space-based weapons and defensive systems already existed prior to Reagan's pronouncement of his policy, but by assembling existing programs under the new umbrella, giving it a name and adding a few new wrinkles, the then-President was able to effectively position himself and his administration in his desired "leadership" and "get tough" roles.[3]

Presto, Getty's Government seized "the communication's agenda to (ensure) that public discussion focused on the government's issues, not those of the opposition parties and special interest groups."[4] With kingly muscle the Crown overwhelmed the public agenda, elbowing aside those with genuine interests and inviting in government advocates, naming the Chamber of Commerce, capital's tootsie, as a dear confederate (the most special of special interest groups):

> Special Interest groups – such as the Alberta Wilderness Association, Alberta Fish and Game Association, Canadian Wildlife Federation, etc. While these groups will never be convinced to abdicate their "watchdog" role over government

policies and actions, their positions can be softened through education and opportunities to participate in two-way communications. Other special interest groups which play an advocate role on behalf of government (i.e., chambers of commerce) may be reinforced through information and communication.[5]

The Crown's choice was to honestly address environmental issues or ignore them by "packaging and promotion" of the status quo with a "few new wrinkles." They chose repackaging and "wrinkles." *Alberta Environmental Protection and Enhancement Act* (AEPEA) was their "Star Wars." Pure Barnum and Bailey, this was "virtual-policy" at its best. Behind the veil it was business as usual for government, and government as usual for business.

The days from 1989 to 1992, with their green plans, round tables, conservation strategies, new boards, commissions and action plans, were busy, risky times for the Crown and capital. Alberta created a new regulatory body under the inspiring but misleading name, Natural Resources Conservation Board, amended the old *Energy Resources Conservation Act*, apparently to provide for the environment and passed its Star Wars bill, the misnamed *Alberta Environmental Enhancement and Protection Act*[6], into law June 26, 1992. The environment would be protected and enhanced through AEPEA's refurbished "environmental impact assessment" (EIA).

Assessing Assessments

As an elixir for environmental ills, EIA presumes that if only decision makers had better information on the effects of certain projects they would make right decisions for the environment, and all would be well. Some are doubtful. Giagnocavo and Goldstein see it this way:

> Whereas before industrial developers had a virtual carte blanche from the state to expand, now they have to submit to such procedures as environmental impact assessments, control orders and monitoring by appropriate environmental officers. While in theory these seem to be progressive developments, in practice they have become nothing more than costly legitimization projects . . . environmental regulation has become nothing more than a licensing system for polluters.[7]

How does EIA work?

EIA selects a few proposed projects or activities for intensive consideration, generally those posing threats to human health and safety, economic interests or, less certainly, the environment. For a few of those, EIA appears mandatory (but it may not be); in others, discretionary; and in many, exempted. Taken together all the projects subject to EIA form a minuscule part of the activities causing ecosystem and environmental decay in Alberta.

To illustrate EIA's limited application, decision makers for a project under the new regimen, the Natural Resources Conservation Board (NRCB), the Alberta Energy and Utilities Board (EUB) or joint Federal Provincial Review Panels, are to consider the EIAs prepared under AEPEA. AEPEA was proclaimed in effect on September 1, 1993. During the four years following its proclamation, NRCB held public hearings on only three projects that together had capital costs of just in excess of $100 million. All were approved.[8] In the same period, the EUB considered in public hearings only two projects (one, the Cheviot Coal Mine, was a joint review) involving EIAs under AEPEA. Both were approved. Federal-provincial joint reviews considered four projects using AEPEA EIAs (Express Pipeline, Cheviot Coal Mine, Sunshine Ski expansion and Highwood River diversion projects). All were approved. During those four years, the province generated some $300 billion of gross provincial product. During that time only about one-quarter of one percent of that activity has received public consideration using AEPEA EIAs. With modest modifications, all the projects were approved.[9] Also during that period, Alberta chopped its forests (4,000 km²), drilled oil and gas wells (30,000), grazed its public lands, expanded its cities and built infrastructure that penetrates deep into the land. Not a single project was properly reviewed for its contributions to cumulative or comprehensive effects.

EIA employs the Pollyanna premise. Because EIA is project-triggered, the assumption is that "but for the project everything is fine." Only the project is under scrutiny. If approved, the project is OK; if not approved (statistically remote), then everything is still OK, but it might not have been had the project been approved. Regardless, everything is OK.

A project focus invites a reductionist approach. Squinting at the project makes ignoring the world easy. EIA is effectively blind to large-scale, long-term causes of ecological devastation and environmental degradation. Proper cumulative and comprehensive environmental assessments[10] might ameliorate that in modest ways, but none have been performed in Alberta.[11] Broader kinds of assessments—legislative, trade, policy or technology assessments—would assist because they, more than individual projects, influence the degradation of the whole.

Regulators in the EIA process generally do not commission evidence or produce research on environmental issues. They rely on the participants. The process's adversarial heritage also compromises the kind and quality of information that is introduced. At the end of the process, the regulators only need to "consider" the evidence arising from the EIA process and they have no legislated values governing them. Some of the best are sceptical of this process. Dr. David Schindler, a world-renowned scientist who sat on the review panel for the proposed Alberta-Pacific Pulp Mill denounces them: "Every one of these things is done as though it were on another planet. There is no learning and most would not pass a scientific peer review."[12]

AEPEA'S SCOPE

Are claims that Alberta's petroleum industry is the most environmentally regulated and responsible on the planet gaseous bluster? The EUB's record in granting 200,000 well-drilling licences is that it refused scarcely any (about 11) on environmental protection or public safety grounds after public hearings involving EIAs.[13] Under AEPEA, it is business as usual.

Like oil and gas, most forestry occurs on Crown lands using Crown resources. For that reason what is commonly called "government regulation" of forestry is mostly the management a resource owner might require of an exploiting tenant/manager/operator. A normal shopping mall lease has more stringent and demanding terms than an Alberta Forest Management Agreement. In one case it is good business, in the other, excessive government regulation.

Superficially NRCB appears to have jurisdiction over forestry, but it considers the "facility" not the forest. NRCB reviews pulp or sawmills, but not their demands on forests and FMAs. Forestry practices employ the usual props of round tables, steering committees, public information meetings and such, but decision making occurs elsewhere, behind the veil wrapped around government and industry. Occasionally public statements issue from behind the curtain:

> "One of the things that pleased me most was when I learned that (sic) Daishowa's philosophy: a flower grows and a petal falls and fertilizes the ground so another flower will grow" said Fjordbotten.[14]

Albertans had to listen to the minister's ecological nonsense, but they had no say in grants of Denmark-sized land to Daishowa and Al-Pac, a scale not unlike Charles II. The public will have little input into the upcoming Forest Management Agreements, those proposed for GAP or solicited for the Footner Forest.

Government involves itself deeply in agriculture: developing and operating land and water projects, product development, market promotion and industry stimulation. What in agriculture is subject to EIA? AEPEA's Mandatory Activities list stipulates nothing directly. Indirectly, dams higher than 15 m, water diversions of more than 15 m^3 per second, water reservoirs of greater than 30 million cubic metres, pesticide manufacturing plants and chemical fertilizer manufacturing plants are on the mandatory list. Some agricultural activities may attract AEPEA's attention through associated activities but strictly agricultural activities get no consideration. For public health and safety issues there are volumes of regulations. For environmental matters, it is nearly hands-off. That is the way it was before. Despite recent green initiatives, that is the way it remains.

"Environmental law" is usually little more than an amalgam of public health, safety and resource management legislation. Its purpose is to protect contemporary humans from their own activities.[15] It has little to do with protecting non-humanity or future humans. Assurances that it does so are little more than legislative legerdemain. John A. Livingston sees it this way:

> EIA is a grandiloquent fraud, a hoax, and a con. Others have seen it as both a boondoggle and a subterfuge . . . . EIA may not be good science, and may not be conservation, but it is excellent business.[16]

Those who remember the 1970 *Environment Conservation Act* and the Mackenzie Valley Pipeline Inquiry must marvel at our backward lurches to the future.

WHO REGULATES REGULATORS?

Government delegates some decision-making functions to the regulators, who, they say, decide these matters in the "public interest." Legislatures cloak them in autonomy as unbiased and objective decision makers, but the regulatory body is shaped, guided, moulded and managed by the Crown. They fill it—with purposes, information, resources and people.

Are regulators independent and guided by the public interest? Manipulation occurs in many ways in pliable systems, some subtle, some direct. Regulators review discrete projects. As with EIA, this frames the process to provide little answers that avoid big issues.[17] Information on the project and the regulated industry[18] are composed by the applicant and extruded to regulators through its filters of self-interest.[19] Questions important to the public interest—public costs and benefits, cumulating socio-economic and environmental impacts, resource and land degradation issues, and the future—are rarely addressed.[20] More frequently now, the regulator's position reduces to this—what is good for the applicant is good for the public, "private interests" displace the "public interest." The "public interest" is an endangered species in the regulatory zoo.

Crown and capital claim that the regulators are without bias because they are independent of government and private interests.[21] The illusion of independence is maintained through careful selection of those who make the decisions. Determining "who" decides the issue approximates the power to determine "what" is decided. To be appointed, a candidate's spiritual, ethical, political and social values ought to be conventional, consistent and shallow. Philosophers, clerics, paleolithic people, socialists, deep ecologists or Jainists, fundamentalists other than from the Chicago School of Economics, need not apply.

Future prospects may ply some regulators' minds while they regulate. If, after a full and illustrious career, government and industry decide a particular regulator has been helpful, he might retire to more distinguished or remunerative jobs in the regulated industry (often hiring himself out to massage his former regulatory body). Sometimes he ascends to the Boards of Directors in regulated companies or consults to "special interest groups" like mining, oil and gas, forestry, banks or others of capital's interests. Few end on boards of the so-called "special interest groups," the organizational gulags who lobby for the poor, the discriminated against, the sick or the land itself.

Within the regulatory matrix, industry has the best and brightest managers and massagers. Their big-firm, big-bill lawyers adroitly bend and ply plastic systems to their client's advantage. Like comfortable courtiers attending in the chambers of a favoured aristocrat, these agents supplicate with the Crown's selected, business-vetted regulator to deliver happy decisions. The rumpled and harried public interest advocate comes late to the process, most often with few resources, filtered information, and no prestige or position. The public interest stands scant chance.

There is little risk to government and capital in this show. First, not much is at stake. Only a few projects are subject to intensive regulatory review. Second, if the project is important to those with influence, there are methods of ensuring it proceeds whether within the regulatory regime, sidestepping it or overstepping it. If the Crown wants the project, it proceeds—as surely as the Oldman River dam dams the Oldman and the Al-Pac pulp mill excretes industrial ooze into the Athabasca River.[22] Both projects were recommended against by federally demanded review panels, panels notable for their independence and integrity, but both projects were ultimately built. Third, even if regulators deny the application, government and capital (and impressionable environmentalists) parade the decision as proof of regulatory independence. It is conclusive, they say, regulators are not captives.[23]

For the most part, regulators produce the decisions expected of them. Some call this "capture" of the regulator by industry. Captured regulators are as predictable as their education, selection process, employment contracts, institutional information flows and ambitions. Sometimes, government and industry, or industry itself may be divided. In those cases, regulators make hard decisions but they are becoming less frequent as the Crown increasingly submits to capital, leaving the public interest (such as it is) further unattended. It seemed like a natural progression when in February 1996, Alberta farmed out much of its environmental monitoring and regulating power to industry, the target of its regulation.[24]

LAWLORDS

The bedrock of Alberta's law is that of the tribes of England.[25] It is another exotic. This tradition contains the captured memory of millennia of gods, kings, empires and customs. It carries forward the vestiges of Abraham, Moses, Christ, Charlemagne and William the Conqueror. Case and statute capture John Locke's spirit and mind. Its purpose today is as clear as it was last century when the law helped take the west from the Native people. It is the law of capture and exploitation, of the consumption of Earth and the subjection of other tribes. Its entrapped metaphysics—attitudes toward nature, paleolithic peoples and the future—have changed little since then.

Courts remember medieval practices through the complex of costume, hierarchy, discipline, protocol and literate contest. In this jousting, the supplicant's hired courtiers, barristers, thrust and parry to curry favour with the local regent of the Crown, the judge. Courts have a pecking order in which the litigant's power and prestige, the lawyer's reputation and the resources dedicated to litigation aid mightily in establishing the merits of one's case. The Crown appoints judges based on their commitment, excellence in these inherently conservative institutions, often with an eye to their fealty. As courtiers for the sovereign, judges comprise a powerful class of persons who are dutiful to rulers and ancient notions but not really the land or the people.

The rule of law applies equally to all in theory. The inference is that precise and clear law is applied by objective and unbiased judges uniformly and rationally to produce a just result mechanically and predictably. This may nearly be so in some areas and cases—private property law, commercial, criminal and civil litigation—areas of little concern to the elites or where there is a transcendant consensus. It is not so in those areas that have been historically the purview of the Crown or elites. John Ralston Saul claims that, "Law has become like court etiquette of the late 18th century. Each man goes through the motions of acquiesence. Then those with power of any sort go away and do something quite different."[26] The higher the level and closer to elite interests, the greater law's plasticity seems. In matters of economic development, resource exploitation and nature's conservation, Alberta's courts usually demonstrate little appetite for public participation or land protection.[27] That may be how the process works and it just may be the law.[28] Because law reflects the values, priorities and interests of those who make it, those in political power—as it did during Absolutism, the Squirearchy and the taking of the west—it favours elites.

Courts may not have the regulator's discretion, but it is broad. They find credibility and determine facts, settle procedures, which issues to address or ignore; whether to use broad or narrow based determinations; which procedural, interpretative or substantive tools will deliver which result and how to structure it so it fits neatly together. Courts respond to favoured counsel, firms, parties, demeanours and other tribal messages in ways that may tip their scales. Going to court with non-elite public interest groups is a crapshoot with suspicious dice.

SWORDS AND SHIELDS – ROLE OF THE RULE

The law can be sword, shield or sham. Often the law's power relates positively and directly to the wealth of those employing it. The justice system is adversarial, so the strong overwhelm weak more than the right defeat the wrong. Cynical comments, but what is the record? Did the law come to the rescue of Native people and their claims? Over a century of Indian law suggests that the courts can ignore at will what now appear to be issues of fundamental justice.[29] Narrow, legalistic mechanisms denied remedies to generations of Native people.

Some thought the law might defend the land against the big forestry giveaways announced by the Crown in 1988. Peter Reese, the Sierra Club and Alberta Wilderness Association, took the Minister of Lands, Forestry and Wildlife, Leroy Fjordbotten, to court over Daishowa's FMA and the Forests Act, s. 16 wording that provided for "perpetual sustained yield." In effect, the late Justice McDonald held "perpetual sustained yield" to be whatever the minister decided it was, whether sustainable or not. In that regard, the minister could enter FMAs unless they were such that "'no sensible person could ever dream that entering into this agreement lay within the minister's power."[30] Baring the law's teeth, court costs were granted against the public interest groups, keeping public-spirited people off balance for months.

The Rafferty-Alameda decision of April 1989 created a small disturbance.[31] This decision required the federal government to comply with its own laws, the Environmental Assessment Review Process (EARP). Its timing made life difficult for Alberta's bushwhackers and the dam builders on the Oldman River. To the Crown's joy, the giant Daishowa project slipped through early and easily but, to their immediate consternation, Al-Pac's mill required federal approval.

The Alberta and federal governments appointed a federal-provincial panel to review aspects of Al-Pac and it unanimously recommended against the project. Not to be bullied, whether by a review panel, a trapped and uncomfortable federal authority or any land lovers, Alberta announced a second expert review of the project. When they refused to approve the project, Alberta engaged yet a third gang of reviewers, this time to study proposed technology that might reduce some of the problems. After long, hard shopping the Crown finally got the answer they wanted, even if they were no longer asking the right question. Forests fall, stacks steam, the river loads up and the Crown gloats.

John McInnis, a former New Democratic Party member of the Legislative Assembly (1989-1993) served Albertans in investigating Alberta's great forest giveaway. Later McInnis took employment at the University of Alberta (U of A) as Associate Director of its Environmental Research and Studies Centre. McInnis claims that Al-Pac threatened to withdraw a $12 million offer of funding to the U of A if U of A continued employing him. The provocation behind these threats involved some rather tame comments that "citizen"' McInnis made in a speech in Japan. Mr. McInnis sued Daishowa-Marubeni and Al-Pac alleging they acted to induce U of A to breach his employment contract. Daishowa and Al-Pac counter-sued the public-spirited former U of A wage earner for defamation.

The SLAPP lawsuit (Strategic Lawsuits Against Public Participation) provides a powerful tool to preoccupy, manipulate, divert and drain public interest groups. Legal expense forms a small, necessary and tax deductible cost of industry doing business and obtaining economic advantage. On the other side, the public interest advocate does not obtain economic advantage, only risk of personal economic loss. A legal action, judgement or even award of costs against a public interest litigant might bankrupt them. The absolute and comparative advantages are clear. With a little inappropriate application, SLAPP provides a fine bludgeon for private interests to pummel the public interest.[32]

ZOO-OLOGY
- THE PROTECTION RACKET

If there is little help there, what of Alberta's parks and wilderness areas legislation, its hunting and fishing laws? What of Special Places? Are these legislative regimes not intended to protect the land and non-human nature?

Alberta's fourth-largest industry, recreation and tourism, is founded on the postcard notion of a wild and beautiful land, where bears prowl and wolves howl. Hunting and fishing law and regulation ensure the continued harvest of game animals and fish by sportsmen; certainly an advance over the days of unfettered free enterprise and free markets in wildlife. Provincial parks burst with recreationists and tourists but do they save the land? And what is the value of Special Places? Are they refugia?

To celebrate winning control over its resources, in 1930 Alberta enacted its first *Provincial Parks Act*.[33] Several years after, the first eight provincial parks were established, later numbering approximately 65 parks, significant primarily for recreational values. Legislated protection for land started in 1959 with the *Wilderness Provincial Park Act*, later renamed the *Willmore Wilderness Act*.[34] That gave considerable protection to 5,500 km^2 of Alberta lands just north and east of Jasper National Park. By 1970 that area was chopped to about 4,500 km^2.

In the mid-60s the *Wilderness Areas Act*[35] established three wilderness areas—the Ghost River, Siffleur and White Goat areas. For the first, and likely only time, the legislature recognized that the public interest required that land and non-human nature be conserved and maintained intact, if only in some areas:

> WHEREAS the continuing expansion of industrial development and settlement in Alberta will leave progressively fewer areas in their natural state of wilderness; and

> WHEREAS it is in the public interest that certain areas of Alberta be protected and managed for the purpose of preserving their natural beauty and primeval character and influence and safeguarding them from impairment and industrial development and from occupation by man other than as a visitor who does not remain; and

> WHEREAS to carry out those purposes it is desirable to establish and maintain certain areas as wilderness areas for the benefit and enjoyment of the present and future generations.

These were welcome steps, particularly for the time, but, like several other historical initiatives, turned out to be a mere hesitation on the path of "industrial development and settlement."

Lougheed's Conservatives found several sections in the *Wilderness Areas Act* offensive and deleted them in 1981, ensuring that wilderness areas might no longer be preserved for their "primeval character and influence" but only for their natural beauty, and not in ways that would safeguard them "from occupation by man other than as a visitor who does not remain."[36] The inference was clear; in wild areas man was coming to stay and to take. Nature was dispensable and aesthetics were in vogue. Of great importance was the beauty most alluring to tourist dollars.

During the last several decades, nature advocates struggled to increase protection for fast disappearing lands—representative ecosystems, habitats for endangered or threatened species or "endangered spaces." Devastation laboured on as well, gaining virtually all the victories. Price-led oil booms gutted more wilderness and the forestry swipe cut more again. Amendment of the *Wilderness Areas Act,* in 1981, by adding *Ecological Reserves and Natural Areas Act* to the title, rekindled hopes for some, but only a little land was protected under that legislation. By 1993, the Alberta Wilderness Association estimated:

> Outside of national parks (federal), the Province of Alberta has designated less than 2% of the provincial land base within protected areas. And, incredibly, we actually have less wilderness protected now than we did in 1965.[37]

Others estimated "a tiny 2.48%—approximately 16,366 km²"—was protected.[38] This was plainly insufficient.

Some advocates strategized ways to save relic pieces of what formerly was, an ark or zoo of Alberta wild lands. The project "Special Places 2000" sought protection for the best remnants of some 17 subregions having no current protection out of the 20 subregions contained in Alberta's six natural areas. This project suffered the usual zoo and ark problems. Designated areas would be small, isolated islands with varying degrees of protection. None would be large enough to maintain long-term diversity or systemic integrity, but something is better than nothing. Called "postage stamps 2000" by skeptics, these colourful "postage stamps" would decorate development's envelope. Supporters pleaded with the government's Grandees—the Ralph Kleins, Ken Kowalskis and the Ty Lunds—to save these remnants. The public wanted it. Even the oil industry would sacrifice a few places if certain it could suck the oil from the rest.

Government announced its plan of protection in 1995, saying that "Special Places balances the preservation of Alberta's natural heritage with the other three goals or cornerstones: outdoor recreation, heritage appreciation and tourism/economic development." Neither balanced nor a protection plan, it was multiple-use planning in pale green garb. It used currently classified areas—the provincial parks, wilderness areas, natural areas, ecological reserves—and nominated new areas, but "protection" was hardly their purpose.[39] Government's words clarify their intent. "Did You Know," the government proudly asks:

- That hunting is used as a management tool in some provincial parks and ecological reserves . . . . ? These population control programs help minimize conflicts with surrounding landowners.

- That oil and gas wells currently exist in seven provincial parks, three ecological reserves and 22 natural areas? More than two-thirds of the natural areas permit oil and gas activity.

- That livestock grazing is part of the active management plans in four ecological reserves, seven provincial parks and one natural area? Annually, more than 31,000 Animal Unit Months of cattle grazing are available.

- That Alberta's provincial parks serve over eight million visitors each year?[40]

After ravenously consuming 99 pieces of the pie, the glutton demands balanced sharing on the hundredth, the last piece.

CHAPTER 16

EPILOGUE

his story began at the end of the last ice age. But glaciations also have their beginnings. Long before ice takes hold, thousands of years before thresholds are encountered, those circumstances that favour ice take seed, gestate and grow; their power accumulates. As potent as these may be, pre-threshold changes are subtle, often imperceptible, and the land and life seem strong. Once critical thresholds are crossed the onset of an ice age can be geologically instantaneous, as little as five years some think, and consequences colossal. Ice laminates the land, submerging it to the deeps and stripping it of life. Ice and abiotism take dominion for, what is on human timescales, an eternity.

On this book's timescale, the last 10 to 15,000 years, immense changes of other sorts, anthropogenic in origin, many on the global scale, have occurred. The five to 10 million hunter-gatherers on Earth at the last ice age have grown to six billion, scarcely any of who today are hunter-gatherers. This radical lamination of the human species on Earth is now virtually complete in expanse but not in intensity. Population continues to grow onward to 10 billion or more and per capita impacts elevate ever upward as appetites and human technological powers bound higher and higher.

The Quaternary extinctions eliminated much of Earth's Pleistocene mega-faunal life at the genera and species levels. Since then almost all other large life forms, and many small, have been stripped away, some by extinction and, with alarming and increasing frequency, by extirpation and elimination of populations. In their place have been laminated the new plastic beasts, domesticated animals. These are dedicated not to the Biosphere but to service of the Noosphere. Most arable lands have been stripped of wild flora and fauna, displaced or replaced by domestic plants, resources to feed the Noosphere. Plantations and tree farms increasingly rise up where Earth's forests once grew. Seas are harvested, fisheries stripped to the point of collapse in many instances. Biodiversity is plunging and intact ecosystems are utterly endangered. Earth's atmosphere is being polluted and its climate is changing, loaded with the greenhouse gases and other chemicals produced in the last several centuries of industrialization. Each change changes others. The Biosphere is in full retreat, the Noosphere is in brazen, unconscious advance.

Today's ambition is to pick up the pace of global "development" as the Noosphere confidently goes down a never-before-trodden path with scarcely a thought for where it leads. The fresh new land, Alberta, has been developed and plundered in quick time, so fast and furiously that there has been barely opportunity to reflect on it. In just over one century so much has been stripped and laminated that Alberta is synthetic in many ways. Provincial leaders shrilly exhort all around to take and plunder more, faster. But where does this lead? What prospects are there for the future in a fabricated world in which most are motivated by the ravenous twins, production and consumption?

BACK TO NEIGHBOURS

About six years ago, just after writing the prologue, I moved away. Recently I returned to the old neighbourhood. The house looked content, congenial and happy to see me. Someone else lives in it and the cottonwood still stands. The ash that the girls and I planted on Father's Day some years back, grows, much larger now. The wild rose, the one lovingly dug with my father, our last real interaction before disease took his memory and then his life, is gone. Memories fade, places are lost, but the exotic ash thrives. Things look neat and clean.

The nice neighbours down the street and across the alley and that silly grain elevator birdhouse, pluck full of English sparrows, remain. It is a fine neighbourhood still. Over on the hill I wander and wonder, possibly looking for the bed of gentian, perhaps that swatch of prairie wool, maybe the bones of Holden Caulfield. There are improvements there too. A nature trail now winds up the hillside over the bed of gentian. Too bad about those gentian; no longer part of the Biosphere and all. When asked about them, a neighbour said he did not know them. Maybe it is easier not to know what was. Perhaps the problem is with remembering too much—one can only embrace so many neighbours, whether place, plant, animal, human, past, present or future?

But we risk much to forget the future. The Biosphere is shrinking and the Noosphere is growing in a dialectic that leads in never-before-experienced, never-charted directions. What will this old place be like next century? What of this old world? What new strips and laminates, what new dynamics? What synthesis? What resolution?

And what of mental environments? Illusions rule. Our collective mind thinks that the Biosphere is not being stripped away, that it is still intact and dutifully working for us, helping fulfil our destiny. But this too is a laminate. Crafted over the growing Biospheric void are faux mnemonics of what once was. If these new illusions of what-once-was-but-no-longer-is are the navigation points guiding the Noosphere into the future and our aggregate appetite is the compass, we have passage on a voyage to a strange and dangerous unfoundland, a new *terra incognito* or possibly *terra nullius*. Without a polestar and with only our voracity for a pilot we cross risky thresholds on the way. Once there we may find that nothing inhabits this fabricated future-land other than, perhaps, willful monsters and a haunting echo of Margaret Atwood's words in *Speeches for Doctor Frankenstein*:

> Doctor, my shadow
> shivering on the table,
> you dangle on the leash
> of your own longing;
> your need grows teeth.
>
> You sliced me loose
>
> and said it was
> Creation. I could feel the knife.
> Now you would like to heal
> that chasm in your side,
> But I recede. I prowl.
>
> I will not come when you call.[1]

ENDNOTES

PROLOGUE

1. Harold Innis, *The Fur Trade in Canada* (New Haven, Conn., Yale University Press, 1930; repr., Toronto: University of Toronto Press, 1970), 287-288.
2. Michael Polanyi, *The Study of Man* (Chicago: U of Chicago Press, 1959), 13-15.
3. John Rawls, *A Theory of Justice* (Cambridge: Harvard University Press, 1971), 512.
4. E. C. Pielou, *After the Ice Ages: The Return of Life to Glaciated North America* (Chicago: University of Chicago Press, 1991).

CHAPTER 1
ICY BEGINNINGS

1. Quaternary Period divides into the Pleistocene Epoch (from two million years ago until 10,000 years ago) and the Holocene Epoch (the last 10,000 years, including the modern era).
2. In the "albedo effect," fresh fallen snow reflects some 75% of light (sun's heat energy) into space. Forests reflect only 10%.
3. *Exodus* 14:21.
4. Alfred W. Crosby, *Ecological Imperialism: The Biological Expansion of Europe, 900-1900* Canto Ed. 1993 (New York: Cambridge University Press, 1986), 9-12.
5. Controversy exists over the significance of glaciation's role in these examples of avian speciation.
6. Uncertainty remains over the existence and use of the corridor.

CHAPTER 2
FIRST PEOPLES

1. Digs in Monte Verde, Chile indicate that humans were resident there earlier, perhaps as long ago as 33,000 years BP. This suggests migration before glaciation's retreat and prompts closer examination of other strategies—perhaps by boat.
2. Joseph H. Greenburg and Merritt Ruhlen, "Linguistic Origins of Native Americans," *Scientific American*, November, 1992, 99.
3. S. David Webb, "Ten Million Years of Mammal Extinctions in North America," ed. Paul S. Martin and Richard G. Klein, *Quaternary Extinctions: A Prehistoric Revolution* (Tuscon: University of Arizona Press, 1984) 206-207.

4. Most environmental changes seemed conducive to expansion of diversity, not contraction. With glacial retreat new habitat opened up. Expansion not contraction might be expected?

5. Paul S. Martin and Richard G. Klein, eds., *Quaternary Extinctions* (Arizona: University of Arizona Press, 1984), ch. 27 to 35; Crosby, *Ecological Imperialism* 13-17; Pielou, *After the Ice Age*, 254-261.

6. There is evidence of a miniature race of mammoths that survived until approximately 3700 years ago on Wrangel Island.

7. Olive Patricia Dickason, *Canada's First Nations: A History of Founding Peoples from Earliest Times* (Toronto: McClelland & Stewart Inc., 1992), 32, reports first use of the bow and arrow in North America at about 250 A.D. It arrived in Alberta several centuries later.

8. In what some refer to as "buffalo time", archaeologists age bison skulls according to their size. Early is larger, recent is smaller after making relevant adjustments for specimen age, sex and circumstance.

9. J. Stan Rowe and Robert T. Coupland, "Vegetation of the Canadian Plains," *Prairie Forum: Canadian Plains Research Centre*, Vol. 9, No. 2, 242.

10. Elaine Anderson, "Who's Who in the Pleistocene: A Mammalian Bestiary," ed. Paul S. Martin, *Quaternary Extinctions*, 55.

11. Robert W. Kates, "Sustaining Life on Earth," *Scientific American*, October 1994, 114, in a graph entitled "Height and technological change," notes that pre-agricultural eastern Mediterranean men were 5 foot 10 inches while early industrial European men averaged only 5 foot 7 inches (118-119).

CHAPTER 3
DISTANT RUMBLINGS

1. David Anthony, Dimitri Y. Telegin and Dorcas Brown, "The Origins of Horseback Riding," *Scientific American*, December 1991, 94.

2. Farley Mowat, *The People of the Deer*, (New York: Pyramid, 1968), 74-77.

3. British Commander-in-Chief Jeffrey Amherst directed distribution of smallpox-infected blankets among Native encampments in the aftermath of the Treaty of Paris and the Proclamation of 1763. Dickason, *Canada's First Nations*, 183.

4. *Numbers* 13:17-20.

5. If the Opium Wars of 1841 (England and China) were indicative, the empire did much to force trade in vile commodities, like opium, even if it meant war.

6. Innis, *The Fur Trade in Canada*, 332, describes HBC policy: "the Company met competition by general instructions to destroy furbearing animals along the frontier."

7. Ibid., 287, 288.

CHAPTER 4
BISON BOUNTY

1. Kenneth Norrie and Douglas Owram, *A History of the Canadian Economy* (Toronto: Harcourt Brace Jovanovich, 1991), 271.
2. C. Gordon Hewitt, *The Conservation of Wild Life of Canada* (New York: Scribner, 1921), 119-20.
3. Farley Mowat, *Sea of Slaughter* (Toronto: McClelland & Stewart, 1984), 142.
4. J. E. Foster, "End of the Plains Buffalo," ed. J. E. Foster *Buffalo* (Edmonton: U of Alberta Press, 1992), 73.
5. Ibid., 74.
6. Dickason, *Canada's First Nations*, 199.
7. Ibid., 193. Dickason comments "In 1833 a Peigan chief, Sackomaph, was reported to own between 4,000 and 5,000 horses, 150 of which were sacrificed upon his death."
8. Ibid., 199.
9. Thorstein Veblen, *The Theory of the Leisure Class* (New York: Modern Library, 1912), 2-4, and also, Chapter IV considered these matters in the context of early societies.
10. Foster, "End of the Plains Buffalo," Foster, *Buffalo*, 74.
11. C. Gordon Hewitt, *The Conservation of Wild Life in Canada* (New York: Scribner, 1921), 121.
12. Lennard's Carrying Co. v Asiatic Petroleum Co. Ltd [1915] A.C. 705, 713-14 H.L. Viscount Haldane asked "Who is really the directing mind and will of the corporation" to determine who fundamentally was responsible for the corporation's actions. This work sometimes uses those words in a broader sense, to speculate on whose interests are being attended to when an action is undertaken.
13. Foster, "End of the Plains Buffalo," Foster, *Buffalo*, 76.
14. D. H. Meadows, D. L. Meadows, J. Randers, *Beyond the Limits: Confronting Global Collapse, Envisioning a Sustainable Future* (Toronto: McClelland & Stewart, 1992), 187.
15. Tom McHugh, *The Time of the Buffalo* (Lincoln, Nebraska: University of Nebraska Press, 1972), 284, reports that American General Philip Sheridan allegedly submitted to Texas legislators that "Instead of stopping the hunters they ought to give them a hearty, unanimous vote of thanks, and appropriate a sufficient sum of money to strike and present to each one a medal of bronze, with a dead buffalo on one side and a discouraged Indian on the other."
16. Canada, House of Commons, *Record of Proceedings*, March 26, 1877, 990. This is one example of the effects being known. Warnings came from Palliser, others through the treaty process, Commons debates and Northwest Territories Council ordnances. Communications were received from government officials, religious figures, Native people, writers in Canada and America. Ignorance is not the case, intent is.

CHAPTER 5
HUDSON'S BAY COMPANY

1. George F. G. Stanley, *The Birth of Western Canada: A History of the Riel Rebellion* (Toronto: U of Toronto, 1960), 47. Riel's father, Louis Riel Sr., led a Metis demonstration that encouraged the light sentence. Metis took this to mean "Le commerce est libre."
2. Innis, *The Fur Trade in Canada*, 397 claims the "Grand Trunk interests in 1863 acquired control of Hudson's Bay Company."
3. Peter C. Newman, *Caesars of the Wilderness* (Toronto: Penguin Books, 1988), 489.
4. Newman, *Caesars of the Wilderness*, 489.
5. The *Statute of Westminster*, 1931, restricted the Imperial Parliament from legislating on the part of Canada, eliminated application of the *Colonial Laws Validity Act* and allowed Canada its independent foreign policy. The final Court of Appeal continued to be the Privy Council until 1949 and the power of constitutional amendment devolved only in 1982.
6. The enabling legislation for the surrender of HBC lands, *The Rupert's Land Act, 1868*, passed on July 31, 1868.
7. J. Arthur Lower, *Western Canada: An Outline History* (Vancouver: Douglas & McIntyre, 1983), 96.
8. Stanley, *The Birth of Western Canada*, 57. Newman, *Caesars of the Wilderness*, 493 attributes the same comment "sold like dumb driven cattle" to the 1863 sale of HBC controlling interests.
9. "In such a case . . . it is quite open by the Law of Nations for the inhabitants to form a government *ex necessitate* for the protection of life and property, and such a Government has certain sovereign rights by the *jus gentium* . . . . John A Macdonald confidential writing to would be Lieutenant-Governor McDougall on November 27, 1869. Stanley, *The Birth of Western Canada*, 85.
10. Stanley, *The Birth of Western Canada*, 71.
11. Peter C. Newman, *Merchant Princes: Company of Adventurers Vol. II* (Toronto: Penguin, 1992), 75. Earlier (p.69) Newman claims "One of the jurors at his trial admitted 'We tried Riel for treason and he was hanged for the murder of Thomas Scott.'"
12. James G. MacGregor, *A History of Alberta* (Edmonton: Hurtig Publishers, 1972), 85. See R. Brian Ferguson, "Tribal Warfare," *Scientific American*, January 1992, 108 for contrary comments.

CHAPTER 6
TAKING NEW CANAAN

1. Exodus 23:27-31.
2. *Constitution Act, 1867*, s.146; formerly, *The British North America Act, 1867*, 30 & 31 Victoria, c.3. (U.K.).

3. James G. MacGregor, *A History of Alberta* (Edmonton: Hurtig Publishers, 1972), 63.

4. Ibid., 85.

5. Francis Haines, *The Buffalo* (New York: Crowell, 1970), 203.

6. Cecil E. Denny, *March of the Mounties* (Surrey, British Columbia: Heritage House, 1994), 10-11.

7. *An Act respecting the Administration of Justice, and for the establishment of a Police Force in the North West Territories*, 36 Vict., c.35. It was assented to May 23, 1873.

8. Peter C. Newman, *Caesars of the Wilderness* (Ontario: Penguin, 1987), 425.

9. Ibid., 425.

10. Newman, *Company of Adventurers* paperback edn. (Ontario: Penguin, 1985), 256-260.

11. Dickason, *Canada's First Nations*, 45-46.

12. Ibid., 177, 178.

13. MacGregor, *A History of Alberta*, 108, claims that under the treaties "Indians were at least saved from extinction."

14. Douglas Hill, *The Opening of the Canadian West*, (London: Heinemann, 1967), 137.

15. Ibid.

16. *Guerin v. The Queen* (1984) 2 S.C.R. 335. Richard A. Bartlett, "Indian Reserves on the Prairies," 23 *Alta.L.R* 243, 251, states that reserves "comprise 0.95% of the total area of Alberta."

17. McGregor, *A History of Alberta*, 109.

18. Newman, *Company of Adventurers*, 251-253.

19. Rudyard Kipling, "The White Man's Burden," (1899) *Rudyard Kipling's Verse, Definitive Edition* (New York: Doubleday & Co., 1939), 321-322.

20. Alexander Morris, *The Treaties of Canada with the Indians of the North-West* (Toronto: Willing & Williamson, 1880), 296-297, his closing paragraph. Morris was instrumental in the revisions of Treaties 1 and 2, and negotiating Treaties 4 to 6.

21. Newman, *Company of Adventurers*, 243.

22. This right diminishes as the quality and quantity of Crown lands diminishes and suffers other incompatible uses.

CHAPTER 7
TROJAN, IRON, WAR AND OTHER HORSES

1. The American strategy was to purchase Alaska (1867), a nice northwest end piece to their continental sandwich.

2. Notes from Alberta Legal Archives Historical Dinner speech, September 19 and 20, 1995.

3. Samuel Taylor Coleridge, *The Rime of the Ancient Mariner*, Line 197.

4. Stanley, *The Birth of Western Canada*, 314.
5. Ibid., 328.
6. Canada, Statutes, *Canadian Pacific Railway Act*, 44 Vic. 1., Schedule, s.11, assented to February 15, 1881.
7. Newman, *Merchant Princes*, 156, 157.
8. HBC received two of the even-numbered sections in each 36-section township, sections 8 and 26.

CHAPTER 8
WHITEOUT

1. Robert W. Kates, "Sustaining Life on the Earth," *Scientific American*, October 1994, 114. This author relies on Edward S. Deevey, Jr. who earlier plotted human population on logarithmic scales. He observed three surges he believes arose from fundamental technological changes. From one million years ago to 10,000 years ago, toolmaking took Earth's population to five million. Agriculture 10,000 years ago to 300 years ago took the population to 500 million. The scientific-industrial revolution 300 years ago will take the population to 10 or 15 billion.
2. W. E. Tate, *The English Village Community and the Enclosure Movements* (London: Victor Gollancz Ltd, 1967), 88. "It is quite certain at least that there were enclosed in England in some 5,400 individual enclosures during the eighteenth and nineteenth centuries, under nearly 4,200 acts and under the various General enclosures acts, more than seven million acres."
3. Robert L. Heilbroner, *The Worldly Philosophers* (New York: Simon & Schuster, 1953), 23.
4. Clive Ponting, *A Green History of the World* (London: Sinclair - Stevenson, 1991), 129.
5. Galbraith, *Economics in Perspective*, 84.
6. *Ibid.*, 53.
7. Howard and Tamara Palmer, "The Black Experience in Alberta," Howard Palmer, ed., *Peoples of Alberta: Portraits of Cultural Diversity* (Saskatoon, Saskatchewan: Western Producer Prairie Books, 1985), 365-393.
8. MacKenzie King's diary entry of January 10, 1911 comments on the mood of the Laurier cabinet:

   Oliver is strong in his opposition to labour being brought into the country for work on railroads that ultimately is not going to be of service for settlement and favours making restrictions on virtually all save northern people of Europe. I agree with him, but we are about alone in this, others preferring to see railroad work hurried. (PAC, The King Diary)
   Head taxes, legislation, and systemic discrimination kept Chinese numbers low.

9. Howard Palmer, *Patterns of Prejudice: A History of Nativism in Alberta* (Toronto: McClelland and Steward, 1982), 20.

10. Pierre Berton, *The Promised Land* (Toronto: McClelland & Stewart, 1984), 59.
11. Palmer, *Patterns of Prejudice*, 23.
12. Berton, *The Promised Land*, 54.
13. Ibid., 312.
14. Pre-contact populations in Alberta may have ranged higher, as high as 30,000. McGregor, *A History of Alberta*, 207 indicates a population of 6000 in 1914.

CHAPTER 9
SODBUSTING

1. Stanley, *The Birth of Western Canada*, 189. Rates varied in the settlement era.
2. Canadian Wheat Board was established to monopolize grain marketing by Order in Council of July 31, 1919. 36.74 bushels = one metric tonne.
3. Kenneth Norrie and Douglas Owram, *A History of the Canadian Economy* (Toronto: Harcourt Brace Jovanovich, 1991), 484, observes that net farm income for the three prairie provinces declined from 1928 to 1932 from $363 million to a minus $3.1 million.
4. *Report of the Royal Commission on the Economic Union and Development Prospects for Canada* (Ottawa: Minister of Supply and Services, 1985), Vol. 2, 427.
5. Robert England, *The Colonization of Western Canada* (London: King, 1936), 72.
6. *Joel* 3:10.
7. T. K. Derry and Trevor I. Williams, *A Short History of Technology: From the Earliest Times to AD 1900* (London: Oxford University Press, 1960), 671. Tim Fitzharris, "Yesterday's Grassland Tomorrow" *The Beaver* Summer, 1983, 14 of 19 says "Then the introduction of John Deere's mouldboard plough in 1837 opened the entire region to agriculture." Note Clive Ponting, *A Green History of the World* (London: Sinclair Stevenson, 1991) 260.
8. Zero tillage depends largely on chemical herbicides to kill all crop competitors. Erosion is reduced but there are other costs.
9. While the expedition did not actually set foot in Palliser's Triangle, Palliser's expedition claimed that area of the prairies to be too arid for farming. Bounded on the south by the 49th parallel, it followed roughly the lighter brown soil area of the shortgrass prairie.
10. Gross and Nicoll Kramer, *Tapping the Bow* (Calgary: Friesen Printers, 1985), 136.
11. Michael Klassen, "The Last Stand of the Cottonwoods," *Nature Canada* Winter 1990, 38.

12. Sasha Nemecek, "Frankly, My Dear, I Don't Want a Dam," *Scientific American* August, 1997, 20 of 21 reports from a recent *Science* article about the loss of biodiversity "choked off by dams." "Near larger storage reservoirs, the researchers found that the number of species within a given area dropped by about 50%."

13. Provincial government pays capital and operating costs upstream of the irrigation district. In the irrigation district (I.D.) historically it paid 86% and I.D. 14% of capital and rehabilitation. I.D.'s also receive further government grants (dam building is called "environmental protection" in some public accounts), federal subsidies and water rates from farmers. Some years ago the I.D.'s portion was increased from 14% to 25% so that costs are shared between government and the I.D. 75:25.

14. Estimates based on Eastern Irrigation District calculations.

15. Exodus 23:29.

16. W. O. Mitchell, *Who Has Seen the Wind*, Illus. William Kurelek, (Toronto: McClelland & Stewart, 1991), 218.

17. Barton J. Bernstein, "The Birth of the U.S. Biological-Warfare Program," *Scientific American*, June 1987, 116.

18. Rachel Carsen, *Silent Spring* (Boston: Houghton Mifflin, 1987, c 1962), 16.

19. J. Stan Rowe and Robert T. Coupland, "Vegetation of the Canadian Plains," *Prairie Forum: Canadian Plains Research Centre* Vol. 9, No 2, 245 claims the prairie provinces were globally distinguished in their chemical overuse.

20. Canadian Press, *Times Colonist*, May 7, 1996, A6, reports that "In Alberta, a couple of Conservative politicians have called for the mass extermination of the gopher." Some feel they should be exported as pets for the Japanese.

21. One example of many is James A. Young, "Tumbleweed," *Scientific American*, March, 1991, 82, describing the introduction and spread of the tumbleweed in America.

22. Earthworms loosen and aerate the soil, tending to change the micro-organism diversity and mix in soil ecology. That may have larger consequences to native plant, fungi communities, which in turn have their consequences. Some are looking at it with respect to foothills ecology.

23. Paul W. Riegert, "Insects on the Canadian Plains," *Prairie Forum*, Vol 9, No 2, 330.

24. Ponting, *A Green History of the World*, 225-226.

25. Introduced feline distemper now decimates African lions.

26. Canada, Northern Diseased Bison Environmental Assessment Panel, *Northern Diseased Bison: Report of the Environmental Assessment Panel*, August 1990.

27. Alberta, Alberta Agriculture, *Agricultural Statistics Yearbook, 1991*.

28. Lawson G. Sugden, "The Waterfowl Resource of the Canadian Plains," *Prairie Forum*, Vol. 9, No. 2, 307.

29. Ibid., 310.
30. British Columbia's Bennett Dam stopped the spring flooding of much of the whooper nesting and feeding grounds in Wood Buffalo National Park, degrading those habitats.

CHAPTER 10
OIL MOIL

1. Ed Gould, *Oil: The History of Canada's Oil & Gas Industry* (Saanichton, B.C.: Hancock House, 1976), 54.
2. Ibid., 60.
3. Ibid., 76. "Of 57 companies listed, with millions and millions in shares sold, only 12 wells were being drilled in 1915: Two each by Calgary Petroleum Products and Columbia Oil, and one each by McDougall-Segur Ltd.; British Alberta; Monarch; Western Pacific; United Oils of Alberta; Black Diamond No. 1; Federal Oil & Gas, and Southern Alberta Oil." Less than 20% of the oil companies were then drilling for oil.
4. Ibid., 82.
5. Gulf, Texaco, Mobil, Socal, British Petroleum and Shell.
6. Gould, *Oil*, 100.
7. Ibid., 139. Oil and Auto are symbiotic in this hunt, consume and move culture.
8. Peter Foster, *The Blue-Eyed Sheiks* (Toronto: Totem Books, 1980), 35.
9. *National Energy Board Decision GH-3-94*, 26.
10. With specialization, trade is not really free. It is essential, but it is still consensual—one can choose with whom, how much, when and, in the long run, even to reduce dependency. With FTA, the consumer can command trade.
11. B. L. Horesji, "The Hidden Costs of Developing and Exporting Natural Gas Reserves," *Wild Earth*, Winter 1991/92, 28. "An average of two miles (2.9 km) [sic] of access road is built for each well drilled." Thus the estimate is approximately 600,000 km for Alberta. This does not include the public road system (200,000 km), forestry and agricultural road systems, or other private developments.
12. "Oilpatch Must Monitor Itself Closely Or Pay The ERCB Piper," *Daily Oil Bulletin*, November 3, 1994.
13. These are older estimates. Alberta, Alberta Energy, *Annual Report, 1995–96*, 30, claims the oilsands "underlie about 77,000 km²" or 12% of the province.
14. Crown contributions are substantial. "More than $500 million in oil sands research" has been spent in the last 20 years "Oil Sands Company's Share Price Crashes," *Daily Oil Bulletin*, April 1, 1996, 8. Some have reported that Herman Kahn of Hudson Institute suggested the nuclear bomb idea. Foster, *The Blue Eyed Sheiks*, 100, attributes it to M. L. Natland, a senior geologist with Richfield Corp.

15. Alan Boras "Oilsands boost worth $5 billion," *Calgary Herald*, June 4, 1996. "Chretien . . . helped announce more than $5 billion in new oil projects—new and previously pending."

16. Alberta Environmental Centre and WDA Consultants Inc., *Impact of the Petroleum Industry on Cattle Production: Critical Review of Scientific and Other Literature*, April 21, 1995, describes some negative impacts of the petroleum industry on the cattle industry.

17. Canada, National Energy Board, *"Canadian Energy, Supply, and Demand 1993–2010* National Energy Board Report, Technical Report, p.11–5.

18. Clean Air Strategy for Alberta (CASA) claims Alberta has 30% of CO^2 emissions, 24.8% of NO_x and 23.7% of SO^2.

19. Pembina Institute for Appropriate Development, *National Energy Board, Express Pipeline Project OH-1-95*, written submission dated December 13, 1995, 5. The ratio of carbon dioxide equivalent GHG emissions (CO^2 and CH^4) to produce equivalent volumes is 0.78 for oil sands and 0.07 for conventional oil.

20. Chris Bright, "Tracking the Ecology of Climate Change," *State of the World 1997* (New York: W W Norton, 1997), 78, 79.

21. Foster, *The Blue-Eyed Sheiks*, 61.

22. Harold M. Hubbard, "The Real Cost of Energy," *Scientific American*, April 1991, 36, argues "energy costs society billions of dollars more than its users pay directly". The costs included security, military, environmental and other externalities.

23. Canada, National Energy Board, *Canadian Energy Supply & Demand 1993-2010*, Technical Report, p.7–5.

24. Alberta, Alberta Energy, *Alberta Ministry of Energy Report, 1995-1996*, 31. "The new regime calls for a royalty rate of 25% payable on net revenues after the developer has recovered all costs, and a minimum 1% gross royalty. A return allowance—equivalent to the Canadian government's long-term bond rate—will be applied annually to all unrecovered costs." Note the 25% is on *net revenues* and only *after the developer has recovered all costs* plus the return allowance.

25. Not long ago natural gas costs were less than one-third of electricity in industrial markets and half of light fuel oil, based on energy equivalency. Canada, National Energy Board, *Canadian Energy, Supply and Demand 1993–2010, Technical Report* Chart Figure 4–14 Technical Report p.4–15.

26. Bill Reinwart, "Is Bigger Always Better?" *Daily Oil Bulletin*, May 14, 1997, 4. Others play this theme. John Ludwick, "Export Capacity Key to Canada's Gas Future," *Daily Oil Bulletin* May 19, 1995, 5, after lamenting how competition of many small Canadian producers erodes gas prices, quotes Ziff Energy Group as saying, "If Canadian gas producers were running **OPEC**, the price of oil would probably be $3.50 to $4 a barrel."

27. Alberta Energy and Utilities Board, *Alberta's Reserves, 1998* Statistical Series 99-18, (Calgary: Alberta Energy and Utilities Board, 1999) iii.

Remaining natural gas reserves for 1998 are 1,239.9 billion cubic metres and production was 137.1 cubic metres. Assuming those production rates, nine years of reserves remain.

28. In the early '80s as much as 55% of provincial government revenues came from fossil fuel, then it went down to about 20% or $3 billion per annum. The Crown's nonrenewable resources revenue increased for fiscal year 96/97 to $4.396 billion and for 97/98 to $4.125 billion.

CHAPTER 11
BUSHWHACKING

1. Initially there were three zones, Green, Yellow and White but the Yellow Zone was later dropped. The term 'zone' was also changed to 'area'.
2. Government of Alberta, *Alberta Provincial Ecoregions*. Strong and Leggat and Alberta Conservation Strategy Project,"*Our Dynamic Forests: The Challenge of Management*" (Edmonton: Environmental Council of Alberta, 1990), 5, use different classes and categories.
3. "Alberta Conservation Groups Saddled With Court Costs," *Brazil of the North* (New Denver, B.C.: Canada's Future Forest Alliance, 1993), 12. *Our Dynamic Forests: The Challenge of Management*, (Edmonton: Environmental Council of Alberta, 1990), 22-23, a discussion paper for the Alberta Conservation Strategy has a similar but denatured message.
4. Alberta-Pacific Forest Industries Inc. "Letter of Transmittal" for Al-Pac Environmental Impact Assessment to Honourable Ralph P. Klein, Minister of Environment, May 8, 1989.
5. *The Economist* ranked Mitsubishi as the World's largest business in 1995 with global sales of US $175.8 billion. This is about twice Alberta's Gross Provincial Product.
6. Alberta Conservation Strategy, "*Our Dynamic Forests,*" 7. Others indicate that by 1993 some 97.1% of Softwood AAC and 77.4% of hardwood AAC had been allocated. *Alberta Forests-Some Facts* (Edmonton: Alberta Forest Service, 1990), Pub No. 1/371, indicates that about 96% of softwood AAC is committed and 82% of hardwood, or 90% together.
7. Manning Diversified Ind. estimates of 265,000 m3 (presumably coniferous) together with GAP's 320,000m3 deciduous and 480,000m3 coniferous make 1,065,000m3 of a total 22.1 million m3.
8. Government of Alberta Press Release "GAP and Government have Agreement in Principle--EIA and NRCB Review is the Project's Next Step," September 9, 1996, No. 96--109.
9. Alberta, *Daishowa Canada Co. Ltd Forest Management Agreement*, Order in Council No. 424/89, August 3, 1989.
10. Industry seeks longer, nearly full-cycle tenures.
11. FMAs penalize companies that fail to take their AAC.

12. Anthony Johnson and Vicki Barnett, "Alberta to introduce log policing system," *Calgary Herald*, March 10, 1995.
13. Vicki Barnett reported that "More than $3 million worth of Alberta timber was trucked to B.C. in a randomly selected 48-hour period last week, provincial statistics show. A total of 1,352 logging trucks were stopped at five Alberta checkpoints set up by provincial Motor Transport Services during a two-day period last week. . . ." in "Alberta lumber tab hits $3 million in two days" *Calgary Herald*, March 1, 1995,
14. Joanne Helmer, "Pincher MD axes logging rules," *Lethbridge Herald*, September 27, 1995, A1.
15. *Our Growing Resource: Alberta's Forest Industry...Meeting Global Challenges* (Edmonton: Alberta Forest Products Association, 1992), 14.
16. The Crown claims that on average about 1000 forest fires occur each year in the province. This has resulted in an average yearly loss of nearly 50,000 hectares during the period 1986 to 1995. Approximately 45% of fires are caused by people.
17. "Of concern with respect to pulp mills are dioxins, furans, chlorinated phenols, and 300 to 1,000 other chlorinated organic compounds. The toxicity and other properties of less than 30 of these are known, but a few of those that have been studied are very toxic." Alberta, Alberta Environment, "The Proposed Alberta-Pacific Pulp Mill: Report of the EIA Review Board," March 1990, 21.
18. The Alberta-Pacific Environmental Impact Assessment Review Board, *The Proposed Alberta-Pacific Pulp Mill: Report of the EIA Review Board*, March, 1990, recommended against the mill at least until further intelligence had been obtained, including river studies (and proper review of FMA).
19. B. Dancik et. al, "Forest Management in Alberta: Report of the Expert Review Panel," (Edmonton: Alberta Energy/Forestry, Lands and Wildlife, 1990) 11. "Plans for rapid expansion of lands under FMA disposition, from three million hectares in 1986/87 to a projected 19 million hectares in 1997/98, have coincided with recent announcements of budget cuts in the department. This situation has raised doubts about the ability of the department to do an adequate job of stewardship on FMAs and Crown forest management units". Since then it has worsened significantly. Much information about the FMA forests are gathered by the FMA holder and held as proprietary.
20. John McInnis, former MLA and Alberta Environment critic on Japanese Investment in Alberta's Taiga Forest, argues that "In Alberta, over the last five years, stumpage collections averaged less than one-third of the government expenditure on forest management." John McInnis, Speech Notes, February 25, 1994.
21. Larry Pratt and Ian Urquhart, *The Last Great Forest* (Edmonton: NeWest Publishers, 1994), 6.

22. Government of Alberta Press Release, "Alberta Sells its Investment in Millar Western," April 1, 1997, No. 4690. Government of Alberta Press Release, "Alberta Receives $260 Million for its Al-Pac Loans," May 15, 1998.
23. A. Nikiforuk and E. Stuzik, "Great Alberta Give-Away," *Globe and Mail*, 1989.
24. *Environment Network News*, Nov/Dec 1995 estimated pulp costs for an interior BC pulp mill of $25/m3 while in Alberta pulp operators paid the Crown, $0.26 to $0.70/m3. "Canada has the lowest overall stumpage rates in the world, according to 1990 FAO [Food and Agriculture Organization] statistics collected by Dr. Minoru Kumazaki, Professor of Agriculture and Forestry at Tsukuba University in Japan" claims International Press Release, November 15, 1993, entitled "Canada Accused as the #1 Ecological Dumper of Forest Products in the World."
25. Aggressive provincial competition for Capital's favours during recent decades results in strong government competition, driving resource prices and environmental standards lower.
26. Pratt and Urquhart, *The Last Great Forest*, 48-49.
27. That which doubles every 9 years, becomes 2 to the 11th power or 2048 times as large in 100 years. During this time the forest has merely replaced itself.
28. Presently about 20% regenerates naturally. That will reduce to 15%. Another 20% is seeded. The remaining 60% is planted (75 million seedlings). *Our Dynamic Forests*, 16, observed that from 1975 to 1985 36% was planted seedlings, 27% seeding and 37% was left to natural regeneration.
29. Reforestation has about a 70% success ratio.
30. *Royal Commission on the Economic Union and Development Prospects for Canada* 1985, Volume 2, 443 reporting on the submission of the Association of British Columbia Professional Foresters, Vancouver, September 8, 1983.
31. Attributed to Harry A. Merlo, Lousiana Pacific's CEO in Manitoba, by *Canadian Dimension*, April-May 1995, 58. Merlo assures "I've understood how precious our God-given resources are, and how important it is never to waste them. The lessons I learned from my mother ... I have not forgotten for a single day. And as head of the Louisianan-Pacific family, I apply those same lessons. I was raised to believe that wasting resources was a sin. And we've always run Louisiana Pacific with that attitude."

CHAPTER 12
WHITE MAN'S CARESS

1. MacGregor, *A History of Alberta*, 85.
2. Ibid., 127, MacGregor estimated the 1881 White and Metis populations to be 1,500.

3. Aberhart's attempts to manage debt, control banking and issue "scrip" or funny money, were declared invalid by the federal government or ruled *ultra vires* by the Supreme Court. Alberta's *The Accurate News and Information Act, The Bank Taxation Act,* the *Credit of Alberta Regulation Act,* these and others under the umbrella *Alberta Social Credit Act* were declared *ultra vires.*

4. This is part of the puzzling global decline in amphibians. Andrew R. Blaustein and David B. Wake, "The Puzzle of Declining Amphibian Populations," *Scientific American,* April 1995, 52.

5. Two million walleye fry were planted in 1997. An arctic grayling introduction program was reestablished. Of Alberta's 59 species of fish, eight are introduced, but interbasin transfers are frequent and displacement usual for many species.

6. Government press releases indicate caribou populations range from 3,500 to 7,000 animals, a range that indicates much about their level of knowledge. Gossip has it that there may be fewer than 1,000.

CHAPTER 13
STRIPS, LAMINATES AND BIOMES

1. Jim MacNeill, Pieter Winsemius, and Taizo Yakushiji, *Beyond Interdependence* (New York: Oxford University Press, 1991), 58-61.

2. Brian L. Horejsi, "Some relationships between wildlife habitat loss and ungulate population decline with application to the Yukon," Report of Western Wildlife Environments Cons., Calgary, 1997.

3. John Terborgh, "Why American Songbirds are Vanishing," *Scientific American,* May 1992, 98.

4. City micro climates have temperatures that are several degrees warmer than in outlying regions and rains come from the sprinkler.

5. The realm of impacts must be at least as large as trade's realm, the trade area. With global trade then there are global impacts. Pollution's realm is often global as well.

6. Introduced diseases of animals are often overlooked. The Wyoming population of wild black-footed ferret, found in 1981 after eight years without one being seen in the wild, was decimated by canine distemper in 1985. Ten survivors were captured, forming the basis for a captive breeding and release program.

7. In Wood Buffalo National Park the nearly wild and nearly natural herds of plains bison are under threat from far away cattlemen. Because cattle introduced their exotic diseases to buffalo (brucellosis and tuberculosis) and now cattlemen wish to eliminate these diseases, it is recommended that the buffalo be eliminated. See *Northern Diseased Bison,* Report of the Environmental Panel, August 1990.

8. W. E Rees, "The Footprints of Consumption: Tracking Ecospheric Decline," *Trumpeter*, Winter 1997, 2, discusses ecological footprinting. In part, it attempts to determine the resources required by each person. A city requires from 300 to 1000 times as much productive land as it actually occupies to maintain it. Thus Calgary needs from 150,000 to 550,000 km2 of productive land dedicated to its purposes. If so, in the long run, because Alberta lacks that much productive land, Calgary requires more than Alberta to sustain it.

9. Rounded and with altered titles, taken from Table 1.2.2 "National and Provincial Summary Statistics," *Human Activity and the Environment, 1994* Statistics Canada, 1995, 30.

10. Swift fox are taken for reintroduction from American populations.

11. Although it does not make significant difference in result, white tail deer are not included in the calculation.

12. Nicholas Georgescu-Roegen, *Energy and Economic Myths* (Toronto: Pergamon, 1976), 56.

13. Donella H. Meadows, Dennis L. Meadows, Jorgen Randers and William W. Behrens III, *The Limits to Growth: A Report for the Club of Rome's Project on the Predicament of Mankind*, 2nd Ed., (New York: Signet, 1974).

CHAPTER 14
ROADKILLS ON THE HIGHWAY TO PROGRESS

1. *An Act for the temporary Government of Rupert's Land and the North-Western Territory When united with Canada* (assented to June 22, 1869) and *The Manitoba Act* (assented to May 12, 1870).

2. W. F. Lothian, *A Brief History of Canada's National Parks* (Canada: Minister of Supply and Services, 1987), 10.

3. Ibid., 48.

4. Jon Krakauer, "Rocky Times for Banff," *National Geographic*, July 1995, 54.

5. Banff-Bow Valley Task Force, *Banff-Bow Valley: At the Crossroads Summary Report* (Ottawa: Minister of Supply & Services Canada, 1996) 27, 49.

6. Steve Chase, "Klein supports takeover idea on feds' parks" *Calgary Sun*, April 26, 1996, 42. "Klein said he's sure Alberta could find private companies to run federal parks just as the province has already found corporate stewards to manage provincial parks."

7. Richard H. Grove, "Origins of Western Environmentalism," *Scientific American*, July 1992, 42.

8. David H. Breen, *Alberta's Petroleum Industry and the Conservation Board* (Edmonton: UofA Press, 1993), xxviii.

9. Grant MacEwan, *Entrusted to My Care* (Saskatoon: Modern, 1966).

10. Today policy and program environmental reviews are considered visionary.

11. Statutory definitions of environmental conservation (ss. 2(d) and 3.) are broad enough to include ecological considerations, but the focus is on resources and direct economic effects.
12. Recital to *Wilderness Areas Act.* These acts were assented to in this order, March 31, 1971, April 16, 1971 and April 27, 1971.
13. Meadows, *The Limits to Growth.*
14. The conference's first principle was "Man has the fundamental right to freedom, equality and adequate conditions of life, in an environment of a quality that permits a life of dignity and well-being."
15. P. S. Elder, "The Participatory Environment in Alberta," (1974) 12 *Alberta Law Review*, 403.
16. 1973, Statutes of Alberta, c.34, assented to May 10, 1973.
17. There are three or more discretionary points. The Minister has a discretion ("in the opinion of the Minister") in determining the triggering event; he has a discretion in issuing an order ("may . . . if ... it is in the public interest to do so"); and he had discretion over what is to be included in the report. One author feels there to be no discretion for socio-economic assessment or consideration of the economics of the public interest in such projects. As well the scope of the environmental assessment was narrow. See P. S. Elder "Environmental Impact Assessment in Alberta" (1985) 23 Alberta Law Review, 286, 298.
18. Alberta, *The Environmental Effect of Forestry Operations in Alberta,* (Edmonton: Environmental Council of Alberta, February, 1979).
19. Thomas R. Berger, *Northern Frontier Northern Homeland: The Report of the Mackenzie Valley Pipeline Inquiry,* Revised Ed., (Vancouver: Douglas & McIntyre, 1988).
20. Government expenditure on conservation is small. Far more is spent on human health and safety in relationship to the environment--to ensure that humans are not poisoned through their own activities. This includes regulation of industry, keeping it within thresholds of pollution and destruction that are tolerable to the public. The art is to maximize sustainable or long-term negativities. It ensures economic growth and development, political control and utter long-term natural decadence. Much is spent on comprehensive exploitation, finding ways of taking from the land through multiple resource usage. Some is spent on science and technology to find other ways to exploit, some aids recreation and tourism, and much is spent on big resource projects like dams. Some is spent on theatre and puff.
21. Breen, *Alberta's Petroleum Industry,* xxviii.
22. World Commission on Environment and Development, *Our Common Future* (Oxford: Oxford University Press, 1987), 43.

CHAPTER 15
THE SALVATION BAND

1. September 1989 document attributed to the Communications Committee on the Environment, Alberta Public Affairs Bureau, entitled *Action on Environment* and subtitled *A Proposed Strategy on Environment Communications for the Government of Alberta*.
2. Ibid., 3.
3. Ibid., 7.
4. Ibid., 9.
5. Ibid.
6. Alberta, Statutes, 1992, E-13.3 (assented to June 26, 1992).
7. Cynthia Giagnocavo and Howard Goldstein, "Law Reform or World Reform: The Problem of Environmental Rights," 35 *McGill Law Journal*, (1990), 350.
8. Vacation Alberta or WestCastle Project was approved subject to conditions, one required the establishment of a Waterton-Wildland Recreation Area surrounding the expanded ski-hill and relocated golf course. Natural Resources Conservation Board Decision No. 9201, December 1993.
9. Energy Resources Conservation Board, *Decision D 94-8* September 6, 1994, 35, the Whaleback decision, did not involve an AEPEA EIA.
10. AEPEA, s. 47(d) requires a report to contain "a description of potential positive and negative environmental, social, economic and cultural impacts of the proposed activity, including *cumulative* , regional, temporal and spatial considerations" (emphasis added).
11. EUB Decision D94-2, 10, contains a treatment of the evasion of the obligation. The argument over who should do it, government or industry was resolved by dispensing with the requirement, while approving the project.
12. Andrew Nikiforuk, "The Nasty Game,"[http://www.carc.org], January 1997, 2. Dr. Schindler sat on the Proposed Alberta-Pacific Pulp Mill Review Panel.
13. During the period 1975 to 1995 only 11 applications for well licences were denied or cancelled after public hearings for reasons of environmental protection or public safety. About 100 thousand wells were licensed during that period.
14. Jack Danylchuk and Scott McKeen, "Flowery praise for Daishowa project," *Calgary Herald*, September 23, 1990.
15. AEPEA addresses 'release of substances' into the environment and contamination, conservation and reclamation of sites after use --clean up your mess, clean and safe water practices, hazardous wastes and waste management issues, recycling and such matters.
16. John A. Livingston, *The Fallacy of Wildlife Conservation* (Toronto: McClelland Stewart, 1981), 33.

17. Judith B. Hanebury, "Environmental Assessment as applied to Policies, Plans, and Programs," *Law and Process in Environmental Management* (Calgary: Canadian Institute of Resources Law, 1993), 101, 104. "A project-based environmental assessment process is narrow in scope. It is a reactive procedure that aims to ameliorate the projects biological and physical site-specific effects. More widespread effects such as global warming, ozone depletion, and acid rain do not readily lend themselves to a site specific analysis."
18. Industry is usually self-reporting but also very powerful in determining what is required to be reported. Aggregate non-economic costs and externalities associated with the oil and gas industry are nearly impossible to obtain.
19. Industry and government share funding EUB activities.
20. Cumulative assessments are not done, proper public interest evidence is not presented in matters to be decided in the "public interest", socio-economic impacts particularly as they involve public economies are nearly nonexistent and when they get in a corner on the deficiency of evidence, regulators say it is "implicit" in the application.
21. Some equate government with the public interest. It is rarely so. Government has its own interests. Sometimes it corresponds with the public interest but not necessarily. More often it is an extension of the political and economic elite's interests.
22. Al-Pac and the Oldman River dam are examples. Sometimes there are direct appeals to Cabinet. *A.G. Canada v Inuit Tapirisut* [1980] 2 S.C.R. 735. Sometimes big projects are done in small pieces that seem to evade the obligation for review and compliance. Some argue that is what is happening in the Westcastle.
23. *ERCB Decision D 94-8*, the Whaleback decision, denied Amoco's application to drill on unexplored montane lands. The application was denied as premature--they must await a proper land-use plan for the area. Some took this postponement to be a denial on environmental grounds, thereby validating the entire regulatory process. Government and industry cheered this interpretation. In 1999 portions of the Whaleback received Special Places status.
24. Larry Johnsrude, "PCs pass environmental powers to industry," *Calgary Herald*, Tuesday February 27, 1996.
25. English law of the day became the North-West Territory's law on July 15, 1870.
26. John Ralston Saul, *Voltaire's Bastards: The Dictatorship of Reason in the West* (Toronto: Penguin, 1992), 335.
27. Donna Tingley, "Going to Court," *Law Now*, May 1992, 12. In respect of litigation over Alberta forests: "What has been achieved? To date, none of the actions has resulted in the remedy sought by the environmentalists. None of the activities viewed as objectionable has been halted by the

courts." The few cases that got to the Supreme Court of Canada may have enjoyed success in law but not on the ground, i.e., the *Oldman River Dam*.

28. The lack of class action law suits, the difficulty of status or standing, the intimidating and expensive process, the lack of substantive principles and rights in the law, the record of decisions, all recommend against the public attempting to advance the public interest through the courts. Much of this is a problem of legislation, because Canadian legislation is often enabling or structuring legislation, but void of principles or rights.

29. Thomas R. Berger, *A Long and Terrible Shadow: White Values, Native Rights in America* (Vancouver: Douglas & McIntyre, 1991), presents the larger picture of Aboriginal justice in the Americas. Saul, *Voltaire's Bastards*, 326 argues the law's pliability in the hands of the judiciary by recording the United State's Supreme Court flip-flops on slavery, child labour and discrimination, all based on interpretation of the Bill of Rights.

30. *Reese v. Alberta (Minister of Forests)* (1992) 85 Alta.L.R. (2d) 153, 180.

31. *Can Wildlife Fed. Inc. v. Can (Min. of the Environment)* [1989] 4 W.W.R. 526.

32. For example, see Christopher Genoval, "Daishowa Tries to Gag Critics," *Alternatives Journal*, Spring, 1997, 12.

33. In 1930, the same year, Canada enacted its *National Parks Act.*

34. Alberta, Statutes, *Wilderness Provincial Park Act* 1959 S.A., c.95. The name changed in 1965.

35. Alberta, Statutes, *Wilderness Areas Act*, 1971 S.A. c. 114.

36. Alberta, Statutes, *Wilderness Areas Amendment Act*, 1981 S.A. c-76, s.3.

37. Alberta Wilderness Assoc., "AWASSOC Newsletter," Summer 1993.

38. George Newton, "2001: A Parks Odyssey," *Environment Network News*, May/June 1992, p.3.

39. E. A. Bailey, "Parks for Profit," *Environment News*, Spring 1995, 5, claims that the Crown does not want to pay for it. In three years the provincial parks budgets were reduced by 30%. Many parks are being put under private control, privatized. The trend is to grant lands and monopolies over land to be used as parks.

40. These were the first four items contained under a Special Places heading entitled "Did You Know" taken from Environmental Protection's web information site, June 30, 1997.

CHAPTER 16
EPILOGUE

1. *Speeches for Doctor Frankenstein*, originally published in *Animals in that Country* (Oxford University Press, 1968).

INDEX

refugia, 3, 7, 59, 89, 141, 142
regulation and regulators, 146-153, 160-162
reservations, 57-59
Ricardo, David, 71
Riel, Louis, 43, 44, 52, 54, 66, 67, 74, 110
robes, 25, 30
Royal Commission on the Economic Union and Development Prospects for Canada (MacDonald Commission), 118
Royal Commission on Energy (Borden Commission), 96
Rupert's Land, 21, 26, 39-44, 49-51, 56, 61, 62, 67, 72, 76, 79, 107, 143
Rupert's Land Act, 121

S
sabertooth tiger (*Smilodon*), 9, 14, 15, 135
Sarcee, 30
Sayer, Guillaume, 39
Schindler, David, 159
scimitar cat, 9
Scott, Thomas, 43
shadows, 127-129, 133-135, 138, 139
shrub ox, 8, 14
Sifton, Clifford, 73, 74, 79
sloth, 8, 9, 14
Social Credit Government, 148, 149, 155
Special Places, 165-167
Squires and Squirearchy, 50, 55, 69, 70, 122
stag-moose, 8
Stoney, x, 93
strip (discussion), 132-139, 169, 170
Suncor, 99
Sunshine Ski expansion, 158
Sustainable Development, 152, 153
Syncrude Canada Ltd., 99

T
tar sands. *See* bitumen.
techno-biomic change, 132-142
teratorn, 9, 15
Timber Quotas, 109, 118
treaty, 54-59, 62, 76, 97
Treaty of Tordesillas, 1494, 19
Trudeau, Pierre-Elliott, 97

Turner Valley, 94, 95, 98, 103, 135, 147
Tyrrell Sea, 5

U
United Farmers of Alberta (UFA), 122
United Nations, Environment Program 152; Stockholm Conference 149, 151
Universal Time System, 65, 66
University of Alberta, 164

V
Van Horne, William Cornelius, 144
Vernadsky, Vladimir, xviii
Voluntary Challenge and Registry, 101

W
Wa-Pa-Su, 27, 94, 99
Waterton Lakes, 93, 94
West, Stephen C., 112
Western Accord, 97
Weyerhaeuser, 116
Wilderness Areas Act, 148, 165, 166
Wilderness Provincial Park Act, 165
Willmore Wilderness Act, 148, 165
Wisconsinan Glaciation, 2, 11
wolfers, 34, 53, 93
wood muskox, 8, 14
World Commission on Environment and Development (WCED), 152, 153
World Conservation Strategy, 151

Y
Yellowstone Park, 31